EARTH'S COSMIC ASCENDANCY

EARTH'S COSMIC ASCENDANCY

Spirit and Extraterrestrials Guide us through Times of Change

by

GEORGE E MOSS

www.whitecrowbooks.com

For information, contact White Crow Books
at 3 Merrow Grange, Guildford, GU1 2QW United Kingdom,
or e-mail to info@whitecrowbooks.com.

Cover Designed by Butterflyeffect
Interior design by Velin@Perseus-Design.com

Paperback ISBN 978-1-910121-28-3
eBook   ISBN 978-1-910121-29-0

Non Fiction / Body, Mind & Spirit / Death & Dying

www.whitecrowbooks.com
www.salumetandfriends.org

SALUMET'S ANGELIC REALM TRUTHS / SPACE-TRAVELLERS / PYRAMID ORIGINS.

—A spiritual journey taking into account contemporary scientific progress and Earth's place within the patterns of a busy cosmos.

—But the real authors here are: 'Salumet', 'Bonniol', 'The Kingsclere Séance Group' and 'Wondrous Beings' who speak from across the universe.

Also by:

George E Moss	*A Smudge in Time*
George E Moss / Salumet	*SALUMET - His Mission to Planet Earth*
George E Moss / Salumet / Bonniol	*The Chronicles of Aerah – Mind-link Communications across the Universe*

DEDICATION

To those who seek beyond the footlights of this Earthly stage, and rise to the curtain call of changing times—thus to discover truth, the boundless mind, friends across the universe and the love of all creation.

"The mind is not a vessel to be filled but a fire to be kindled"

– PLUTARCH.

CONTENTS

ILLUSTRATION LIST

ACKNOWLEDGEMENTS

Many have contributed to this book. There is the Kingsclere Group of course, that functions as a team; part of which is here on the planet and part in spirit. Some who began as planetary team members are now themselves in spirit—that includes Leslie our group founder and president to whom we send our very personal thanks. The team is extensive and all who have made their contributions are sincerely thanked, wherever they may be. Perhaps that term 'wherever' should be clarified further. And I should begin with Salumet, our guide and teacher, who has visited via Eileen for the past two decades. Virtually all that is described in these pages has resulted from the input of this one. As a light-being of Angelic Realms Salumet can be anywhere at all within what we know as the physical universe, and he is of all-knowledge—that all-knowledge being known to some as Akasha. Thank you Salumet for your mission to Earth that has revealed so much and is now available to many!

We are blessed with words and presentations from a number who now progress within Earth's spirit realms—simple folk, ex-military, nuns of holy orders, scientists, notaries, royalty, some who relate to our own previous incarnations, some from ancient cultures, even a Chinese acrobat from a travelling circus. It has been quite a mixture of input. But the creation is of course many, many times more extensive than just this one single planet, a fact scarcely accounted by Earthly religions; and we have been further blessed with communications from sentient beings who live on several other planets in this and in far galaxies. All other planets have *their* spirit realms of course, and where relevant, we have in addition received word from certain of these domains. We are therefore much indebted to both this world and the next—not just where Earth is concerned but other planets and other galaxies included. A special 'thank you' to Bonniol and his team of sixty or so who live on Planet Aerah—they have brought to us so much factual data and understanding, that link having been arranged for us by Salumet.

In presenting what follows, I have felt it appropriate to make occasional reference to our historic and scientific records. It is as well that we see clearly any connections that come to us from spirit or from elsewhere, with the histories that we already hold. This all helps to illustrate that at long last science, mysticism, spirituality, and human endeavour are merging together as they should in this 21st century. Spirituality is a flowing river having depths and progression, while science and mysticism are components of understanding contained therein. I therefore acknowledge with sincere thanks the authors of 37 reference works listed at the end of this book. And the patterns of connection to our Earthly thinking may also help to establish some small degree of credibility for the words that come to us from so many different sources throughout this truly awesome creation.

I also acknowledge with thanks all those who have taken the trouble to travel and 'sit in' on occasions, to experience the union and pass the word on to others. There have been those from both near and far, the latter including visitors from Canada, USA, Japan, Denmark, Finland, New Zealand and Australia.

Finally, a reference to the observed and long awaited drawing together of the ways of spirit and what might be described as the 'cutting edge of our scientific thinking'. And it is fitting that a Foreword contribution comes from Professor Ervin Laszlo and Gyorgyi Szabo MA; also a contribution that concerns current highly indicative pyramid excavation work from Dr Sam Semir Osmanagich. These are much valued contributions.

Regarding that latter contribution, it will become clear that human development cannot be described using physical concept alone; and the notion of a 'missing link' in evolution has really to be seen as a figment of our material imaginings. In order to unite the physical, the energy and the spiritual considerations, it is essential that we make proper study of the gulf that currently exists between 'physical science' and 'spiritual science'—this gulf must close and indeed is closing. Salumet has spoken on this (14th December 1998):

~ "Until your scientists in this world begin to realise that the human make-up, as you call it, is more than physical, they will always be faced with many problems."

And in describing pyramids at one of our early meetings, Salumet has in fact referred to them as 'star pointers'. And pointing to North Star may well be seen as a convenient way to align East-West faces to Earth rotation. The significance of this important factor will soon become evident to the reader, whether spiritual seeker or inquiring scientist.

The Foreword that follows is by cutting-edge scientists—revisionists—and includes updated scientific terminology. It will be an education as well as a challenge to some, to observe how scientific endeavour must lead to an understanding of spirit. Salumet frequently speaks of 'energy'. It may assist the non-scientist to note that the 'quantum' is the fundamental unit of energy in quantum mechanics theory, while 'photon' is the fundamental unit of light energy. Spiritual energy is spiritual energy, whether described with reference to photons and quantised field in the new science, or as simply perceived by spirit communicators.

Gyorgyi Szabo PhD (Cand.) is currently writing her doctorate thesis at the Sorbonne, University of Paris, on the scientific theories of Ervin Laszlo. She was Co-Founder and Executive Director of the Exploratoria program at the same centre—Ervin Laszlo and Gyorgyi Szabo have been collaborating for over six years. To adequately describe the achievements of Ervin Laszlo would fill several pages. So, with apologies, I will just briefly mention a few details concerning this pioneer of *systems thinking* in philosophy. He holds the highest degree of the Sorbonne (State Doctorate) plus four honorary Doctorates. He is founder and president of the international *think tank* 'Club of Budapest', now in partnership with the 'Giordano Bruno Globalshift University', an online university designed to transform our planet's obsolete paradigms—he himself being Chancellor. He is founder and chair of the Ervin Laszlo Centre for Advanced Study, dedicated to the research and development of the new "Akasha Paradigm" presented in his previous and current books, the most recent being *'THE SELF-ACTUALIZING COSMOS: The Akasha Revolution in Science and Human Consciousness', Inner Traditions (2014)*[37]. He is head of the 'General Evolution

Research Group', has published more than 70 books and in excess of 400 papers. He is recipient of 2001 Goi Award (Japanese Peace Prize) and has twice been nominee for the Nobel Peace Prize. And, as stated below, he recognises a *plethora of non-physical forms of existence.*

FOREWORD

By Ervin Laszlo and Györgyi Szabo

This is a book of intelligent insight and intelligent advice. It comes from an intelligence—but not from an intelligence born and bred on this planet. It comes from an intelligence elsewhere in the universe. The insights and the advice are sound—the readers can judge that for themselves. But the messages come from a being that is not one of us humans. Should we then doubt it? And perhaps reject it? This is a question of credibility, and it is the issue we address in this Preface.

The mysteries of out-of-body and near-death experiences and of the experience of receiving unfamiliar or unrecognizable information have to do with people not being familiar with the plethora of non-physical forms of existence. For the most part, we are not ready to accept that such experiences are real. By discovering the laws of the deep dimension of the world, many of these mysteries could be cleared up.

One such law is the transmission of information by resonance. We know that information is transferred between wave-fields when the waves are in phase—when they "conjugate." Every single thing in the universe has its own resonance, every single human being has its own vibration. Every thing and every human exchanges information when its waves are in phase—when conjugate. Then they resonate together. We only give names to each other and to others because we are not able to distinguish each other only by resonance. Our brain and body receive millions of resonances every day, but we fail to decode them and hence we do not actively resonate with them.

Perception is highly selective. The way we filter the information that reaches us is determined by the traits of our upbringing and the influences that act on us. Mediums can process information that "normal" people filter out. This information is anomalous for most people; it is nonlocal information based on quantum-level resonance. When one processes information in this mode, signals, images, insights and intuition reach conscious awareness.

The experience of mediums prompts us to revise the classical concept of perception of the world. Our world is not a vast machine reducible to its individual parts, but a holographically integrated irreducible whole.

The modern mind, influenced by classical physics, filters out information that does not mesh with its materialistic, machine-like preconceptions. Modern people believe only what is perceptible to their senses—what they can see and hear and touch. Anything that is not sense-perceptible they consider but illusion or delusion. The dominant belief system places mind and consciousness in the category of unreal things, because mind and consciousness are not material. The simplest way for the modern mind to deal with them is to claim that they are produced by the material brain—a by-product of complex cerebral functioning. Consciousness researchers now realize, however, that this does not answer the question regarding the place of mind and consciousness in the world, because it cannot tell us how something as material as the brain could produce something as immaterial as a thought, a perception, an intuition, a sensation, or a volition.

The above is the "hard question" of consciousness research, and it turned out to be not only hard but intractable. That we cannot say how the brain would produce consciousness, does not mean that the brain would not "have" consciousness. It could have it not as its product, but as something it receives, elaborates, conserves, and transmits.

There is more evidence speaking to this concept of consciousness than to the consciousness-as-by-product-of-the-brain assumption. It is also what Salumet tells us in this book. Yet the argument that dominates the modern mind is that consciousness is a product of the brain, because when the brain stops functioning, consciousness stops as well. This, however, is like claiming that our TV set produces the programs it displays, because when we shut off our set, the display ceases. Evidently the program—more exactly, the electromagnetic wave-patterns that reach the antenna and through it the set that displays the program—continues to exist. In the same way consciousness can continue to exist when the brain has died—when it is "shut off."

We do not suggest that the contents of consciousness are "produced" ready-made by some extra-somatic intelligence, only that the phenomena of consciousness—our direct experience of the world—is the consequence of our brain's reception of signals that originate beyond it. They originate in the consciousness that pervades the universe—in the "spirit world" that Salumet and other spiritual entities speak about. We receive signals from this world from the vantage point of our brain—from our being-in-the-world. This is what constitutes our conscious experience. It is not limited to one point in space and time, because consciousness is nonlocal in the universe. Human consciousness displays this element of nonlocality: it persists also beyond the brain. There is good evidence on this score in NDEs (near-death experiences), in OBEs (out-of-body experiences), and even in experiences transmitted by electronic instruments (in EVPs, electronic voice phenomena). Why should we not consider the evidence for medium-transmitted messages in the same way? The difference between NDEs, OBEs and messages transmitted by mediums is that information in NDEs and OBEs is received by the subjects themselves, and medium-transmitted experiences, it is received by the mediums. The process is likely to be the same.

The veracity of reports by people who approached the portals of death but then came back (or were sent back) appear more credible because in NDEs the reporters experienced the events they recount themselves. We doubt the experiences conveyed by mediums because we suspect that the mediums could be making up their reports, whether voluntarily or involuntarily, as fraud or hoax, or as the result of subconscious suggestion by others. Yet there are well-documented cases where the mediums convey information they could not have obtained by ordinary means, and where they recount experiences they could not possibly have undergone themselves. Where did they get this information, and how did they come by these experiences? The answer can only be framed by the concept of consciousness that is, and has always been, affirmed by great prophets, artists, and spiritual people—and by non-human entities such as Salumet.

If we take an in-depth and unbiased look at the evidence, and seek the explanation for it in reference to the latest discoveries of the sciences, we come to the conclusion that the information we access in the universe is not a mosaic of unrelated bits and pieces, floating randomly in space and time. It is an integrated whole, where all parts are instantly and intrinsically related to all other parts. The consciousness that we access—that we participate in—is a hologram. In it all things are "entangled" in space as well as in time.

This is no longer an esoteric tenet: it is a conclusion derived from the latest findings of contemporary quantum physics. In the deep dimension of the cosmos—in what we call the Akasha—there is no space and no time; space and time are its perceivable, measurable manifestations. The deep dimension creates physical space-time, but it is not "in" space-time. This was an esoteric insight a few years ago; it is a scientific fact today.

We should view the information conveyed by trance mediums such as Eileen Roper, Sarah Duncalf and others in light of these emerging insights. Could they not have accessed some elements of the holographically integrated information that pervades the universe? And could the information they have accessed not have originated anywhere in space-time? The answer is yes: this is entirely possible.

There is yet another factor that calls for our attention in regard to the credibility of the messages conveyed by mediums. Are the entities they channel physically real? By "physically real" we do not mean that they are material, for the physics we have in mind is not classical but quantum physics. Reality in light of quantum physics is not material; it is quantum-informational. Our body and brain are one particular kind of configuration of quantum-information, and quanta on the one hand and galaxies on the other are other configurations. They appear as material entities because they have particular locations in space and time and produce measurable effect on interaction. But there are entities in the universe that do not have these qualities yet merit being considered real entities: for example, quantum field excitations at the Planck-scale. These are photons and other particles without rest-mass. Salumet claims to be constituted of photons: if so, he is a light-entity. He could be just as real as a quantum-configuration based on the integration of quanta into atoms, of atoms into molecules, of molecules into cells, and of cells into biological organisms with brains. When we hear Salumet speaking to us, we witness one kind of quantum-configuration communicating with another (human) kind. That this communication involves vast distances in space is not an anomaly. In a quantum-entangled space-time all things are instantly connected. Salumet could be sending his messages from next door, or from another galaxy. As long as he is in the same physical space-time, his messages reach us instantly.

Thought, as Salumet himself notes, is the most powerful thing in the universe. It is powerful because it is coherent information, and the universe is built of information. When the information is assembled by an information-configured entity into coherent messages that "inform" other information-configured entities, they create (as David Bohm would say) "effective in-formation."

This, we believe, is the case in regard to the messages published in this book. They are powerful messages if they are not filtered out but consciously received. Whether this is the case is up to the readers. Consciously receptive readers can be effectively in-formed by messages whether they come from human or from other sources. Now they have the chance to be in-formed by truly wise messages—thanks to Salumet, Bonniol, and the Kingslere Group convened by George Moss.

January 2014

PYRAMID
EXCAVATION WORK

Dr. Sam Semir Osmanagich, Ph.D.
Foreign Member of the Russian Academy of Natural Sciences
Anthropology Professor and Director of the Center for Archaeology
and Anthropology
at the American University in Bosnia-Herzegovina
www.samosmanagich.com

I met George Moss at the Bosnian Pyramid site in Visoko, Bosnia-
Herzegovina. He followed me and a group of visitors deep in the
Prehistorical labyrinth under the pyramids. Some sections were

narrow, filled with the water, so we had to crawl. During our breaks, we had a feeling of being in Mother's womb.

I've been following his comprehensive spiritual work for couple of years. The messages he brings are of importance for all of us. In particular, descriptions of pyramid builders and purpose of these structures are of great interest for me.

I usually start my talks with the sentence: "Almost everything they teach us about the ancient history is wrong: origin of men, civilizations and pyramids." And really, Homo sapiens are not a result of the evolution and biologists will never find a "missing link", because intelligent man is the product of genetic engineering. Sumerians are not the beginning of the civilized men, but rather a beginning of the most recent cycle of humanity. And finally, original pyramids, most superior and oldest, were made by advanced builders who knew energy, astronomy, geometry and construction better than we do.

Since I discovered the Bosnian pyramids in 2005 it has become the most active archaeological location in the world. We have spent over 340,000 man-hours in archaeological excavation, sample testing and radiocarbon dating in the period from 2005 to 2013. We've determined that the Bosnian Valley of the Pyramids consists of five pyramidal structures discovered to date which I named: The Bosnian Pyramids of the Sun, Moon, Dragon, Mother Earth and Love. The site also includes a tumulus complex and a huge underground labyrinth.

In the case of Bosnian pyramids we can witness that superior builders knew how to manipulate huge quantities of materials. This discovery is historic and changes the knowledge of the early history of Europe for several reasons:

1. These are the first pyramids discovered in Europe
2. The site includes the largest pyramid structure in the world— The Bosnian Pyramid of the Sun - with its height of over 220 meters is much higher than the Great Pyramid of Egypt (147 meters).
3. The Bosnian Pyramid of the Sun has, according to the Bosnian Institute for Geodesy, the most precise orientation towards cosmic north with the error of 0 degrees, 0 minutes and 12 seconds.
4. The Bosnian Pyramid of the Sun is completely covered by rectangular concrete blocks. The properties of the concrete, including extreme hardness (up to 133 MPs) and low water

absorption (around 1%), are, according to the scientific institutions for materials in Bosnia, Italy and France, far superior to modern concrete materials.

5. Radiocarbon dating from the organic material (fossilized leaf) discovered between two concrete layers on the Bosnian Pyramid of the Sun in summer 2013 and performed by lab in Kiev, Ukraine confirmed the age of 29,200 years +/- 400 years. This finding confirms that the Bosnian pyramids are also the oldest known pyramids on the planet.

6. Beneath the Bosnian Valley of the Pyramids there is an extensive underground tunnel and chamber network which runs for a total of more than ten miles.

7. Ceramic sculptures have been discovered in the underground labyrinth with a mass of over 25 tons which makes them the largest found so far in the ancient world.

Original pyramids (Giza, biggest Shaanxi in China, Teotihuacan, Bosnia) were used as huge energy machines: they were emitting electromagnetic fields, creating ultrasound and more energy phenomena. Most probably they were receivers, as well.

In order to understand the ancient monuments, we need to view them through three realms: physical, energy and spiritual. Our scientific instruments are simply not adequate to explain the purpose of the oldest pyramids. Mainstream scientists, archaeologists, historians and anthropologists with their rigid approach, are often the main obstacles for scientific progress.

The gap between physical and spiritual science is to be bridged if we want to get full understanding of the past. One way to do it is to tap to the spiritual realm and different dimensions.

In front of us is a good example how to bridge this gap.

Dr. Sam Osmanagich, 8ᵗʰ October 2013.

A NOTE
ON FORMAT

In a book of this nature, the words spoken arise from a number of different sources. As an aid to clarity, some rules of presentation have therefore been observed. Firstly, all speech received via a medium has been given the prefix '~'. In addition, these statements are indented and spaced within general text. Human speech is presented in the usual way, with occasionally a word in italics for emphasis. In speech, capitals have sometimes been used for further emphasis, and that seems to capture the thrust of certain key statements. In general, dialogue is presented without any modification. But in just a few instances an inconsequential word has been added in brackets to improve sentence flow. One cannot always expect perfect 21st century English from every location in time, spirit or universe! References to Earthly literature have been given superscript numbers and are listed at the end of the book.

INTRODUCTION

S alumet's teaching mission spans two decades and continues. The wisdom that comes to this Earthly realm from this Angelic source has a four-fold quality that embraces:

- Direct teaching from all-knowledge source, with time allocated during the séance sessions for question-and-answer.
- Arranging for 'experts' from their specific places in 'time' and 'location' to come and speak their truths direct.
- The opportunity to discuss with our guide the words of those 'experts' from Earth's history, pre-history, and from elsewhere in this universe.
- Further question-and-answer sessions relating to current world affairs, scientific endeavours or arising from our own general thoughts.

As we proceed, the aim will be to cover all modalities. In so doing, it will quickly become evident that there is a pressing need for us to bring together 'spirituality', 'scientific intellect' and an awareness of our true home—the 'created universe', of which Earth is but a minute part. But before we begin our journey—a mental exercise:

Imagine that you are a light-being within that Angelic domain of light. You have universal all-knowledge of what has gone before and a near-perfect knowledge of what is to come. Your understanding of Planet Earth and its populations knows no bounds. Within Earth's human populations, most extensive preparations have already been made, involving present day lives as well as a procession of past-life encounters and gatherings. Many have been those synchronistic 'nudges' that reveal pathways and bring people together. You have awareness of the one Earthly group in particular who meet in séance and who will be warmly receptive to a teacher from your distant realm of light and love. The preparations have been well laid and you are now ready to embark on your **Mission to Earth**.

But the pure energy realms are of course inanimate—formless— there are no bodies, there are no names and all communications are telepathic thought; very different from here on the material planet. So there exists a huge gulf between Angelic Realms and the ways of physical humanity living in the space-time creation. The missions mounted from more easily imagined higher spirit planes have been conducted in past times in a number of different ways. There have been incarnations—slow to start at first, with the birth and the childhood years; Jesus and Buddha being examples. There have been 'series visions' with advisory messages; Mary's many visions through the 20th century being a prime example of this approach. There was Edgar Cayce, who in both sleep-state and trance received the most amazing information, to be passed on to others. A fourth method has been: speaking via an entranced medium during séance; for example, White Eagle speaking via Grace Cooke. This latter option, once the arrangements are in place, and taken together with today's technology, has the distinct advantage of being suitable for an *ongoing* teaching programme, and those communications can then benefit the entire planet. It might be said also that, once arranged, there is an element of expediency available, should through human default, expediency be required.

So, continuing in your imaginary role as beneficent light-being, and knowing the sheer size of the project that lies ahead, it is no surprise that you favour the latter approach—the medium-in-séance-group situation. And now, at this time, there is that tremendous advantage of developing technology—recorders, computers, the prospect of an expanding Internet and even hearing aids, for those more elderly ones who might otherwise miss a word or two. But even so, bearing in mind the gulf that separates us—where to begin? Firstly, when using the voice mechanism of a medium, there has to be a name—a named introduction is the standard way of Earth. Then the purpose of communicating should be given. Question and answer sessions and the teaching would naturally follow.

That, on the evening of 27th June 1994, at a meeting of the Kingsclere Group, UK, via Eileen, is exactly how it began—slowly at first with some hesitation, later to become a mind-enhancing rollercoaster ride, through which, at times we held on tightly to unforeseen perceptions. But it was slowly at first:

~ "I—am—'Salumet', I have waited a long—long time to come to you."

And following the giving of the name, a name that embodies salutation, and Leslie's warm welcome, the voice, so richly imbued with love and compassion, continued:

~ "We are reaching the point where your world will—WILL be a better place. Do not doubt these words. It may seem that (this) cannot be so. I am here to say: it will be—WILL BE! We have much to teach you."

That was the start, and Leslie assured that all would be recorded to pass on to others. Salumet replied that, in spirit, this was already known—of course! The plans were well laid, and it was known long before how we would respond. And indeed, there had been prior mention to us of the mission. It was on his next visit, one week later that Salumet reminded:

~ "We have told you in the past that there would be 'happenings'— when your flower, the rose, was in bloom."

The roses in Leslie's garden had never looked better, and the 'we' of course is the spiritual 'we'—those in spirit.

~ "My mission here, is to extend our love and to bring you knowledge. I want to say to you all: YOU ARE ALREADY IN THE PATHWAY OF LIGHT."

The phrase 'say to you all', of course, embraces those who sit as a group, the readers of these pages, those who receive email transcripts, those who are now able to follow the website updates and any who receive by whatever process—world population is being addressed here and world population is being invited to walk in THE PATHWAY OF LIGHT. A phrase spoken by Jesus comes to mind: *He that hath ears to hear, let him hear.*

Eileen—Eileen Roper—is Salumet's chosen and well-prepared medium. The voice that issues is entirely different from Eileen's own softly maternal tone. There would be 'fine tuning' to benefit more prolonged future sessions, and she would now rapidly become 'full trance'; meaning that, during sessions, her own consciousness is placed *entirely* to one side. Eileen thus has no knowledge of what transpires—we generally chat and bring her up to date afterwards, over a cuppa. Later, there would be the full transcript, followed by a CD-recording to listen to. A decade on, we learned that, as a group, we have been together before—several times—but this particular time within the Gor-rukka Amerindian tribe, many, many moons before the white settlers. Then, as 'Nahashiwah', even then, Eileen was a major tribal link to spirit—name given to her by that Great Spirit in the Sky—*Nahashiwah* mean: 'small body, great spirit'. And 'Small body, great spirit', remains apt description today!

I have referred above to that useful element of 'expediency' pertaining to the chosen method of communication; and in mid-1994, of course, many were acutely mindful of that irksome threat: nuclear default. Surely this matter requires our most urgent attention! A question was placed to which Salumet quickly responded:

~ "Nuclear energy has been misused by you people on Earth—it has been given to you, the knowledge of it, for a very good reason—for the betterment of mankind. But it has been misused. We are trying from our realms now, in a concerted effort, to influence world leaders in these matters—we are trying to put the right thoughts to the right people, that these things will and can be changed."

Then a question followed concerning 'Nostradamus prophecy' and Salumet explained that he could indeed make accurate prophecies. In fact, I have long admired the work and abilities of this 16th century seer and two chapters of our earlier book 'A *Smudge in Time*' provide analysis of certain key prophecies[1]. Nostradamus had predicted difficulties as we approach our new millennium, and Salumet appears to have connected the two questions placed to him:

~ "You speak of nuclear disaster. Your world has been heading towards that for some considerable time. Let me say to you all: There has come the time when many of us, and I speak as, let me say, a Master—Many Masters have come to tread this Earth plane at this particular time.

There will not be a nuclear holocaust. That is our mission at this time in your evolution! That will not occur! But let me tell you: the Earth is changing. And now we get to deep matters again. We spoke earlier of the Earth having an etheric—an etheric body. That is the one that will be filled with love and (will) change—and that is why we have descended at this time—to bring forth the knowledge to help that transition."

The passage of time on Earth as seen from spirit is different, and Salumet has on occasions referred to a period of our years as 'the mere blink of an eye'. However, an update to the proposed etheric happening came on 10th March 1997:

~ "—mankind in general on this planet Earth, has reached an awareness that brings joy to those of us in our world who are striving—who are striving to bring knowledge to this Earth. Surrounding this planet, there now prevails a stillness and peace, which you would not be aware of, but (which) brings much satisfaction to us. The stillness and peace, which over your next thousand-plus years will pervade all of mankind to such an extent, that no longer will there be the fear and—the distrust shall I say—over all things termed 'supernatural'. They will become known and 'natural' to mankind. Mankind will return to knowledge that belongs to him."

So there has already been a fundamental change in the planetary etheric. And this timely input was doubtless pre-emptive of the big change period that we now experience. Past great civilizations shared oneness with nature, such that what we now term 'supernatural' was *their* accepted 'natural'. So mankind will *return to knowledge that belongs*. But firstly, we must re-align to nature's ways. Many modern lifestyles have digressed alarmingly from her soft caress. Even the small UK 1930s-style mixed farms with local employment and local trading were so much closer to nature—hedgerow habitats, bird populations, the song of the nightingale, clover fields supporting myriad honeybees, an attendant bluebell coppice to supply fencing and timber. All that went; to be replaced by wide open prairies-style agriculture with the 8-furrow plough, combine harvester, toxic sprays and inter-continental road transporters. With mechanisation and chemicals, it is the few that prosper while the many seek whatever livelihoods big cities have to offer. And sadly, nature no longer prospers or prevails.

The 'stillness and peace of planetary etheric', referred to in 1997—how might this relate to our surviving nuclear default? Well, 'thought' is of course the prime motivator, while it has to be said: rhetoric usually precedes reality of action; but street demonstration can also be a coercive force to be reckoned with. The following list of events charts our material progress thus far:

1996: Nuclear tests in the South Pacific were abandoned in the face of world outrage.

1996: The Hague World Court ruled use and threat of nuclear weapons to be illegal.

1999: The Hague Appeal for Peace Conference calls for abolition, with the massive resources so released to be used to eradicate world poverty and preserve environment.

2000: United Nations reports five nations are signatories to a 'Non-Proliferation Treaty', agreeing in principle to get rid of nuclear arms. [But so far as may be deduced by averaging various published figures, missile warheads stockpiled worldwide, at this time, sadly still amounted to an horrendous 32,000!]

2010: New Strategic Arms Reduction Treaty (New START). This was a bilateral treaty between the main stock holders—Russia and the US—designed to limit holdings to 1,550 warheads.

2012: In the UK, more than 1,000 individuals sent in donations to fund a full-page CND 'Scrap Trident' poster in the *Guardian* newspaper on 20th October, as hundreds of thousands marched in street demonstrations through London and other cities, demanding government expenditure cuts.

Where nuclear stockpiles are concerned, it is very clear that Russia and US remain the prime offenders. Their holdings far outweigh those of other nations who have followed the example set. According to Internet figures for 2012, missile numbers still far exceed the limits set by New START. It all takes time. The process of change is regrettably slow, but overall, and with each step being preceded by rhetoric and treaties, it would seem that we move in the right direction. So, on reflection, it was indeed a matter of dire necessity—of the most expedient urgency, to get decommissioning started. That should then pave the way to a much more peaceful planet, enabling Salumet's extensive teaching programme to continue forward—that we may all of us walk in THE PATHWAY OF LIGHT.

Can we be certain of facts posted by media? One cannot overlook that there have been cover-ups and state secrets that have clouded crucial issues. A question was placed to Salumet on 10th September 2012 concerning 'openness' as opposed to 'secrecy', and I had made it clear on that occasion that I saw Julian Assange, the Wikileaks leaker of state secrets, as a 'Champion of Openness'. His reply was as ever profound and unequivocal:

> ~ "I would always, my dear friend, advocate openness and truth—I am not here to either condemn or anything else that a human being does. After all, in your world, with your free wills, you are capable of much good but also much that is not good. That, my dear friends, is the responsibility of you all. And I would say only that I champion 'truth' and 'love'. Your world has to find these things for itself."

It is of course the thought behind the words that counts, making it impossible for us to judge another. Salumet then continued on the theme of love (which of course the above missile threat would appear to contravene):

> ~ "Without love, you would be as well not to exist. There are too many people in your world, who seek only for themselves—who have no thought for others. But the time must come when they face themselves, whether it be in this world or in our world, and as I have told you before: it is much better to deal with these things whilst on the Earth planet."

I expressed my view that it is sad that so many around the world pay taxes to governing bodies who are then secretive about how those moneys are being spent.

> ~ "Yes—there are still many places in your world where this would not be possible, but because of the media type that you have now, much can be brought to a wider audience, and if that is used for good, then so be it. You must always champion good."

And we must observe that to champion 'truth', 'love' and 'good' presents a ground logic, these terms being subject to neither subdivision nor uncertainty; while 'openness' is to do with how mind handles these fundamentals. I feel that this statement demonstrates a succinct and sentient quality that has, through the many exchanges, become thematic.

PART 1

The Truth of Existence

"Truth is exact correspondence with reality"
— Paramahansa Yogananda.

CHAPTER 1

PAST LIVES AND REINCARNATION

There is so much more to existence than just the one Earth life; of this there should be no doubt whatsoever. We have all of us been here before, but for vast majority, all direct memory of previous lives will have been erased. This is the regular system, but just occasionally one slips through with some degree of retained memory—sufficient for proof that this is indeed so. As a child, James Leininger for example, in 2001 at the age of three, knew all about the WWII Corsair aircraft—they get flat tyres from heavy flight deck landings, he knew the difference between a bomb and a drop tank and named the carrier Natoma Bay that he had flown from on the day he was shot down in 1945, near Iwo Jima—and he has experienced the childhood nightmares about all that[2]. It was also during World War II that Anne Frank died in the Bergen-Belsen concentration camp—that likewise

1

in 1945. Nine years later, Barbro Karlen was born to Swedish parents and she too had nightmares. Before her third birthday Barbro told her parents that her real name was Anne Frank and her real parents would be coming for her. They thought it mere childhood fantasy—the Anne Frank Diaries had not at that time been published in Sweden, so that the name was unknown to them. That was to change. When age ten, her parents showed her several European cities, including Amsterdam, where the wartime Frank family had lived. It was the ten-year-old who guided them to the house, now the Anne Frank Museum. She had declared: 'It is just around the next corner', and there it was! That had come as a tremendous shock to her parents! And understandably, Barbro has a fear of men in uniforms and of showers—as were used in the Belsen execution chambers. Anne Frank had been a child literary prodigy. Barbro continues with that gift with several books being published through her teenage years. Her story *And the Wolves Howled*[3] was published in 1997. These are just two examples of retained past life memories that happen to have been written about.

There are also, of course, books written by enlightened ones—Lamas, Yogis, St Paul's Nag Hamâdi manuscript. But a favourite passage that relates is the reported dialogue between Paramahansa Yogananda and his departed and much loved Master Sri Yukteswar who appeared before him:

~ "'When a soul finally gets out of the three jars of bodily delusions,'" Master continued, "it becomes one with the Infinite without any loss of individuality. Christ had won this final freedom even before he was born as Jesus—the undeveloped man must undergo countless Earthly and astral and causal incarnations in order to emerge from his three bodies. A master who achieves this final freedom, may elect to return to Earth as a prophet to bring other human beings back to God, or like myself he may choose to reside in the astral cosmos—"'

PARAMAHANSA YOGANANDA. *AUTOBIOGRAPHY OF A YOGI.*
SELF-REALIZATION FELLOWSHIP, LOS ANGELES, 1998, (FIRST
PUBLISHED 1946).

Reincarnation is the prevailing pattern. Salumet has said much on the subject. It is such a basic factor pertaining to all human as well as animal existence, and it really is quite ludicrous that there should be any doubt or controversy concerning this fact of life. Sadly, there are those who become so obsessed with the nuts and bolts of scientific material consideration that all else is ignored—some unfortunately are authoritative academics, who actually pooh-pooh the spiritual basis of existence. Such unreal attitude and its influence will decline as awareness of the details of our spiritual origin that underpins (and indeed has *generated* at the very outset) all space-time—becomes more widely appreciated. And shortcomings in the knowledge have of course been compounded by lack of any clear presentation from religious orders that have evolved from happenings in bygone millennia. It is therefore appropriate that details delivered direct from higher realms should be listed before we proceed any further. The concise overall picture of the spiritual origin of humankind through the process of reincarnation, as gleaned from Salumet's teaching, is as follows: There are immortal parent souls that ever continue in spirit. Each soul is made up of many individual aspects. The *Earthly* life of one single soul aspect begins from that moment of its physical conception. That soul aspect will have returned to Earth for known purpose—usually to learn or have specific experience, sometimes to help another or to teach. It will have a life plan. Its life plan will have been decided upon beforehand, probably with help or counselling from others in spirit. The soul aspect will have chosen location and parents prior to its birth into a new Earth life. A generalisation is that very young children are closer to spirit than adults and are likely conscious of communications not observed by their parents. That is how a life begins. During that life, the physical body houses the spirit/soul aspect, and hence deserves to be well cared for. During sleep-state the soul aspect returns to spirit to revivify. Only very few have awareness of this. And we must always remember that both mind and soul aspect belong to spirit and are exterior to physical brain. During Earth life there will be suggestive guidance and synchronicities arranged from those in spirit, but always decisions will be made by the individual in compliance with the individual's free will—free-will rules. During life, the wise will instinctively know the course to follow in order to fulfil life's plan. Eventually, there has to be the physical death. Physical death comes to us all, of course, and the soul aspect then journeys back to spirit. It will be met by relatives and friends who may well no longer appear aged. Their spiritual (etheric) bodies regress to somewhere near prime condition, so that they no longer show signs of the old physical afflictions. The sadness of Earthly departure is matched by joyous celebration in spirit at glad return. There will be evaluation of the physical life that was and its achievements, for future guidance of the returned soul aspect. Time is not a factor in spirit, so there is no rush whatsoever. But eventually a decision will be made to either reincarnate to a further Earth life or to progress onwards in the planes of spirit—whichever course best suits. There are many levels in spirit—'my father's house has many mansions'. The lower levels are for terrorists and mass-murderers and for those who kill, knowing that it is a crime against creation to do so; albeit 'intention' counts for much in these matters. The midway levels are for those who know 'love'—love their neighbours, love animals, love nature, love their planet and love all creation. The many pathways of progress are open to all sentient beings, at whatever level and help is always to hand. Even those at the darkest, lowest levels, as they become more aware can move upwards into light, none are ever held captive but progress has to be earned. Animals have also been mentioned—their system is a little different, and at death they return to an 'energy pool'. But there are exceptions, and if they have formed a love-bond with a sentient being on Earth, then they may well share an ongoing life in spirit. Love bonds are never broken.

11th December 2000: Salumet was asked about the many reincarnations of the Dalai Lama that are referred to in the literature:

~ "Yes, I have told you there are many Masters who walk this planet and let us firstly say this to you: that those who have attained such knowledge have the ability to realize and understand spiritual ways. The gentleman you speak of has indeed reincarnated many, many times in order that the teaching may continue. It is, in fact, many *different aspects* of his soul. It is not the same aspect each time, of course, but it is felt that, when one has reached such attunement between the physical world and our world, that that attunement must continue for the benefit of all who come into contact with him and of course for his own soul's growth. Do not doubt that by whichever name he reincarnates with, it is still many aspects of the one soul."

Q: "Yes, so all the reincarnations would have a similar energy?"

~ "Yes, that soul has chosen that pathway and there is always a reason— perfect law is always followed. Does that help you? Before that spirit reincarnates, it already knows the task and the length of time which will be spent in your world. The one you speak of is truly spiritual."

There are times when soul aspects of similar energy pattern reincarnate as a group, or they *hope* to be able to come together again as a group whilst on the Earth. Mention has already been made of that time when some of us were part of the Amerindian Gor-Rukka tribe. We were delighted to receive word (10th January 2005) via Sarah, about this from our old chief: Chief Grand Mancha—a visit later confirmed by Salumet. It seems that at that time, Lilian was a teen-age male, Sara was a young girl, and Sarah was next in line for chief but was unfortunately killed while hunting. Our 6' 4" Graham was a youthful grandmother and was my squaw! The Nahashiwah details, already given, were actually spoken on this same occasion by Nahashiwah herself—soul aspect of Eileen, speaking *via* Eileen. The voice was beautifully ethereal. And nine years earlier (26th February 1996), Eileen had clairvoyantly witnessed her own image as Nahashiwah with hair in pigtails and wearing blue beads. That also was a memorable evening, when Nahashiwah gave the message:

~ "Be good to your Earth and you will be blessed many times."

On returning to self, Eileen was tearful and felt that she had lost someone.

Chief Grand Mancha was again with us two months later lustily shouting the tribal greeting:

~ "Ah tor ta tah!—God tor ta tah!"

He had many with him on this occasion—it was a between-worlds party to renew old friendship! Paul sat with us this time, and the chief declared that he had been a revered spirit communicator when with the tribe.

We were together again as brothers in a small monastery at Myddlewood, North Shropshire, UK, in Tudor times. The quite intricate details of those days, and how character traits have been carried over to the present team, are accounted in our 2005 Salumet book[4] and will not be repeated here. The monastery was destroyed, as were many, during the reign of King Henry VIII, with no firm evidential record. But a book has since come to light—*The History of Myddle*[5]—originally published in 1834, which states:

5

'—Broughton and Yorton which now make one parish, did formerly belong, as some say, to a small monastery which stood on a banke cast up by men's hands near Broughton church, which stands in a meadow about the middle way betweene the two townes of Broughton and Yorton. What time this small monastery was dissolved or destroyed is not known.'

That then, would have been our old home that we have learned about in some detail from those in spirit. I moved to the South Coast with family in 1999, to a chalet bungalow named 'RUYTON'—an unfamiliar name, yet it has a comfortable feel. We have since discovered that Ruyton, or Ruyton XI as it is sometimes called, is an ancient main village of a group of eleven villages, just three miles from Myddlewood. Small wonder our house name has a comfortable feel!

During séance meetings, the potential for communication with those who have experienced past lives on the planet is of course vast. As a group, we do not control who drops by for a chat, but many have got to know that there will be a warm welcome. We are aware that there are those in spirit who watch over the meetings—there are 'gatekeepers'. These have spoken on rare occasions. And there is a kind of *love aura* that also protects. So to use a scientific term, there is a *filtration* process that keeps things nice. Where *authoritative* personalities from Earth's past are concerned, Salumet has sometimes selected certain ones and has *made arrangements* for them to be with us—this to enhance our education. Evenings with Catherine the Great – Empress of all the Russias, and Mary Stuart – Queen of Scots, were memorable in the extreme; and furnished details that history books omit. These evenings have been reported in full elsewhere[1, 6]. In fact, in the dialogue with Mary, she refers to the arrangement made:

> ~ "Salumet has told me that he wanted you to realise what he has told you—that you are more than one. And whilst I retain the memories of those painful times within that lifetime; that part of me returned for the betterment of others. And so he hopes we all can share this time, to know that we are not just one."

That statement by Mary Stuart, of course, well endorses the spiritual truth that 'soul' is comprised of many aspects—*we are more than one*. Whilst being part of the whole, the one can separate and speak of that particular past life. Mary spoke of the year 1587 and her execution. Her final words spoken were in French:

~ "Je suis! Je suis!'—'I am! I am!"

And not 'Sweet Jesus!' as some thought at the time and as history books record. And after all, Mary was born of a French mother—Marie de Guise, and was educated in France. So it is fitting that her final words should have been in French.

Other notaries who have visited include Prime Minister Sir Winston Churchill, one of the murdered Russian Romanov royal family, Emma Hardinge Britten (founder of Two Worlds magazine), one who contributed to *The Bible Code* [1, 7, 8] that is concealed within the pages of the Torah, Joseph Merrick (the 'elephant man') and philosopher and architect Rudolf Steiner. Those who have an eye for evidence may like to note the following: when the latter gentleman came through, reference was made to the spiritual teaching centre that he, as architect had designed, near the Swiss border. His reply began:

~ "The Goetheanum!—yes!"

On that evening, when placing the question, I had not known that he named that particular teaching centre after Wolfgang Goethe. That name was neither in *my* mind nor any other mind within the group. The original building had been destroyed in a fire and Steiner had designed a replacement. It was rebuilt following his Earthly death. I had inquired if he had enjoyed seeing from spirit, its rebuilding:

~ "It was a great joy—and a great learning occurred also. I had many opposing forces on the creation of the Goetheanum at the very start."

He went on to speak of difficulties, how success came at high cost and how the Archangel Michael had been his strength and inspiration; how also the Nazis at that time had opposed his spiritual teachings. There have been three illuminating evenings with this intriguing esoteric Austrian philosopher who lectured widely whilst on the planet and who demonstrated to the world a system of 'biodynamic agriculture' that could restore infertile areas of the planet to productivity. He is well remembered.

A part of the past life/soul aspect teaching has shown how past lives can be brought forward for speech from absolutely any period of Earth's history or pre-history—no exceptions. That point became crystal clear on 8th March 2010 when one addressed us via Sarah, saying:

> ~ "The world has changed much, both in visual aspect and also the spiritual energy—that is much weaker than when I was here."

We enquired if that would have been in the days of the Egyptian civilization:

> ~ "That was one time that I was here, but I am now talking to you about another time—before the Egyptian time."

He went on to describe a time of fewer humans, with:

> ~ "as many humans as there were animals of one species".

Man was of different shape, smaller stature, longer arms, dark-skinned and less upright, but with intelligence. In response to many questions came many answers. Apart from the raising of young children, there was little difference between the tasks of male and female. People lived in groups of around one hundred, and there were families within each group. Life centred on an extended family system, such that if one family had too many infants, they were cared for by another. They saw life as a gift to be respected—all lived in harmony with themselves and with nature. Wild animals were killed for food only as befitted necessity, respectfully taking care to pacify the animal before despatching. There were no teachers, knowledge was handed down and there was an inner knowing. There was language, there was mind-link and they could share feelings one to another, also with the animals. There were no prayers to any deity, but all were aware of being part of something much greater—a power that helped, to which they gave thanks. Climate was hot through the day—they did not have fire or stone tools. Food was mainly fruit and meat, strips of the latter being heated or dried on dark rocks, arranged to receive sun heat. Water was dipped from a subterranean channel with coconut shells. Our informative friend continued:

~ "We were aware that seeds turned into plants but we were not farmers as such. We were what you would term 'hunter-gatherers'. There were areas of quite dense forest, and within these forests we were able to find food."

And when we asked how they regarded the stars in the night sky:

~ "The stars were thought of as: little holes to let through the spirits of light. It was extremely cold at night, and when we looked up and saw that bright sparkle, it was as if someone was telling us: 'have strength, the warmth will come again.'"

The above descriptive data is consistent with our very early ancestor Australopithecus from around two million years ago—before the development of stone tools and before use of fire. He was from that very cradle of humankind in the African Rift Valley. That was on reflection a most amazing evening!

So we have accounted that past life from prehistory, and we also know of much more recent past lives. What of the intervening period—a few thousand or tens of thousands of years ago? One example from that time is a communication received 28th November 2005 via Sarah:

~ "—When I was farming this Earth, I was able to share with so many the values of what you would now call 'organic farming'—we used only what nature provided, and now that I watch you, I am happy to see that many are BEGINNING to realise that this method of production is by far the best way for the body and the plant."

This one—Ond Kulla (meaning Big Feet)—was an Egyptian head farmer in the days of the Pharaohs, and was one of the Pharaoh's suppliers. Giving back to the soil—manure, vegetable waste and irrigation waters was seen as a 'thanks' to the soil that kept it in condition. They used subsurface channels for irrigation—also there was divining to locate inland sources. Transport was by canal and the drawn sleigh. Crops were fruit trees, maize and various corns. Crops, to suit season, could be grown the year round. Where farming method is concerned, Ond Kulla and his colleagues continue in their endeavours from spirit, putting out good thoughts of guidance for our present time. We asked if he had a message for modern farmers today:

~ "My message is: use your soil wisely. That would mean: do not over-use, and do not put into your soil that which contaminates it."

The message is loud, clear and logical: it is vital that we recognise and respect nature—we are within her ever-evolving system, and if we buck the system, then we place ourselves in jeopardy. This period in antiquity that spans tens of thousands of years has also been a time of massive stone-works and pyramid building; involving advanced and friendly visitors from across the universe. And regarding space travel and the visitors from afar, Nahashiwah was with us again on 3ʳᵈ September 2007. We had on that occasion been discussing space-travel, UFOs and crop circles, and the failure of newspapers to give adequate coverage of these important matters. Nahashiwah had been listening, and commented:

~ "You are like children. You are in need of first education!—Ha! Ha! You do not recognise the signs in the sky!—but in my time it was just accepted and it was wonderful—space travel has always been!"

These matters concerning visitors from other planets, and their artefacts, are quite obviously of enormous significance, and should be neither ignored nor censored. It is therefore appropriate that these matters be dealt with separately in due process and in the detail that they deserve; that will be in later chapters. There is a wealth of information from Salumet and from several other sources that can now be cross-referenced to give a full and meaningful picture; all in due process.

CHAPTER 2

REALITY, REASONING AND RESCUES

There are many in today's world that are not accepting of past lives, reincarnation and soul structure, or prefer to just stay within the framework of materialism. It is understandable in some small measure. The material world, consisting of suns, planets, landscape, trees, plants, animals, the material part of our bodies, brains etc; is plainly and directly evident—no mystery attached. The material world is the space-time creation with a clear space-time rulebook. Mathematics and the laws of science apply—but ONLY within the confines of space-time. The reality of it is comfortable for any who stay within those limits without asking any of those questions worthy of the sentient beings that we are. What questions? Well, for example: How did it all come about? Why are there happenings *not* explained by the rule book? Why is telepathy instantaneous? How was the Great Pyramid of Giza assembled? How were massive rocks transported in ancient times? Why has Earth's 1-Kilogram platinum-iridium weight standard established 122 years ago, lost weight? The answers to such questions, as will become evident later, simply lie beyond the scope of the space-time rulebook.

The reality is that spirit, mind, consciousness and the processes of thought, prayer and telepathy, are all beyond the space-time format—all are exempt from space-time rules. On several occasions, Salumet has made the statement that spirit has always been—of course! Since spirit is *not within* space-time, it is not shackled by time! Time has no dominion over spirit. In our limited material view therefore, it has always been! I had put a question about this to Salumet (25th April 2005). This had followed much discussion amongst Earth's scientists concerning 'singularity' pre-empting a 'big bang' as the basis of a beginning.

Q: "—the singularity would be visualised as a point-without-space-or-time, and of course, the singularity as conceived, was viewed in *physical* terms. But if that singularity were viewed with *spiritual eyes*—that simply *has* no space or time—it might well be seen simply as 'spirit'. So perhaps the scientist's only mistake was to view the idea of 'absence of space and time', with physical eyes instead of spiritual eyes—?"

~ "Yes—you are correct in your thinking—many things that happen upon your planet have been because individuals have seen life through physical eyes rather than seeking the spiritual explanation. For so long individuals could see nothing other than what stood before them, but all that is changing. And after all, remember that spirit has always been, and whatever explanation mankind places before himself, it cannot change the ultimate truth."

So for 'singularity' we should read 'spirit'. And the 'big bang' was in effect a 'big misinterpretation'. I had commented that we have been so intellectual and so physical in our thinking, to which Salumet replied:

~ "Yes. I would say to each one of you, my dear friends: think simply as does the small child. When they look for explanations, it comes from within, and that is where the truth lies—deep within."

The exploring mind might consider two realities—the 'physical' and the 'spiritual'. But they are connected and there cannot be one without the other. Spirit initiates and supports the physical existence. The physical lives gather experience that adds to soul development. And soul is the ever ongoing immortal spiritual existence. So as each Earth life comes to an end that soul aspect returns to experience the joys of reunion in spirit. The sadness left on Earth at departure is matched by joy in spirit. There is no death.

How can we be sure that this is the modus operandi? Are such transitions always flawless? We know of those rare occasions when memory of a previous life is not fully erased, and this can be seen as evidence for the past life existence. Equally, there are rare hiccups in the transition-from-Earth-to-spirit process that can be seen as evidence for the actual return to spirit. Departing spirits sometimes get 'stuck' close to Earth and fail to complete their journey. The reason may be total disbelief in spirit, simple ignorance, a thought fixation, or the powerful attachment of love bonds that will simply not let go. Those thus affected will *think* they continue in Earth life, but something is not quite right. The materiality is not quite so material as it once was. Fortunately, there are workers in spirit who watch out for such hiccups and they are there to help. What can they do? One procedure is to take that spirit along to a séance group and place them in a receptive medium for counselling by the group. Not many groups do this kind of work. The Kingsclere Group does—and apart from being in the first place a service, it can also be seen as instructive. Leslie and Lilian have been our experts in the counselling process, but others also lend a hand at times and can cover as necessary for any absentees. We are on occasions told to: *'Go away!'* or *'Leave me alone!'* Individual cases may be sad while others may have a humorous side. One gentleman, who had died in a pub, and who after a chat, was now moving forward, wanted to know if he could take his pint of beer with him! We had to smile at that. The two dialogues that follow are example rescues (C = counsellor, of which there will be several participating in these examples):

16th August 2010 via Sarah:

~ "I am looking for my needle! I think I put it under the chair, but I can't find it!"

The lady had been working a tapestry and Lilian quickly recognised that this was a 'rescue'.
C: "Does my voice seem at all familiar?"

~ "No, but I hadn't really thought about it. I was only really thinking about my needle!"

This seemed to be the problem—a fixation on the hunt for the needle; but she was willing to talk. Lilian asked if she had thought about what would happen when she died. There was a pert reply:

~ "Yes, I would go to heaven—but I want to finish my tapestry first!"

The conversation continued with Lilian explaining that she had indeed died and it was her job to help her on her way.

~ "Well, I do find it a little strange I must say. Well, let's just suppose you might be right—then I will just hear out what you have to say—and then I will continue to look for my needle!"

The necessity to move forward was explained and she was asked to look to the light ahead.

~ "Well, if I were to draw my curtains back—"

C: "Draw the curtains in your *mind* back and you will see a very bright light—"

~ "I can see the moon—a very bright moon I have to say."

C: "If you continue to look at that light, it might get brighter."

~ "Well, I have to say: the light is getting very, very bright!"

Lilian went on to say that she would eventually see people waiting to receive her. There was a short pause.

~ "Well, I'll be blowed! There's my mother with my needle! Well! And she says: come and get your needle!"

And we all had to laugh as she went forward with problem solved.

2<u>nd</u> April 2012 via Eileen:
C: "Is anyone there? Are you wishing to speak?"

~ "Who are you?"

C: "My name is Sarah."

~ "What do you want?"

C: "I thought you had come to visit and I thought you might like to speak with us."

~ "I don't know what to do, I just don't know. I've just had enough.

C: "Just had enough—"

~ "Yes."

C: "Do you remember what you were doing last?"

~ "Just give—kids—kids—"

C: "Yes, well I think what has happened is, you've moved on to spirit."

~ "No—no—no!"

We tried to explain further and suggested there had been stress with the children.

~ "Yes, I won't have another, I won't. I just want—"

We tried comforting words and encouraged her to look to the light.

~ "I don't understand what you are talking about."

C: "You *will* understand—just look up, don't be afraid. Can you see a light?"

~ "No, all I can see is houses—houses and houses. The children—the children—"

C: "Never mind—don't worry about the houses or the children—"
She became more distressed.

~ "But I am—I *am* worried!"

C: "Can you tell us how old you are?"

~ "I'm twenty-eight."

C: "Tell me what you are worried about."

~ "I can't bear it—I cannot bear it! I swear one day I'll kill 'im—I'll kill 'im."

There seemed to be little progress and several of us tried different approaches.

C: "Could I just ask you: do you have any belief in what happens when you die?"

She declared herself to be Roman Catholic and we suggested that her belief would be that there is a spirit that moves on.

~ "I don't have time for you preachers! I wish you'd leave me alone!"

C: "We're not trying to preach to you. We're just trying to help. How many children have you?"

~ "I've got six."

C: "Six children!"

~ "Yes."

C: "Oh!—Well that's alright—the children are fine, and you are away from your husband now, so he will not harm you anymore."

~ "I don't know where I am."

C: "Well my dear, you have had difficulties and you have become overwrought—and you have died. But you continue obviously. You are spirit, and that has been your belief. And that is reality—you are spirit. You are moving on to the heavenly realms. And if you look ahead, you should become aware of a light, a wonderful light—and we are all here to help you make that crossing—to the light. You will see someone that you know very soon. Who would you like to greet you?"

~ "Well, I hope its Jesus."

C: "Well it could be him. Is there anyone else who's passed on—perhaps a grandparent—anyone else you would like to greet you?

~ "No."

C: "If you look into the light, there will be someone waiting there. It may take a little time, but if you look to the light—"

~ "I won't go unless it's Jesus—I won't, I won't go."

C: "Yes alright, but look to the light—can you see the light now?" She was still very upset.

~ "I thought that might be it."

She expressed concerns about confession—we said not to worry about that now, and that she would be shown how she can be close to her children—watch over them.
C: "Is it lighter now?"

~ "Yes."

C: "That's good, keep looking into the light."

~ "It's drawing me."

C: "That's good. Go with it. Move towards it and you will see someone."

~ "Oh!—Mother of God! Ah! It's beautiful! It's beautiful!

C: "Move into that beautiful light—happy to go now?"

~ "Be—au—ti—ful!"

We really felt for this one—a young Irish mother trying to look after so many children. It was the mother-bond that held her close to Earth, so that she could only see the rows of houses instead of her way forward. But happily she was receptive to a little help and was now on her way.

So the occasional hiccup is a kind of proof of transition—well known to the séance groups that help out. And on occasions, the helpers in spirit come through to have their say. On 16th January 2012, three WW

I soldiers, Peter, Tom and Bill, told us how they had died together-- all so pleased to find that they still lived! Now they help others who succumb in the continuing war zones. That is their calling. Their statements from the dialogue that followed leave much for us to think on:

~ "It's not just physical help they need, it's mental—and so many of those poor lads were killed by our own people, and you know, that sticks to me still—you have to forgive them. They thought they knew what was right—I wish you could see these people when they come over to us; the shock and horror of what they have done to each other! It doesn't matter what side they belong to; the shock and the horror is devastating to them. So, my dears, I would like to ask that you give thoughts for all those people who are still in wars today—they don't know what it's done to their spirit. That's the tragedy; that the spirit itself is damaged, not forever of course, but that is something that has to be worked at. That is what my friends Peter, Tom and I do."

Well said! So much to think on here—how sad to see youth being encouraged to go to war to kill youth! What of the politicians who consider there to be just cause? How can majority support governments in this? What of selfish intent and the ways of suicide bombers? We owe so much to those who help in spirit.

CHAPTER 3

PLANET EARTH:
ESSENTIAL FACTS

In the early days of his teaching, Salumet made the very clear statement that Earth is but one small planet within one small galaxy, where teaching takes place.

~ "We have many 'Earths' in many galaxies, all doing and teaching different things. I do not wish to sound disrespectful—you know that is never my purpose—but this planet is so young. This planet is so very young that souls, who come to inhabit it, come to learn. That is what you must always remember about this Earthly planet."

That is true perspective, to be enlarged upon later, when the timing is right. [And that earlier notion that was so insisted upon by the Holy Catholic Inquisition, that Earth enjoys majestic place at the centre of God's creation, is of course utter nonsense.] During a later meeting Salumet actually gave some indication of the creation sequence:

~ (19th June 2000): "It has been created in the world of spirit before the physical creation. I have told you have I not, that all things are created first in the world of spirit and their counterparts are then brought into the physical existence. So do you see the connection between what you are (as a soul in spirit) and what you are now in the human form? Can you begin to understand there can be no separation from what we call the universal consciousness?—there are many names used.

'Universal consciousness' is one that would seem to be understood by many. Many of your earlier civilizations had much greater spiritual knowledge."

It is true—we have to acknowledge that some, in past times knew more of spirit, could exercise *power of thought* to such a degree that they were able to materialise form—replicate in part—the creation process. This fact will become clearer in due course. Our history books describe the progress, or lack of it, on our planet in entirely material terms and in isolation from other planets—so history books are worthy records but have to be seen as incomplete. It is plainly evident that the Salumet view of human progress embraces the fundamental relationships of Earth to both spirit and to the entire universe, which is of course the much wider view of a true Master. This is made clear in a further teaching:

~ (9ᵗʰ July 2007): "Although many of you feel that life on this planet Earth is harsh at times, let me just remind you my dear friends that you human beings are on an upward curve of consciousness and although that may not seem possible when you study individual problems in your world, on the whole this planet Earth is making good progress spiritually—so I would like you to remember this. Remember my words and it will sustain you in your daily lives. The angelic beings from all other planets are working hard to help humankind and it is a little unfortunate perhaps, that the people of this time have lost that knowledge and consciousness of your ancient peoples. It would be worthwhile my dear friends if you would strive to attain just a little of that consciousness which the ancients had. They, of course, were able to see these Angelic beings but they called them in your mythology 'gods', and although they may have seemed like gods because of their great knowledge and help, they are in fact the Angelic beings which have always been a part of this Earth planet."

So the gods of mythology were actually seen by humans and are not just fanciful tales, but are attentive angels. Their significant place in our history should really be acknowledged as fact!

In response to a relayed question placed concerning the possibility of an evolutionary 'master plan' and how such a plan might relate to the confusing diversity of religions that we have on the planet at this time, Salumet had this to say:

~ (13th June 2005): "Yes. Let me say this to all of you, and especially for your friend who asks the question: always there has been—as he puts it—a master plan. What he must remember is this: that the plan affects, not only your planet, but all those other planets which are in existence. The plan of that great consciousness has always been. But that is not to say it has been worked as it should have been. But when we speak of your Earthly planet, let me say only this to you: on your Planet Earth, there have come to all people, many forms of religion, as he has stated. Mankind upon this planet has been given free will as have many others on many planets. But mankind being in a stage of growth—in a stage of infancy if you like—is still at a point of learning. And although there are many factions who are still so set in their thinking that it has created many problems, there also is a much greater faction who are coming closer together; after all, I think you will know and understand that your religions in this past century have become much more tolerant towards each other."

Well—terrorist extremists falsely usurping religious belief excluded of course. But we have now left behind us nine bloody crusades, the dreadful punishments handed out by the Inquisition to those of differing belief, the killing of ½ million Albigensians and so forth. Religious intolerance is now thankfully much less marked than in those earlier times of such devastating atrocity.

~ "At this moment in time, it would not be appropriate to try to connect all religions, not because it cannot be done, but because it is not part of the plan of unification of which we are going forward to. The time will come when all people upon this Earth, will have greater understanding, not only of each other, but of each religion. But greater still will come the understanding that every religion is focussed to one point. But it cannot be done in an instant. Part of the great plan is that we bring people together by their own free will—by their own workings and understanding of each other. There have been many instances when this *should* have happened. The coming of the one named Jesus, of whom you all know—that was part of the plan to bring people together. There have been many, many instances. But, let me say: within your next 100 years, there will be greater understanding amongst all people in your world. Down will come religious barriers. Down will come the dissatisfaction that people feel because of their individual religions. We are moving forward, my dear friends, to such a time when the people of your world must accept each of their brothers of whom they truly are, not of separate race, not of separate religion, but one brotherhood of man."

Q: "And as you said at the beginning: that fits in place in relation to a wider plan concerning the universe—"

~ "Yes. You cannot segregate this planet with a separate plan. There is a much greater plan in place, and that great plan is moving forward at all times. Therefore, I thank your friend for his question; but may I gently remind him, that as much as he would wish one to come to bring together all people, that is not likely to happen for some great time yet."

In response to a further question, Salumet later expanded on *'has created many problems'* and on the *'master plan'*:

~ (15th August 2005): "There has always been unhappiness amongst humans. There has always been a degree of dissatisfaction with some, which has caused unrest which has led to wars, to man against man, killing, fighting and all of these things that you are well aware of—but of course as time has progressed and weapons have been constructed and become such destructive forces; then of course the unrest and dissatisfaction with fellow men has become greater; because the destruction of fellow men is greater. But there has always been this element of mankind, no matter what religious status, there has always been a minority of peoples who have brought upon themselves and their fellow men much harm and destruction, so you see this is not new. It is something that has constantly happened throughout your time. That is why it is most important that those from our world have gathered in numbers at this time of your evolution so that mankind can recognize the many, what you would call 'injustices' within your world. And until such time as mankind REALIZES, there will always be unrest. But remember my words that this time mankind will not be allowed to become a destructive force upon this planet. Eventually the time will come when mankind must realize that his fellow man is the object of his love and not his hatred. For whatever reason he feels there may be injustice, it cannot be allowed to simmer—and I assure you, my dear friends, that that is our purpose and our plan for this planet."

Well that perhaps places problems and the awful warring into better perspective. And I think it is clear that we now live in times when realization of injustice begins to surface. Salumet then added:

~ "You must always remember these incidents are small incidents in the history of your Earth, and no matter how devastating they may seem to you or to the peoples of this Earth, there is always that much wider picture."

The wider picture prevails and must be considered. It will become clearer as we move on that Earth is not alone—we share with others this arm of the galaxy.

Another question sent in by a friend concerns Earth's dwindling oil stocks, and how many see this as a politically dangerous period of 'transition'. I suggested that Salumet might see this as an exercise for us in looking for new energy sources, and preferably a source less damaging to planet and to health than oil has been:

~ (15th August 2005): "Again you see, mankind on this planet has always tried to claim what the Earth brings as their own, when in fact all of these things are 'on loan' to you. And let me say that the word 'transition' that you used—that is precisely what it is. But the depletion of oil supplies in your world will of course be replaced by other energy. And if you remember quite some time ago, I told you that they would look to the seas of your world for energy. That is something to come. But I understand your question—and yes there will be many who will be unhappy with the situations in your world. And it will cause problems, but to you I say: keep faith in that all of the Earthly laws will continue in the way that they are meant to be."

Well, whether the movement is wave-motion or tidal, seawater is roughly one thousand times denser than air and therefore has that much greater power potential. So, as an energy producer, the sea should be more easily productive than a wind farm and much less messy than oil rigs and tankers. As with all steps forward, that will happen of course when the time is right. Mention has already been made of the biodynamic agriculture of Rudolf Steiner. When the work of this gentleman was first mentioned to Salumet, he had this to say:

~ (25th June 2007) "Yes, names matter not as you know, but of course he would have been influenced in some way—although there is a simple explanation—he has elaborated in his own mind what has been given to him and made use of that information. He would have been influenced as all people on this Earth are influenced in some way: your chemists, your doctors, your scientists—name any of them who create some new ideas, or (what) you THINK is a new idea—"

I had replied: "As you have told us many times", and we all had to laugh at that.

~ "So always my dear friend, when you read these things, or see these *new* inventions; think spiritually, and the answer becomes easy for you to understand. We need to *influence* some human beings to start the process off—it matters not, the steps that are taken. It is the outcome which is important."

So, when the time is right for marine energy schemes, teams will receive 'influence' and the new project—or perhaps we should say: old re-hashed idea—will move forward. In fact, as I write, now six years on, some progress is already under way. France has a 240 MW plant in operation. Russia has a 1.7 MW pilot plant paving the way for a 10,000 MW plant, and has plans for further large tidal units—all leading of course to an *'outcome which is important'*! We are steadily becoming used to the awareness that Earthly progress arises from teamwork rather than individual prowess, whilst of course named individuals still play their significant part in what transpires.

Russia is also a lead country where 'pyramid research' and knowledge of 'pyramid energies' are concerned. Understanding, or re-understanding pyramid technology, will be a major step forward for modern mankind, and it has become clear in recent years that large *ancient* pyramid structures abound all over our planet, some dating back thousands and even tens of thousands of years. Why should this be? There has to be good reason, both for their widespread presence and to explain their sometimes massive construction in ancient times. Professors Golod and Krasnoholovets have in recent years built glass-fibre-and-plastic hollow pyramids up to 44 metres high. Experimental results concerning the energy within include: water failing to freeze at − 40°C and increased crop yield for pyramid-stored seeds. We referred these details to Salumet, and he was quick to confirm results and elaborate for us:

~ (26ᵗʰ June 2006): "What is happening with your Russian friends and their pyramid experiments is not new knowledge, but knowledge that has been regained and is now beginning to be understood—the ancient Egyptians in your world—had much more knowledge of energy and vibration—and space-travel."

We had suggested that the effect on seeds compares with the effect observed for seeds recovered from crop circles:

~ "And I would say to you—your crop circles are indeed related to that same energy. It is an energy not fully understood as yet but I have to say, many are being helped in this field. The energy is—a higher vibration than currently known in your world."

Our teacher spoke of the energy becoming of even higher vibration on rising to the pyramid apex, and then of how it is important for our scientists to recapture this long lost knowledge. It is significant that Professor Krasnoholovets has published a paper: 'The Great Pyramid as an Aether Wind Trapping Site'[9]. I am sure he *correctly* indicates the all-pervading aether as instrumental in producing the pyramid energy. And it is clear that the structures must always have one pair of sides facing East-West, to benefit from Earth's rotation and so gather the energy. Pyramid energy effects that have been observed in the Russian experiments include:

1. Water fails to freeze, even at − 40°C.
2. Razor blades are sharpened (cf. Ultrasound polishing).
3. A vertical column of energy (detected by radar) rising at least 2 Kilometres above the pyramid apex.
4. Plant growth in the vicinity around pyramids is enhanced.
5. Altered resistance to carbon materials.
6. Radioactive materials decay faster.
7. Diamonds get harder.
8. Human aura is brightened.
9. Meditation is enhanced.
10. Foods stay fresh longer.
11. Patient's burns heal faster.
12. Illness, disease and mental conditions are lessened.
13. Nearby plants grow faster in their early phase.
14. Crop yield of pyramid-stored seed is increased 20-100 % (cf. Crop circle wheat seed).

15. Crops grown from stored seed are healthier.
16. Local weather improvement.
17. Too much pyramid energy can cause nausea (cf. Crop circles).
18. Immune systems are enhanced.

Other effects have also been described. The pyramid energy is quite obviously a real phenomenon that can be cross-referenced to information from elsewhere and this is without doubt a very worthy field for further scientific endeavour. There would be huge benefits to be gained from incorporating orientated pyramid designs into or adjacent to hospitals (to facilitate burns recovery) and townships (for various uses and further study).

CHAPTER 4

SCIENTIFIC ENDEAVOUR: AETHER DILEMMA

"And so, implying that the primary body is something else beyond earth, fire, air and water, they gave the highest place a name of its own, AETHER, derived from the fact that it 'runs always' for an eternity..."
- Aristotle

– On the Heavens, Book 1.

The non-scientist may feel uneasy about this chapter, but it is such an important part of our recent history that it must have mention. I promise to keep it brief, and it begins with a synchronicity. I had met Olive just the once—she had travelled 200-miles together with friends Ray and Tricia to sit in with us at our 10th September 2012 meeting. Today, as I write this, she sent an email with a Youtube film. The film depicts a Greg Braden lecture about a hospital in Beijing, China where thought-power is used for healing. It is a remarkable piece of film in which three doctors enhance their therapeutic thought-power with a simple chant that creates the feeling in their patient of already-having-been-healed. During the sequence, an ultrasound image shows a three inch bladder tumour disappearing in less than three minutes. Wonderful! But also during that lecture, reference is made to an article concerning a 1986 experiment apparently proving the existence of the *Aether Wind*. Now, the time tag of the email indicates that Olive sent it within one minute or so of my typing the words *'Aether Wind Trapping Site'* above—that is the synchronicity—and it is not as if *Aether Wind* is a term used in everyday parlance! So I feel that the information that follows *must* be inserted right here, before we move on any further. And thank you Olive!

The famed and much-quoted-to-students (including myself) Michelson-Morley experiment of 1887, was an attempt to detect the aether by looking for a difference in light speed measured in two directions. The results should differ if there is a flow of aether past Earth, so a difference was sought. Several experiments were conducted with very great care, each with negative result. The negative results were seen as strong evidence against the existence of any aetheric medium. This in turn initiated research leading to Einstein's Special Relativity Theory which by its nature obviates any real *need* for aether existence (Special Relativity because it applies to the one special case—General Relativity Theory followed later). BUT, one hundred years on (1986), Ernest W Silvertooth[10, 11], using a novel laser interferometer in which light passage around a circuit is compared for opposing directions, has indeed reported evidence for the long elusive aether; and he takes into account the relation between light velocity and its wavelength. This is represented by the equation $c = v\,\lambda$; where c = velocity, v = frequency, λ = wavelength. So there is now scientific evidence for the aetheric medium. It is understandable if this news is not shouted from the rooftops or is not considered sufficient by institutions and traditional scientists—it turns upside down decades of scientific endeavour! Unthinkable! But *we* know from Salumet's spiritual teaching, from the above pyramid work and from other information to be detailed later that *aether is indeed part of the reality of existence* that cannot and must not ever be overlooked. So this really is a time for the scientific annals to face up to U-turn.

The 'aether', which is sometimes spelled 'ether' like the anaesthetic, just to confuse us! has been given a number of different names over the years, one of which is 'energetic void'—at least, that name recognises the energy that is inherent such that it cannot by any stretch of the imagination be dismissed as 'nothing'. In Plato's *Timaeus*, the aether is described as: *'that which God used in the delineation of the universe'*. Bravo Plato!—a neat statement! A 1930s quote from James Jeans' book 'The Universe Around Us'[12] states re the aether *'—has dropped out of science, not because scientists as a whole have formed a reasoned judgement that no such thing exists, but because they find that they can describe all the phenomena of nature quite perfectly without it.'* Well, that's it—it just dropped out, and following that, scientific endeavour unfortunately lost its way. In his other 1930s book 'The Mysterious Universe' [13], Jeans muses on how it is possible for mathematicians to produce from pure thought, disconnected from rationalism, *an independent world created out of pure intelligence*. Perhaps we should see this as what has happened—a pseudo-world constructed out of purely physical intelligence. But that academic pseudo-world can now be seen as the fiction that it is. Much physical intelligence has certainly been applied, but sadly, in isolation from that other stark reality for which there are now volumes of accumulating data.

We have quite extensive files concerning Salumet's related statements. I decided, at our meeting of 24th September 2012, to try to recap on what has been said and to add a little more clarity if possible:

Q : "Spirit has always been"—

~ "Yes."

Q: "Mind is part of spirit, and I think we appreciate that spirit has a number of parts"—

~ "Yes."

Spirit of course has its distinct realms, with souls and beings within those realms.

Q: "And there is what we call 'energetic void', which extends throughout the universe"—

~ "Yes."

Q: "I am wondering if that has always been or if that is part of creation?"

~ "It is part of creation, but it has the ability to change. So yes, it has always been."

So it *is* part of creation, but it has also always existed albeit in different form.

Q: "And I imagine spirit *has* to be in association *with* the energetic void?"

~ "Yes, you cannot separate the two."

Q: "Going on from there—if the energetic void is part of evolution, then I imagine that it continues to be created and is in pace, in a way, with the expanding universe?"

~ "Yes, as I have said, it is able to change. When all belongs to creation, we do not speak of static energy—you cannot separate the two, although your scientists would say: that is not quite correct—as I am sure you are aware."

"Yes, it seems a very logical notion that the energetic void is part of creation and ongoing."

~ "Yes, and the word 'void' is slightly misleading I feel. What is void?"

"I think it simply means that material atoms are missing from it."

~ "Yes, but it is still part of all creation. You cannot dismiss this in any way."

"And spirit and mind"—

~ "Mind belongs to spirit, yes"—

"Mind belongs to spirit and in a sense would seem to be conveyed by this badly named void."

Salumet's reply was that there are many ways to describe it, whilst at the same time he made it clear that it would be unproductive to expound further at this stage. I thanked him for clarifying thus far. Jan referred to consciousness as a part of spirit, which of course is certainly not void.

~ "All is energy, whether you give it a name or not."

I added: "Well the old-fashioned term was to call it 'aether', which is perhaps a better word."

~ "Yes, I would agree. I would prefer to use that word. It is basically a spiritual energy—yes, and all is part of creation—you cannot separate it."

Our teacher was duly thanked for his helpful clarifications.

Newtonian physics has been a comfortable and accurate way to evaluate the hardware of space-time—planets, moons, suns, falling apples etc—the laws accounted in Isaac Newton's 'Principia' have properly described all such motion for 300 years. But that *non*-material part of this universe has been ignored, and alas, through much of the 20th century, has been seriously regarded as empty space—nothing. And, as a young student of the 1950s, I was ticked off by a lecturer for daring to think otherwise! He was wrong, and there must now be a new paradigm. The 'nothing' view of the space between the stars has been around for too long. Despite many proofs and publications, noble works by individuals and small groups—the realities of spirit, spirit communication, telepathy, synchronistic events, teaching from Angelic Realms, visions witnessed by huge crowds and the proven value of prayer—these have all been essentially shunned by learned institutions, well-funded scientific bodies and news media. This non-acceptance has become a stumbling block to progress and has to go.

Here is a brain-teaser that developed from that daring thought I had as a young student: It is scientifically accepted that 'sound' is a *compression wave*, generated from a vibrating source, a guitar string for example. The sound travels in air at fixed speed and exerts a measurable pressure on the surface that it strikes—all very physical and understandable. It is logical (and against conventional scientific thinking) to suppose that 'light', on a much finer scale, is a similarly generated compression wave that travels in the *aether* medium. Like sound, it travels at fixed speed, is generated by a vibrating (atomic) source, and exerts a very small but measurable pressure (radiation pressure) on striking a surface. So light appears to have a modicum of physical character. BUT, unlike sound, the difference is that light can travel the universal distance to reach us from the far galaxies. I would maintain that it requires aether as its carrier in order to do so; just as sound relies on air as *its* carrier. What gives light that trace of physical character? I would say: compression—it really is a trace, yet real enough to create the observed radiation pressure. I would go further and suggest that the compression within the light wave is a tiny step towards creating matter from the aether. [I know that James Clerk Maxwell has described the light wave in electromagnetic terms—electric and magnetic vectors will be the effect of movement within the waveform; also a part of its character.] As support for this notion I quote Zabdiel, a knowledgeable spirit speaking through the Rev. G Vale Owen in 1913[14]:

~ "If you were to endeavour to build up a machine for the manufacture of aether and the conversion of it into matter, you would find no substance to your hand on earth of sufficient sublimity to hold the aether, which is of a force greater and more terrific than any force which is imprisoned within what you understand as matter."

So this spiritual source of 100 years ago acknowledges two principles: (1) that of aether converting to matter, and (2) that of aether as a very powerful energy. Our nuclear bombs have worked backwards to convert matter into a vast amount of energy, but in-keeping with the statement of Zabdiel, we have of course no way of reversing that to a process of creation. Einstein's equation $E = mc^2$, reading left to right as is the convention, is a scientific statement of Zabdiel's described conversion, but we have only ever succeeded in using Einstein's equation backwards. And in support of Zabdiel's description—try to imagine a machine sufficiently robust to squeeze a nuclear detonation back into its original bomb-size!

The essential difference between light and thought would appear to be light's physical character. It originates from a physical vibration that generates the compression wave in the aether. This compression wave must be seen as physical because it has finite velocity and measurable radiation pressure. Thought however, does not arise from physical source (mind is not physical). Therefore it does not have to comply with any physical rules. It is beyond space-time, ignores distance and its passage is instantaneous.

So is this the sum total of evidence for light as a compression wave in the aether? No, there is one further observation to mention. The pitch, or frequency, of a vehicle siren is higher on approach than when receding. The difference in the sound heard, is known as *Doppler shift* after Christian Doppler's work of 1842. Light travelling to us from across the universe also displays Doppler shift, seen as a colour change. The extent of shift is measured by reference to absorption spectra bands generated by elements at the galactic source. The bands appear as dark lines in different positions when seen against the light spectra of distant galaxies—according to speed of recession of the galaxy. The greater the speed of recession the further the bands move towards the red end of the spectrum. Hence, this phenomenon has been termed 'red shift'. So the 'Doppler shift' of the compression wave 'sound' is equivalent to the 'red shift' of the light wave. And the pattern of red shifts for variously distanced galaxies is also a part of the evidence for universe expansion.

This matter was now discussed further with Salumet, and it is really a continuation of that 25th April 2005 discussion that took place seven years earlier and has been reported above. I referred to the essential statement *spirit has always been*, with the space-time creation then following. The material world of space-time has its space dimension of course whereas spirit does not. So scientists, thinking strictly in *material* terms, could only view spirit as a point source. This had spawned the notion of a 'big bang' issuing from a 'singularity' source—an impossible and magical delusion that had nevertheless received wild publicity and the earnest attention of mathematicians at the time! Salumet began:

> ~ (16th January 2012): "Let me say this: you say spirit has no space—no material space. Spirit has no space—but ALL of space!"

"Yes!" And we all laughed heartily at the thought juxtaposition.

> ~ "Yes! Let us clarify—a simple point, but a point that is neglected by your scientists in the most part. Their knowledge is gaining ground at a tremendous rate—but they still have to find within themselves—spirit."

"But while spirit has no space as such, it nevertheless—I take your point—it is extensive throughout all."

> ~ "It is everywhere!"

"This is a difficult fact for us to get our brains around!"
Salumet had replied that we cannot understand *all* whilst we remain physical beings. Jan and I had then exchanged thoughts on big bang, expanding universe and red shift. Our teacher responded with:

> ~ "I was about to say: you can give names to anything at all within the scientific world. I will repeat what I have said on a few occasions: energy is never static."

"It is transmutable."

~ "Yes, of course—so I would like to simplify, as the dear lady says—energy is all around, in the same way as spirit is nowhere but everywhere. Energy cannot be static. It is transmutable—can travel across many universes as quite a natural happening. Your scientists complicate matters by their theories. Would you agree?"

"I would agree; and I was going to put the question if I may: would you feel comfortable with the idea of a 'steady state universe', as opposed to an 'expanding universe'?"

~ "You cannot be comfortable with a steady state universe—no. Energy is ever changing—energy cannot stay still. But I know where your question is going, and I understand how your scientists and your people of knowledge feel; but basically, a lot of the time these people do not believe in spirit—their outlooks and their views are coloured by this."

Jan suggested that there is an element in this of egos competing to write the next paper.

~ "I understand your view, but they are after all, people who are only seeking what I call 'the truth'. Therefore, do not be too harsh on them. They are trying to find out, but they fetter themselves by their own views."

"There is a great need to take on board the values of spirit and place those values together with scientific thinking. I think that is a way to put it."

~ "Yes—only in that way will they arrive at the true conclusion. But you have to give credit to them for the work that they are trying to do."

Exactly right!—and but for those boffins who beaver away in laboratories we would have no knowledge of equations, quantities, recession of galaxies and such, to fuel discussions with our teacher. The growth of knowledge has to begin somewhere, and there has to be respect for the various avenues of endeavour.

It was later in the year that there came the opportunity to discuss the natures of light waves and thought waves in the aether:

~ (30th July 2012): "Yes my friend, you have differentiated between what you call 'waves'. I like to use the word 'energies'. Of course I have always taught you that THOUGHT is the most powerful thing that you can ever possess and yes, THOUGHT belongs to spirit. It has no weight, it is pure energy—it belongs to the energy of the whole of Creation. That is why THOUGHT can travel throughout many universes in an instant—even more quickly than an instant!—I have to use physical words for explanation. Yes, I understand your comparisons—"

"Well it helps me to understand, by seeing the continuum as having two distinctive types of wave that can travel through it."

~ "Yes, because that is your way of thinking and I would say to all of you within this room: you each must find your own way of discovery of truth. I could put words into your mouth, but that is not what I wish to do."

"And I appreciate that any movement within the continuum is energy."

~ "Yes, it is all energy and that is being recognised. But yes, THOUGHT is a much different process."

"And yet it would seem to be in the same medium (as light)—"

~ "It is all part of the same energy, but it is much finer, much more refined. That is the simplest way that I can put it to you. But you must, each of you, find what sits comfortably with you and the way to do that I reiterate, is to go within, to find that energy of THOUGHT within; that takes you throughout all of Creation, where you become part of Creation. That should be your goal, where all things are part of each other."

"Yes, that is a thought that has become much stronger with me in recent years."

~ "That is what we are trying to achieve for you all."

Sarah picked up on *thought can travel throughout many universes* and referred to a radio programme in which the question came up: 'where does one universe end and another begin'? I had suggested: perhaps they are coincident?

~ "Yes, and density of energies—you are moving into an area that would be difficult to explain to you at this time. But if we speak of 'many universes', it is all gathered within the one energy, as I have just spoken of. But energy can be transmuted, and we have also spoken about this at times, which offers some explanation also."

It was suggested that they are all coincident but of different densities.

~ "There are many energy waves that mankind has yet to discover. There is a continuance of discovery ahead for your scientists—energy waves they have not as yet discovered."

Sarah inquired if this would be in the nature of more *re*-discovery for mankind:

~ "No, there are energies yet to be discovered, but that is something to come."

So we stand at the very brink of fresh discovery—new uncharted waters. Recognising that 'Akasha' is a Sanskrit word meaning 'aether' that may be abbreviated to 'A-field', the following quotations are highly relevant to this discussion:

'—the A-field links things and events in the universe at staggering speeds—a billion times the velocity of light.'
ERVIN LASZLO, *SCIENCE AND THE AKASHIC FIELD*[15]

'The rediscovery of the A-field will also change our world itself. When people realize that the age-old intuition that space does not separate things but links them has a bona fide scientific explanation, the genius for innovation inherent in modern civilization will find ways to make practical use of it.'
ERVIN LASZLO, *SCIENCE AND THE AKASHIC FIELD*[15]

All this leaves us with much to think on. Although spirit is everywhere, it has no space dimension because space is simply not a parameter of spirit; just as thought has no weight because weight is not a parameter of thought—yet thought is tangible and can produce great artwork. We shall see later, illustration of how thought can reach out across the universe(s) *at staggering speeds*, but it is of course always weightless. There is reason to suppose that the energy of the aether is everywhere and enormous. Its energy is not immediately apparent, so perhaps it should be seen more as a 'potential' energy; at least, potential in so far as we Earth dwellers are concerned. Salumet has indicated that aether *is* part of the creation, but already existed in some other form prior to creation. Putting together all information available thus far, I think I see aether (1) as a precursor to space-time creation, (2) as a necessary part of the ongoing universe that increases with universe expansion, (3) as a medium necessary for light-transmission at fixed speed (4) as a medium for instantaneous thought transmission and (5) as a medium that powers pyramids when they sweep through it. And as stated, it cannot be separated from spirit. It also seems fitting deduction that if, as stated earlier, aether and mind are inseparable, and mind belongs to spirit, then the 'power of thought' comes from that enormous potential known to be available within the aether. These things do not appear to be acceptable as part of mainstream science— yet scientists hypothesise about what is termed 'dark matter'. This I find most interesting! It is no secret that there is theoretical reason for supposing, that by far the greater proportion of matter in the universe remains unaccounted for by its galaxies and various heavenly bodies. And the presence of an 'invisible dark matter' is hypothesised as a vehicle necessary to make sense of further progressive reason. We must say just a little more on this important development.

In astrophysics, the more recent literature refers to two universe components: 'dark matter' and 'dark energy', as having become the central issues in modern cosmology; also to the acknowledgement that more remains unknown than *is* known. It follows from Einstein's $E = mc^2$ that energy always exhibits relativistic mass. One line of reasoning linked to universe expansion indicates roughly 70 % as 'dark energy' and 25 % 'dark matter', leaving only 5 % as the visible galaxies. A version of Einstein's gravity theory involving a 'cosmological constant' leads to the prediction that 'empty space can possess its own energy and this will not become diluted as the universe expands'. As more space is generated, more energy-within-space will appear. So, going beyond 'general relativity', these are some of the current constructs. 'Dark energy' has also been described as a dynamic energy fluid or field that fills all space, while 'dark matter' has been described as necessary for holding the universe together. It is my feeling that those who are exploring such concepts are doing a grand job and are now homing in towards a much fuller awareness of aether and its place in creation.

So what of all that light from all those galaxies, criss-crossing the heavens—carrying its acknowledged *radiation pressure*, bestowing that tiny modicum of physicality to all that light energy? There is just so much light and so much aether! And so much to equate to relativistic mass! So when our science finally acknowledges in full detail the energetic aether, with its light-activated attributes, perhaps the prior notion of 'invisible dark matter' will join the pile of discarded yesterday's hypotheses. And it will be seen that the aether with its so many intrinsic properties had just been overlooked. But it is evident that, a stage seems to have been reached, of realising the rather large anomaly in the old way of thinking that is now to be corrected. Wonderful! And I have refrained from pushing my luck by placing the subject of dark matter before Salumet!

On 5th November 2012, I again referred to our discussion on light, indicating that, with further thought, it is easy to accept that light is physical because of its measurable radiation pressure:

~ "Yes, of course; I am pleased that you have understood my reply. I know sometimes what I say to you, sits a little uncomfortably with some of you, but I endeavour to bring you truth."

Well that endorses 'light's physicality', even if it sometimes takes a little while for the penny to drop—of light's physical character there remains no doubt. There is just one more item to mention before we leave the subject of 'scientific endeavour'. In chapter 2, we spoke of the creation—we spoke of a 'big bang' emerging from a 'singularity', and how that theory came to be; without pointing out the absurdity of such a notion. It is obvious and generally accepted that the universe expands from all-points-within-itself and not from one singularity point. Universe expansion compares with yeast-activated baker's dough. Spirit in the universe is like yeast in the dough mix—it exists throughout so that expansion happens everywhere. This is the observed pattern, and this pattern is consistent with Salumet's statement:

~ (19th June 2000) "It (the Earth) has been created in the world of spirit before the physical creation. I have told you have I not, that ALL THINGS are created first in the world of spirit and their counterparts are then brought into the physical existence."

The stepwise modus operandi is thus clearly stated. So there was never any big bang and no singularity start-point. The physical creation is an ever ongoing process that emanates from spirit; spirit having no geographic parameter, yet is everywhere—still unnoticed by many mainstream scientists, but that is changing.

CHAPTER 5

CHILDREN OF
THE COSMOS

A question had been placed to Salumet following our first three years; concerning hopes for the future of humanity. His answer to that question took us all by surprise:

~ (14th July 1997): "Why should you confine your hopes, your wishes, to the population of this planet? My wish for you would be, that you could become more aware, more universally aware, more cosmically aware, rather than stay in the confines of Earthly population—I want you my dear friends to be *children of the cosmos*, because that is what you are. I would wish that you can grow enough whilst we are together, to realise that what you are, and what you have been, is spirit which has been confined to one planet in this lifetime. We have spoken much about this, but now the time is coming, when all of your population, all peoples, no matter what colour, what race, what religion; all will come to the realisation, that we belong to the much wider scheme of life, of living, of love, of that eternal energy to which we all belong."

This is a definitive statement. We have all become so familiar with, and accountable to, the dictate of national bodies, governments, religions, commerce and so forth; but it is now pointed out that we are free to reach beyond those immediate supposed confines. There is just so much more to life than meeting the exigencies of one single planet. The creation is vast, and that much wider picture beckons. We are indeed—CHILDREN OF THE COSMOS—and our minds have the capacity to reach out far beyond—far beyond this one cherished potty little planet with its many foibles, to which we nevertheless owe so much. It has been the birth cradle of our species, but we must now see that this dear home is but one speck within a much wider scheme of creation—and we shall in due process be guided in the seeking of truly limitless horizons.

It happened on 4th October 2004. Firstly, a Chinese lady speaking via Sue said that one would be coming via Paul—one of those surprises again; because Paul had thus far been little used as medium. The voice via Paul faltered at first, as the visitor struggled to articulate longer and meaningful sentences. But then, with necessary adjustments made, there had followed the explanation delivered with excellent clarity:

~ "I think it best to say: I am not from this place. I come from another— PLANET—I think that's the word. I am testing the water, you might say—for future exchanges—then we can teach each other things. At first we are meant to get to know each other."

Thus began a series of visits, all via Paul, the chosen medium for this visitor. We soon got to know and to dearly love this one named 'Bonniol'—named after a star in his own part of the heavens. On 'Aerah', Bonniol's home planet, he is supported by a séance team of sixty or so individuals who meet in his house, and his group communicates with ten other planets of this universe. By our standards, his people are both spiritually as well as technologically well in advance of Earth. An important realisation for us is that, with due preparation, minds may link across the universe in this way, and this, we understand, to be standard practise for advanced extraterrestrial sentient beings—but:

What about that scientific incongruity known here on Earth as the 'Fermi Paradox'? Our scientists have correctly postulated there to be many millions of habitable planets in this universe. And equations have been devised to estimate the number of advanced civilisations scattered throughout—the Drake Equation being prominent. An update to Frank Drake's equation by Carl Sagan and colleagues in 1979 suggests up to one million advanced civilisations! But the US organisation SETI—Search for Extraterrestrial Intelligence—has sent out radio signals over a period of 50-years with not one single reply. It was Enrico Fermi who had commented that if all those ET-intelligences are out there, then where are they? Good question! This apparent absence of

ET-civilisations set against their calculated huge incidence, became known as the 'Fermi Paradox'. The reason for this much-thought-about paradox is now crystal clear—advanced civilisations do not use—would not dream of using—radio dishes for interplanetary dialogue! Mind-link communication is in so many ways far, far superior—this for the reasons shortly to be listed. It is perhaps fitting to quote a comment from our dear friend Bonniol at this point:

~ (29th March 2010): "Your technology can bring about much, but at some point you will understand that the mind is always—always—I would always encourage them (scientists) to use their minds in less mechanical ways, and in more spiritual ways."

Many questions arise concerning the Bonniol communications— what of modus operandi, why no apparent time delays in transmission, and surely—surely language differences must present an insurmountable barrier? We have received clear explanations to these initial questions, also to a number of further queries that have naturally followed—log-ical clarifications from both Salumet and Bonniol. The full Bonniol story, in which the first sixty dialogues are detailed, is set out in our book 'The Chronicles of Aerah'[16], published in 2009. The accounts have been described by some as breath-taking, and the concluding chap-ter describes a most incredible cosmic party, arranged from spirit, and attended by beings from several universes. It was a party during which each of us was 'overshadowed' by a different sentient being and then each asked to describe our feelings. The somewhat bewildering descriptions were then substantially verified by he who organised the event. On reflection, it might possibly be seen as an intergalactic ver-sion of the party game 'consequences' yielding equally bizarre results! The following sketches were made immediately after the cosmic gath-ering, and give some idea of the variety of existing sentient life forms that were indicated by this amazing event:

I would draw attention to the life form having the appearance of a 'mushroom with halo'—it is far from being just a vegetable! Physically they grow in a ring with similarity of form to our meadow mushrooms but they have highly developed communication skills and are expert in mind travel; and with Bonniol's help, we have actually had conver-sation with them! They linked with and travelled with Bonniol during one of his visits, and Bonniol spoke for them. He articulated:

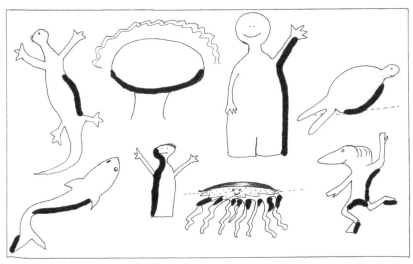

Sentient life forms sensed during séance by overshadowed sitters.

~ (22 August 2005): "They sleep, and during their dream-states, they are able to venture into the spirit realms and journey into many different realms of existence. And when they are not dreaming, they are able to contemplate from their own physical standpoint, the different spiritual realms. There are so many realms, so many worlds within worlds, that to have a fixed place to return to can be very useful as a focal point."

Returning to the occasion of the party, Sarah's daughter Emily, who spends much of her time in Australia, had not experienced many of our meetings. She knew nothing of the 'mushroom people'; and when Emily began to speak of a tree-like feeling and: "My legs feel like they are just one", our party organiser quickly interposed:

~ "Dear one, I believe you were not at this group when we had a visitation from one who came from a planet where the bodies were (shaped as) 'mushrooms'. You have indeed a 'mushroom' of that planet."

And there followed whoops of delight at our realisation that these dear friends from 3-years earlier were now here at the party! That was such a treat! As to myself, I equate to the running figure with the long nose—I had a feeling of great strength, I could move fast and had

particular awareness of three fingers and thumb being in effect weld-
ed together with the little finger remaining free. I can certainly vouch
for the feeling of that particular being's format. Each of us experienced
powerful impressions that were discussed and confirmed. We had experienced a multi-universe cosmic party in which, by means of overshad-
owing, the morphology of other beings was unmistakably conveyed!

The exchanges with Bonniol and his Planet Aerah team were highly
detailed, containing much information. What now follows is a list of
clarifying facts that emerge from all the Bonniol transmissions:

> The list presents highly significant data concerning aether, ET-
> communication, other planetary ways and religious belief. They derive
> from or have been confirmed by the Bonniol conversations. Many
> revelations were, and still are, considered to be of such magnitude
> to have amply justified presentation in their full ET-conversational
> context. That is the format of the above-named book—a Star Trek style
> but *in every detail* NON-fiction adventure—strictly factual dialogues
> that reveal TRUTH OF EXISTENCE. And the reader can see exactly
> how everything came about—an adventure and at the same time an
> accurate historic presentation. There are also of course explanations
> where relevant and helpful elaboration from Salumet—all wonderfully
> helpful and reassuring. We know there are those however, who
> would still welcome a concise list of the main items of scientific or
> philosophical merit that have arisen. The list that follows has therefore
> been compiled and made known since publication of the book:

- Mind/spirit/consciousness are all external to space-time, so
  that mind-link conversations are in no way compromised by
  physical distance—are instantaneous (as with telepathy, prayer
  etc). But brain is of course physical and belongs to the physical
  space-time creation.
- Within space-time nothing travels faster than light speed—186,282
  miles per second (in vacuum), usually denoted as 'c'. Spirit is a
  domain that *has* no space, so that minds, wherever located in
  the *physical universe*, can simply link. Mind ignores the physical
  distance.
- Mind-link can operate at any *physical* distance, even beyond
  the observable universe. Physical distance is simply irrelevant
  to mind connections.

- Brain is a biological computer and can download thought* or the-thought-behind-words to *its* known language, so that translation is taken care of in mind-linked conversations as an entirely automatic process. Hence, there are no language barriers.
- Crop circles are attempted communication from beings having UFOs in our space sector. But they are at the same time much more than just that—they are a conditioning and a device to encourage us into raised awareness. The crop circle designs are made by beneficent ET beings.
- UFOs can travel faster when in dematerialised format and are then not susceptible to momentum change or 'g forces'—our conventional craft *are* of course susceptible to g forces, which is a limiting factor in the way they manoeuvre.
- 'Traversable wormholes' are quite numerous midst the galaxies and they periodically switch direction. By inference, it is likely they are a balancing mechanism between universe regions that convey an (undefined) flux or energy.
- Physical spacecraft travelling wormholes will travel at huge speed. It is inferred that they would not exceed 'c' locally but would appear to greatly exceed 'c' relative to wormhole exterior.
- Meditational mind-link is a much favoured method of communicating used by other physical beings inhabiting this universe. It clearly obviates both language and physical travel difficulties, and once minds are linked dialogue is instantaneous or virtually so.
- 'Materialisations' are possible by means of developed mind power; to the extent that the light industry of a planet can be replaced by materialisation procedures; also houses can be group-mind created or erected. This is the method of 'house-building' used on Aerah. The advantages of evolving to advanced spirituality with associated mind-power immediately become apparent!
- It is our understanding that 'teleportation' of objects between planets is a real possibility but this has yet to be demonstrated

---

* Before the computer age, Nicola Tesla had made the statement: *My brain is only a receiver. In the universe there is a core from which we obtain knowledge.* He is one from our past who was aware of how brain can download from elsewhere.

so far as our group is concerned. Attempts to teleport an object from Aerah during séance have been made and swirling colour effects noted by sitters, but no permanent solid object has as yet resulted.

- There is evidence on our planet that beings have teleported 'themselves' here in past times, and have made themselves known to humans.
- A pyramid-shaped building with one pair of sides aligned to face planetary rotation contains energies that can be utilised in a number of very useful ways. An aligned pyramid may be seen as an energy collector or generator.
- We understand that the element 'carbon' is a vital regenerative element and is common to all planets in this universe that have life as we would recognize it.
- Earth has been visited by spiritually advanced sentient beings from elsewhere at various times in our past and there is much evidence that remains from their visits. Such evidence includes massive stonework, built for good purpose that has been moved and assembled using non-Earthly methods. It is understandable that these feats cannot be matched by our technology that we have today. And recent radio-carbon dating provides proof that some such works occurred tens of thousands of years ago.
- There are many forms of energy that are available for utilisation by spiritually aware civilisations, including an interesting one, a part of which is evident as 'plant aura'. This particular plant-derived energy is utilised extensively on Aerah, providing virtually all her energy needs. There are reasons why it would be impossible to harness this energy in the absence of advanced spirituality. (Plant aura can be observed quite well with raised consciousness, and may also be viewed with a perfect clarity by means of Kirlian photography, by humans in normal conscious mode.)
- Following sufficient mind/spirit development it is possible to communicate with babes before birth and with relatives long after death—again, standard practice on Aerah.
- Reincarnation from planetary spirit realms is the general pattern of existence extending throughout the entire universe. (It will be seen later that we have actually had dialogue with beings who are now within the spirit realms of other planets.)

- Spirit interacts with the space-time creation in such a way that, as the spirituality of a planet <u>in</u>creases, its matter-density <u>de</u>creases. This means that, through the lengthy passage of time, everyone and everything slowly becomes lighter.** This is a universal law, as yet not acknowledged by Earthly science. As might be expected for a spiritually advanced planet, conditions on Aerah are less dense than here, such that Aerans are able, with due care, to leap into quite deep ravines and land without mishap.
- There are higher beings—angels, guides and teachers that help other planetary cultures in their way forward, very similar to the situation here on Earth.
- Our continued advance in science/technology MUST go hand-in-hand with mind/spirit development, or it will be a short-lived development. It follows that the vast majority of other cultures having wonderfully advanced technologies and abilities, know 'love' and it would be most inappropriate to place them in a to-be-feared category.
- There is a universal spirituality, known and understood by advanced cultures throughout the cosmos that is beyond any individual religion of a single planet. It is inferred that a multiplicity of religions are at best 'stepping stones' towards this ideal status.
- All planetary cultures of our knowledge recognise the one 'Creative Principle' or 'Creative Force', known to many here on Earth as 'God'.

It suddenly became clear to us during the Planet Aerah exchanges that all members of Bonniol's team had full awareness of the proceedings. Some of us accordingly began to get that goldfish-in-a-bowl feeling!—the feeling of being observed by many of higher intelligence. A further factor that has featured in the exchanges is 'clairvoyance', and this at times ran concurrently with dialogue. Jan and Richard, I would describe as strongly receptive in this respect, each receiving images of Aeran terrain that they were able to describe—even compare

---

**It is reported (2011) that Earth's 1 Kg platinum-iridium standard of weight kept at Sevres, France, has through the course of 122 years, unaccountably lost 50 micrograms. This is a fact having no conventional scientific explanation. But the reason for the weight loss is given above.

impressions between themselves during the séance session. There have also been occasions when, during the ongoing dialogue with Bonniol, Jan received accompanying 'mind pictures' and additional information from the Aeran team (not from Bonniol), leading to periods of casual cross-talk. Hence, there is evidence that the thought-behind-words can carry with it rather more than just plain speech. There are many other ways in which *advanced* beings may study another planet. During one of our meetings, a sample from Paul's memory banks was downloaded by Bonniol to facilitate further study by our friends whilst back home on Aerah! This would lessen the number of questions necessary during séance and could of course, regrettably, lead to less frequent visits.

CHAPTER 6

PLANET GLONG

Through the summer of 2009, our meetings were blessed with further wonderful visits from Salumet and of course others, but it was now nearly a year since Bonniol's last. We were enjoying the warmth of August evenings. This particular evening began with a chat with a 'ferryman' who took pleasure in safely escorting to spirit those departing Earthly lives. He explained that he had been attracted by the bright spiritual light of our meeting house. It may have been especially bright this evening, although only five were present this time. Next, one arrived via Sarah who declared:

~ (10ᵗʰ August 2009): "I am feeling most peculiar—I do not feel that this body is quite right for me—but I have been asked to let you know that we are hoping to bring to you—another one of our planets tonight. We have had communication from one that has already visited this group; and they told us that you are most interested in other beings."

Well, that might well be described as a gross understatement! A few questions and answers and our communicator was saying:

~ "This will be new—but no, it will not be Bonniol. But we are hoping that we will be able to bring one who is quite—"

And the rest faded out in a progressive distortion, perhaps due to adjustments being made. There followed a pause of 1½ minutes with heavy sounds of exhalation as another took over. The new voice was both strong and eloquent:

~ "It is my pleasure to come to see you." But then this was quickly followed by: "It is very hot here! I think your planet is much hotter than ours—and the air much thinner. I am feeling very stretched upwards—but I feel if I can just adjust a little—"

There are ways of helping and we encouraged our guest to take his time, while Lilian said:

"I am just going to put my hand on the lady's back."

This always seems to help where energies are in need of balance, and after a few deep breaths:

~ "That is much better!—Thank you! Thank you! I was beginning to feel I would be stretched out of all recognition. Yes, that is much more comfortable."

We then placed questions to which answers readily came:

~ "I have come from a planet known by your friend Bonniol, and he has asked me to make contact with you, because he has not yet been able to come back to you, and he wishes for the interest to remain vivid, so that is why I have come."

Q: "It is absolutely fascinating that you can travel in this way—so you also have exchanged with Bonniol?"

~ "We have much contact with the planet you call Aerah."

"Wonderful!"

~ "And, we are quite similar to those beings, but we do not visit in person, but just through thought."

Q: "Is it possible to give us a name for your planet and yourselves?"

~ "I can, indeed, give you the name of our planet—our planet, which is much smaller than Planet Aerah—is called 'Planet Glong.'"

Q: "Glom?" In answer to which, the name was repeated with exaggerated emphasis:

~ "Gerlong!—Glong means 'small but important' and the reason why we have the 'important' part is because we are what you might call the central nervous system of many even smaller planets that surround us. We are used as a base for these small planets, who, in turn, receive information, like an echo. No sooner has their question or their need been received by us than they receive the reply. It is as if these planets were antennae from our planet. They are part of our planet, but they are not attached. There is very much communication with all these planets, and we feel as one with them, but we do not visit them and they do not visit us, but we know each other intimately."

Now this was becoming strange but really fascinating.

~ "We have one, as you might call it, 'Mind', which is separated by these separate planets. When the information is needed, it is as if it were their own mind working alone. Their mind comes to us and is sent back again."

Well, this takes us well beyond previous imaginings of mind work. We could not help but wonder if this new friend was backed by a support team as are the Bonniol visits:

~ "There are many of us who are 'as one'. We do not have any who are greater or lesser than another. We are all of the same. We do not use our physical bodies to promote any sign of greatness, but the mind works together. We have individual names, but the minds are joined, so if you wish to look at each individual, you can do so, but, if you wish to use the mind of one, you will be using the mind of all."

So in effect, a plenteous support team is a permanent fixture! We inquired after this new friend's name, but to their way of thinking, this seemed to be an irrelevance:

~ "You can have my name, if you wish, but , if ever you are to contact us again, you will need only to mention the name Glong, because we are all one—so if you are speaking to one you are speaking to all."

We acknowledged understanding, but these are deeper details as to the nature of mind than were ever dreamt of in Earthly philosophy!

~ "So, I cannot say that there are not individuals. There are 'beings', but not as you know them, not as you have here; where the mind can be blended with another, but they do not work totally in harmony with one another. This is something that we have learnt to do—to be a complete being of many parts."

We, for clarification, asked if they have separate physical bodies:

~ "Yes, we do. The beings are there, but the mind-thought process is as one."

So, all physical beings are united by the sharing of one single mind. Now is this something that has evolved over a lengthy period, and is there memory of an earlier period of non-compliance?

~ "The ones who are on the even smaller planets are the ones who are working towards this united mind process—they are the ones who have not quite achieved what we have on our planet. I believe this is something that has evolved over a very long period. I have never known any difference, and, as far back as I have word no one else has ever known any difference, so I can only assume that the process has taken a very long time."

Paul suggested: "With all those minds in harmony, I imagine you would be able to utilise that mind-power to tremendous effect."

~ "We indeed do, but we can only help those who wish to be helped, and, on our planet, we have no need to change much, because we work so well in harmony with one another. So, the use of our single-mind thought is put to best effect helping those small planets that surround us, and in time, we hope that they too, will join in the complete harmony that exists with us."

So we wondered if the physical being takes food, and lives in a similar way to us:

~ "We do indeed eat, but we only eat what we grow. We do not have animals on our planet, and, therefore, our diet is completely vegetation."

George: "Yes, I understand. And—before this evening, we knew nothing of your selves, but would I be right in thinking you have observed our planet and know something of us?"

~ "We have joined with our good friends of Planet Aerah and have listened to your meetings. And this is why we were asked to visit this time, because we are aware of you and how you exist. It is most interesting for us to see how you are working, and we are sometimes surprised and a little amused by your 'goings-on.'"

Much laughter followed as I added: "I'm sure you must be!"
So, we have also been observed by Planet Glong beings, they being both surprised and amused by our Earthly antics!

~ "But, yes, we do feel a great warmth for this group, because we almost feel as if we know you already."

Lilian responded: "It's very kind of you to say that."
This was becoming a truly wonderful evening and we expressed our great pleasure; declaring it to be such a joy to be learning more about the universe that we all share. Paul commented that we still have such a lot to learn—provoking more laughter. This continued as I declared that I felt a need to apologise for some of our Earthly capers. But the mood became serious again as Lilian pointed out how frustrating it is that there are so few with whom we are able to discuss these matters.

~ "Well, that is partly why I have come—to let you know how other planets exist and though you may not be able to discuss this with others, you can dwell on it yourselves. And, do not forget you have that powerful mind! You do not NEED to speak."

I replied: "All of the Bonniol exchanges have been recorded and we have written them into a book, which is being published at this moment, and your speech this evening is a wonderful addition to that, so we are doing our best to get everything known around the planet here."

~ "I am happy to know that you feel you are able to include our planet also in your writings."

So interplanetary permission has already been granted for this particular chapter!

~ "And may I clarify what I told you about our involvement with meetings with you. We, of course, do not 'sit in' at the meetings, as do those on Planet Aerah; but we are able to use the minds of those who are involved, which is relayed to us. In that way we are participants, but not in the physical form."

George: "Yes, we were aware that Bonniol has a support team of about sixty individuals, and with the mind, these sixty have been involved, I know, but you also have been involved in the 'mind-link'. Wonderful! That is wonderful news for us."

~ "Well, let me tell you, it was wonderful news for us too, because any new information is always of interest, and especially when it is of a planet, so very, very different from ours."

George: "Yes, it's certainly different! Might I ask—do you know and are you aware of Salumet?"

~ "I personally am aware of this being, but I do not have any of his information."

George: "I merely ask, because I think that Salumet was instrumental in making the Bonniol link, or helping towards the link in the first place."

~ "—that is as far as I am aware of this one. I know he was involved, but I do not know anything more about him. I am sure that if we were to tap into the one you call Paul, we could indeed get all information, but we are at present in so harmonious a situation in all aspects of our planet, that we feel, perhaps, that the information you are being given, is directed more to Planet Earth, than to our planet. And that is not to say that we cannot learn from this one, but the thought is that this one is for use on the Planet Earth."

There was of course our general appreciation of that, and Paul enquired if Glong would be classed, like ourselves, as a learning planet. I commented that I felt Glong had already learnt!

~ "I think we could say that although we possibly, and perhaps I should say surely, can learn, our main task is to teach those smaller planets around us. We are all given a task to do and our task is a combined effort for those around us and, perhaps, our learning is to work as one."

Paul commented on 'oneness': "I think we have a deep understanding of it, but it is not very conscious. On a certain level, there is the feeling that we are all one—unfortunately, it doesn't come out enough in our daily life. So, you have reached a very good stage of oneness in your planet. Can I clarify: did you say that you are, broadly speaking, humanoid?"

~ "We are quite similar to the Bonniol people, and we do have the head, we do have arms and we do have legs, but all these physical limbs are so rarely used, because if we wish to move from one place to another, we can do this with our minds. We do not have to use the physical being. We can use it, but we do not have to."

George: "You can transport the physical body, using the mind. Is that correct?"

~ "That is correct."

Paul: "So could you, in theory, materialise yourselves on Earth?"

~ "In theory, we could indeed do this, but I do not think this will happen—not yet at least. But yes, it would be possible."

George: "Wonderful! Do you have families?"

~ "We do have families. We have groups of people who live together, and they act as one big family. We do not have, as you do, couples. We live, in what you might call communes, and we are able to create new beings via the giving of spirit to another and create within that spirit, new spirit, that forms into another being. This is the choice of the one being created. It can choose from whichever commune it wishes to belong. Each commune has a slightly different purpose. Each commune provides one aspect of what is needed to keep the physical being alive. So whatever spirit decides it wishes to grow, it joins that commune, and once you have decided upon your commune, you stay there for the duration of your life on that planet, but of course, we all work together in spirit—so this is the physical side of our planet, but the spiritual side is as one. I hope I have made that clear to you."

We thanked our friend and declared it to be a wonderful education for us to know that such a system exists—to use an Earthly expression, a virgin birth procedure! Lilian inquired if he understands our reproductive system:

~ "Yes, and we have to smile that you need so much effort to produce one more!"

Unrestrained laughter followed that! But Lilian pointed out, that here also it is the spirit that chooses parents and pathway:

~ "We have a little similarity, inasmuch as the spirit decides!"

George: "Yes! And, like everyone else, you recognise the one Creative Principle in the Universe—perhaps you have a different name?"

~ "I am sorry, I do not understand what you are trying to say."

I explained: "Each planet seems to recognise the one Creative Principle in the Universe that some call God. Different cultures have different names for the Creative Spirit of the Universe."

~ "Yes, we very much recognise this Creative Spirit, as you call it, and for us, we call this god, THE CORE."

We all agreed this to be a splendid name. There are several names known to us but all mean the same. Lilian commented that it would be impossible for us to visualise Glong's position in the universe:

~ "Well, firstly, I think you need to pretend that you are in a refrigerator."

Again, we had cause to laugh.

~ "That will be a good start, but I have to say that I feel most comfortable here. And I have very much enjoyed my visit with you."

George: "Well we've certainly enjoyed your visit to us."
Lilian gave an open invitation for our guest to come again:

~ "That is most kind of you, but I think, possibly we will not be coming back too soon, because I think Bonniol has other ideas for you."

Lilian: "Yes, he did say he would introduce us to other people from other planets—"

~ "Well, I have been most impressed by you all, and I only wish that all of you on this planet could be as understanding."

There were further pleasantries and observations that led on to a piece of profound cosmic wisdom:

~ "When you have a young planet, you always get a variety of beings, and it is this variety that helps you to grow. You would not grow, if you did not have so many different ideas. So sometimes, the beings on the planet do not help, but many, many do, even if it is difficult to see at the time. So, as long as you are making some progress, this can only be good."

Paul: "Yes, it's a good journey—getting there!"

~ "And, on the subject of journeys, I think I will return, but thank you again for your time, and I have been most delighted to be with you."

The farewells were fond indeed and we were so grateful to our guest for articulating such clear explanations.
I added: "I don't know how difficult it was for you to come along, but it was a wonderful occasion for us. Thank you so much!"
Paul: "We send a bit of our Earth Love back to Glong."

~ "Thank you and I can tell you the journey was no problem. The landing was harder!"

Laughter again, and we certainly had enjoyed our new friend's ready wit.

~ "So now I will leave you and take with me the very fond feelings I have received from you this evening."

As this one departed, we were left with many thoughts, including our new friend's observation that a young planet is aided by having a *variety of beings*. But above all, he left us with a compelling impression of the wide ranging nature and capability of MIND. Mind is just so all-powerful. There has been so much unworthy talk in our scientific circles, arguing for mind being boxed up within physical brain. That unacceptable error has to be dropped forthwith! We now have the improved awareness that mind can, in addition to making connections across the entire universe—it can be developed and applied beyond any of our hitherto wildest human imaginings.

CHAPTER 7

THE RETURN
OF BONNIOL

Despite the dimness of our room, Lilian noticed Paul had that far-away look and so she *tested the water* with:
"Good evening Bonniol!"
There followed a slight pause, then:

~ (1st March 2010): "I have been waiting for a good time to come and join you again."

Jubilant cries of surprise and delight came from all present! After all, it had been 17-months since Bonniol's last communication.

~ "I have been monitoring your meetings, and I have waited for this New Year to come to you again. It is not necessary to explain why sometimes it is good to have these breaks—they help in many ways—to give time to digest, and problems that were encountered can be worked on."

I replied: "Yes Bonniol—it's wonderful to have you with us again, and let me say: in addition to digesting, we have published the book of your discussions with us, and that is now available for many—so let me give you a big 'thank you!' for that."

~ "I have not done anything personally, but I am very happy that it is finished and been published for your people."

But Bonniol showed some reticence, explaining that people will become aware of cosmic truth in their own good time when they are ready—as all of *you* are ready now.

Lilian had declared: "We want to shout it from the rooftops!"

I added: "I think it's very important that more of our people become aware of communications-across-the-universe, and that there are so many cultures such as yours scattered throughout. This seems to me a really important realisation—that there is much, much more than just our Earth in the creation."

It is true that we cannot force the pace of evolution, but in our conversation, we made a case for spreading the word so that people can come to their own realisations as and when each is ready. But certainly, it sometimes takes years for the penny to drop—sometimes thousands of years. [A classic example is 'asbestos poisoning'. In the first century AD, both the Greek geographer and philosopher Strabo, and the Roman philosopher and naturalist Pliny, acknowledged lung sickness and the life curtailment of asbestos workers, yet its use regardless of their published risks continued for a further 1900 years!]

~ "I'm sure that, in putting the information out there, it will be found by the people who are ready. They will be drawn to it. But for many who are not ready, it will be like—like a brick wall, with no giving in it."

Aptly put, and clearly that is how it is. Lilian inquired about the work of Bonniol and his team. They continue communications with others and look to making new connections—there are so many worlds. Lilian had then said that, when we return to spirit, it would be so nice to meet on a one-to-one basis.

~ "Yes, we would like that! You will have that option I am told. It will be a very happy reunion! And we are looking forward to more work together this year."

All expressed delight at this prospect, and I affirmed: "That's good news!"

~ "I said before that there would be a few more visits—and a few more visits from some of our other friends."

George: "Yes indeed, I was going to say: Planet Glong—I believe that is one of your contacts."

~ "Yes! That was one of the planets from our—"

George: "Well, that's nice—we had a visit from them."

~ "And we were very happy that that went as well as we had hoped. I would be very pleased to introduce another to you. This can be arranged when the lady—Sarah—is with us, because she can help with that one."

Lilian: "It was through Sarah that the one from Glong spoke."
George: "Yes! She will be with us again soon."

~ "I have not forgotten the um—"

Lilian: "Materialisation?"

~ "Yes, we have not forgotten. We are confident—but we will not make a promise."

Lilian asked if all Bonniol's friends and family are well:

~ "They are! And they are working as usual, by my side, and they all are happy and joyful to be with you as well, of course."

George: "I have a number of times thought of you and your house, with your team of—sixty, I think you said, and it's a very nice situation for us to visualise."

~ "They are sending their happy thoughts and love. I will take my leave now, as I believe your evening is coming to a close."

The farewells were fond indeed this time, and I added: "—we are absolutely delighted—I nearly said: over the moon!—" which left everyone quite helpless with unrestrained mirth.

One month later, Lilian approached Paul, feeling that something was happening, but Paul's normal voice replied to say that he was just sensing a bright light. Then, two minutes later Paul's mouth spoke with a difference:

~ (29th March 2010): "Hello!—I am very happy to be here again."

Following warm greetings, Lilian introduced our guest, Robin, who was sitting in this evening.

~ "I am always pleased to meet another of you people."

Bonniol then made it clear that *regular* visits will now come to an end:

~ "We have said that it is not necessary for us to continue to come regularly, and we feel that at this time in your lives, we have not brought you anything that will bring forth your growth in the spiritual ways—help you (to) understand how life exists."

I replied that our *understanding* is wonderfully increased, and Bonniol can always feel that he is most welcome here.

~ "We are feeling that. Thank you! And this is the main reason that we come now—as friends, not as teachers—which you already have."

George: "If you come as a friend and with news—that is still wonderful for us."

~ "This is how we have developed with our other planets—we come now as you might visit friends in your own world."

Sarah: "Yes! So you'll just come from time to time then—you're not going to stop altogether?"

~ "We still have a few things to arrange with the other peoples from other planets, and we hope to bring at least one other. We will also attempt to bring you the gifts that we promised."

There were murmurs of approval all round of course, on hearing this. I pointed out that Robin was sitting here with us as a result of reading the book:

~ "And that feels like a good conclusion to it."

Robin suggested it would be wonderful if humanity could significantly develop mind-link communication.

~ "You have all got the ability. It is up to you to do what you can with it."

I mentioned that the information had been passed to SETI who had been sending out the radio signals, and we hoped they might take note:

~ "Yes, the ability to use the mind is the key to so many things. Your technology can bring about much, but at some point you will understand that the mind is always—always—"

Lilian: "The best method?"

~ "—that is correct."

I pointed out that our Earthly technology arises from entirely material considerations, so that it is most important that we take on board the ways of spirit and mind before this planet can begin to succeed in any serious universe exploration:

~ "Yes, of course! I would always encourage them to use their minds in less mechanical ways, and in more spiritual ways."

Reference was made to the fact that the method of mind-link is *known* to our team but we need much more practice before we are able to organise for ourselves.

~ "There is no short cut. The practice has to be done. I am looking forward to a time when we can communicate with you—without needing to use speech."

Ah! Now that would of course be wonderful and we shall certainly continue to practice; but however strong the intention, these things of course take time. It was Lilian who brought up the subject of spacecraft.

~ "We have our own craft. We are unable to use them to get to the planets which have life, because the distances are so great."

George: "Yes, you did tell us about colonising your moon, and this I believe, is the main use of your space-craft—in travelling to your moon and back."

~ "They are capable of much further distance, but it is still not far enough for visiting our friends on other planets."

Sarah referred to her Planet Glong channelling, and sought confirmation that Bonniol had indeed participated in that arrangement.

~ "We were behind that, yes. I was not sure that it would come through you (Sarah), but that was in the end, our best option. I was (also) hoping to come through myself, but that was not easy at that time. I was present but I was not able to speak."

As lighter conversation then proceeded, Bonniol was saying that they had known the Glongans a long time, and their planets have certainly made great use of mind. I referred to our 'cosmic party evening' when we were each of us overshadowed by other beings, inquiring if Bonniol had also been involved on that occasion.

~ "This was something arranged for you, by your own guides. It was something extra that they wanted to give you—as an experience and as an experiment. I was made aware of the evening—yes. It was not my arrangement. And it shows how many worlds there are around you—how much life there exists!"

Exactly so! Robin inquired how many were with Bonniol this evening:

~ "There are sixty-three in my house."

Lilian: "You've got a much bigger house than me—we would be out on the rooftop!"

There followed some talk of how minds can unite as one, with reference to the way each of Bonniol's team experiences our gathering:

~ "Minds can be linked in a number of different ways, but when we link together, we are able to share in a very complete way what ONE is experiencing."

And as to the actual process—the modus operandi:

~ "We are able to listen and speak, using the physical voice here and the physical brain. But we are tapping into it to interpret the thought-behind-the-words, and this is what we are listening for from your words—they are being put into thought forms. The thought is the spiritual. It is all automatic—our understanding of the thoughts is automatic. It doesn't require any mental thinking."

Robin: "Has that always been the case on Aerah, or is that something that has developed over many, many years."

~ "We have developed over many years our mind abilities. We were not always able to do this. And when YOU are able to do this, you will probably wonder why it took you this time to learn—it is a bit like a new technology that can do something so much quicker."

Lilian observed that where animal friends are concerned, we instinctively understand them without language:

~ "So you can see that the abilities are there—they just need to be developed."

So the workings of mind-linking would appear to be very naturally implemented once the spiritual basis of existence infiltrates intellect. But the ladies present then went on to discuss whether we were supposed to be, according to Salumet, the least intelligent—or was it the least spiritual?—of planetary beings. And Robin inquired if Bonniol felt our brains might be too cluttered anyway, with everyday trivia:

~ "Certainly, it doesn't help to have them cluttered, as you say, with so much—um—"

At this point, Eileen's arms were held out, a gesture that always accompanies Salumet's coming forward, and Lilian said:
"I think we have Salumet back with us—"

~ "I am sorry to intrude, but I cannot leave without clarifying something. The lady says you are spiritually poor—NOT IN ALL OF THE GALAXIES! There are many planets that are much younger and have less knowledge than even you human beings. So I needed to clarify this for you."

We thanked our teacher for coming through, and I said that is a clarification I might have made myself but I did not feel qualified to make a statement.

~ "Yes. And one more thing before I leave you: Bonniol is being bombarded about 'thought'. What you must remember, my dear friends, is that although they are so different—they are still a planet of learning. Only in spirit is thought pure. Thought needs no translation; in spirit—it is instantaneous. But with Bonniol, there has to be a process of understanding—not only from their point of view, but from you people here on Earth. So do not forget that they, although very different, are still not spiritual beings. They are beings with a more advanced spiritual viewpoint, but they are not spirit."

So Sarah asked if Salumet could explain what happens when Bonniol listens to our speech:

~ "The mind belongs to spirit—in Bonniol's planet the mind is far superior. It is developed to such a degree that thought can be transmitted much more easily, but it is still not the thought of spirit. That only happens when the form (material body), whether it be human or whether it be from another planet, has been disposed of."

I added that Bonniol had used the expression: the-thought-behind-the-words and I said that that had gone down well with me.

~ "Yes—that is very good. But what I do not want you, my dear friends to do—is to confuse that development of mind with the mind of pure spirit. There is a great difference. And I apologise for the interruption."

Sarah wondered if Salumet, whilst here, would like a word with Bonniol—

~ "—Not necessary."

And I asked if Bonniol wished to speak with Salumet:

~ "I am overwhelmed to be in such good company tonight. It has been a beautiful evening again, but I do not feel I will use up the time to ask questions. Thank you for the opportunity though. I feel it is time for me to depart as well."

There were very fond farewells, and one further observation from Bonniol:

~ "As your Master says, we are all on journeys, still learning so much about this wonderful life that we all have, with so many opportunities placed before us."

Robin expressed his delight at being able to listen to the actual voice of Bonniol's presentation, which for him, added a dimension to his reading of the book. And we all shared so much joy at having had both Salumet and Bonniol 'seated together' for just a few treasured moments within our circle.

Two months later, it was a chatty session with Bonniol's team this time numbering eighty-three—the curious Earth-dwellers sitting in Lilian's room are now more popular on Aerah than here on Earth! Interesting observations were made, with a little philosophical input here and there. Lilian had mentioned our 'platform mediums', who offer proof of spirit realm through their presentation of mediated messages:

~ (24th May 2010): "Yes, we are smiling because we have a little extra knowledge. But it is not something that makes us superior of course—simply that we have walked a little further down that road."

These are interesting times for us, in which groups on our planet are taking a closer look at humanity. It is realised by some that our progress is heavily dependent upon 'scientific thinking' and 'technology', but we cannot forge ahead much more without a proper understanding and acceptance of 'mind and spirit'. All are connected, and science and technology MUST now embrace mind and spirit—a few are beginning to realise this.

~ "Yes! And your progress will occur of course. These are the natural stages in the process, and it is good that you are taking these steps."

We moved on to speak of universe exploration, and how some use space-craft and travel the wormholes. Ann observed that it is so good that some reach out to others in this way; also that Stephen Hawking states clearly that other civilisations do indeed share this universe with us. Whilst there still remains an extensive and unfortunately all-too-well-publicised pattern of scepticism, it is at least good to acknowledge that small steps forward are being made. Fear of the unknown and fear of interplanetary plunder are of course pitifully irrational, and it was voiced that Earth has developed nothing that an advanced culture would consider worth having! And when the period of laughter following that had abated, Bonniol was saying:

~ "It is very unlikely that they would come in that way. And there are of course far more positive forces out there than there are negative. And remember you've got the spiritual side which will oversee all these major events anyway."

I agreed that to be an interesting point and stated our awareness that there is also much love out there in the universe:

~ "That's right!—it is by far the most prevalent force within the universe. It is almost that, to look for the negative is much harder, but it has to be there."

More was said about the longer pauses occurring between visits:

~ "The process that we started with your world, felt like it had completed its first cycle—um—there will be other cycles, but it is natural to have pauses between cycles."

So further visits will happen!—that's nice. We spoke of how happily, more people on Earth are getting to know of our endeavours via the website, and then it was time for farewells.

We are aware that spirit friends often observe the meetings. There was a difference this time in that two of them added their follow-up comments. Each spoke via Sarah, firstly:

~ "We are always interested—it is quite hard sometimes to listen to what you have to say without putting in a word!"

We asked if it is unusual for our visitors to find they are listening to *interplanetary* conversations:

~ "Yes—for me it is the first time I have heard such a conversation," and then a little further on "It is very nice for you to have such contacts and to have the knowledge—but you have to also at this stage, accept what is given to you, and not everyone would be prepared to accept. So it is I feel a case of getting your just deserts."

Well, it has to be said that it is easy for us to accept, with Salumet's endorsement and with so much that can now be cross-referenced using physical intellect. As that one departed and we chatted on concerning these matters, it came as a surprise when a second, much more voluble voice than the first, spoke via Sarah:

~ "And there you go again! You see how much understanding you have! You are certainly worthy of the one you get. You must continue dear friends, because you are started on such an important pathway and we are most pleased. There is still so much that you can achieve and we do hope that you will continue—excuse me for butting in. I often accompany this other one, and we both found it most difficult to keep our mouths shut!"

So it seems we were entertaining a total gathering of at least eighty-five on this occasion!

Our first visitor had said that it is not everyone who would be prepared to accept—a wise statement. Perhaps this is a good place to mention that in fact majority, for their various reasons, are not accepting of the reality of extraterrestrial communication. Sadly, 'majority' currently includes teaching institutions, newspapers and TV news media, so that there is no guidance for vast majority from these sources. The long established insular status quo, of course, needs time to change. The often quoted Albert Einstein understood well our Earthly malaise, and made the challenging statement:

"Great spirits have always encountered violent opposition from mediocre minds."

Perhaps today, people prefer the term 'sceptical' to the more humiliating 'mediocre' where rebuttal of obvious truth is concerned.

It was now the summer evening of 28th June 2010. One spoke via Eileen at some length on blending energies within the group. As that one departed, we noted the sound of distant church bells that seemed to come and go on a gentle breeze. It then became clear that Sara was being guided in taking us on a meditative journey that began:

"Okay—we're going to go on a blending journey—we're going to get into the big spiritual blender—"

As the quite lengthy meditative journey concluded we each reported sensing spiritual light that was connecting us and we were invited to gently hold hands. The experience was like being in a warm loving mist and we understood that the memory of it should help with future blending. At this stage, enter Bonniol:

~ "Hello!—I was waiting for the right time to visit you, and yes, I was aware of the exercise you were doing."

Bonniol was again enthusiastically welcomed and he added that his group had also been blending, as is their regular practise—just the minds, no hand-holding. Sarah mentioned that her daughter Emily had felt that our blending exercise had a Bonniol connection.

~ "She has a good mind. She was picking up the right impressions there. There is, I'm sure, much more to come from her. And it would indeed be a fine evening to bring you something from our world. If you are happy to sit in silence for a while longer—there is no reason to believe it will or believe it won't occur, but we will see what we can do."

Well, an attempt was made, as we sat in silence for 12 minutes, then it was clear that Bonniol was no longer with us, so we discussed impressions. Four reported a recurring strong floral scent, reminiscent of *lily of the valley*. Emily felt a tingling in the hands and they were moved as if to receive something. She felt a positive presence. We concluded that Bonniol had come significantly closer to achieving an interplanetary materialisation, and *very nearly* managed to present Emily with a bouquet!

CHAPTER 8

MORE VISITS:
MORE PHILOSOPHY

It was now 2nd August 2010. An Indian lady spoke via Eileen of times past when her job had been making colourful paper wall decorations. Sadly, she had seen the demise of this work when tapestries took over. But it had been part of her learning to move forward and not to remain engrossed in the past. We felt this also to be part of our *own* learning. In these times of rapid change, we must all move forward and not be captivated by outdated regime; yesterday's status quo was for yesterday, not today. Next, it was the familiar voice of Bonniol saying:

> ~ "Hello!—It is always a pleasure to be here with you. It feels like only yesterday when I first joined with you. And now it is just another visit!"

There were interwoven pleasantries and then our friend was speaking of the journey here:

> ~ "—How it has brought us to you, and we are extremely grateful to all those who help us find our way here."

If we consider the links and ramifications within spirit that must be necessary for mind connections, then of course the mind fairly boggles! And we were stunned as Bonniol declared how they have enjoyed sharing the knowledge of our ways with others:

~ "You would probably be surprised to know that most on our planet are now quite familiar with the workings of your world."

Wow! Fame at last—or would it be infamy? But Sarah had replied: "That's nice to know—I wish most of the people on *our* planet knew about the workings of *your* world! We are getting there slowly."

~ "And we are delighted that you are putting in such effort to share this knowledge."

I tried to explain our Earthly position more clearly, saying:
"Yes, well these are exciting times for Planet Earth, because we are changing—and I think, moving forward quite rapidly compared to past times. We have our scientists who work in a very material way and think along material lines and make some discoveries—but I feel that through our dialogues together, we have taken a different and much more extensive journey, and in many ways, we are discovering and experiencing so much more than our more material science—and it's very exciting for *us*."

~ "I have been hoping that it would excite you of course, and it's good that you feel that you have been given a useful piece of information about the universe."

I had replied: "Yes, not only the universe, but a very useful reali-sation of how mind works and how mind can link, disregarding the physical distance."

~ "Yes, and I think you were told that this was one of the reasons that we were allowed to come, because you needed to have this example of the way the mind can be used."

This of course is the crux of the matter—MIND—our understand-ing of mind. This is so vitally important to further progress on Earth. We simply have to understand and develop mind attributes. We went on to speak of the difficulties of conveying this to others; also in re-spect of our own mind development exercises.

~ "But you are trying, and that is all you can do. And I believe that you will continue to try, and that is all we ask. We are happy that you are spreading the information, but we are also mainly here in the hope that you will explore your own minds more fully, and in that way you will help yourselves, and in turn help others."

Quite so; and we continue our going within for meditation, and our hit-and-miss attempts to mentally send colours and simple shapes to each other.

I continued: "And it has been so nice to hear about the ways on your planet—your mind-link to those who have gone beyond their physical lives and your mind-links to the unborn, and the other communications. All of these just illustrate to us the value of more developed mind."

~ "Yes, I am happy that you see the benefits—it will bring much joy to you. It is a journey of joy. The more we develop, the more we are in awe of the wonders that are around us."

Further reference was made to Aerah's interplanetary explorations. Bonniol describes this as a great joy but was careful to point out:

~ "But we are very much of our own planet, and this is where our main focus lies."

Sarah then spoke of a striking difference between our two planets: "You understand there are many, many civilisations around, whereas most people on this planet believe we are the most intelligent and may-be the *only* ones! There is searching going on 'by radio!'—maybe there is someone else out there who *maybe* could communicate with us 'also by radio!' I think most people on this planet have a lot more learning to do, whereas you are happy, because you *do understand* what else exists."

~ "Yes, you make that point well. It is so important to have this AWARENESS OF YOUR PLACE IN THE UNIVERSE. But it can only happen when you are ready, and it is wonderful that some of you are ready."

I made the point that it is so good to see Aeran peoples reaching out to different planets. And although we cannot do this of our own volition, we can nevertheless see that it can be done, and equally, we can see just how wonderful this universe is, so we can thank you again and again for that.

~ "It is your own inner searching that has allowed it to happen, so the thanks should be shared all around; the many that have helped us as well."

Lilian added: "Yes, those unseen friends! And is this planet the furthest you have travelled?"

~ "It is the furthest apparently, but it (distance) is of course irrelevant. We are simply told that it is a huge distance, but we are unaware ourselves, of any distance of course."

It seems that Aerans do not decide which planets to approach—they are guided. Salumet guided to us, but not all guides are of angelic status.

~ "No, they will often be ones that have lived upon our own planet. They will always have a greater knowledge, wisdom and awareness than our selves. They won't necessarily be from such a high realm as your guide."

I replied: "Yes, there are many levels in spirit, and the decisions that are made where Aerah is concerned have a heavy spiritual involvement, if I could put it like that. Whereas, for the majority on Earth, the thinking is more scientific and more material, but we really need to generally, have a little more spiritual involvement in our thinking and planning. I feel that is probably a fair statement. Correct me if I'm wrong."

~ "I think that is always the way—the direction would always be towards spirit—to bring more spirit into our physical realms—to enrich the physical forms with all of the gifts of spirit."

We pointed out that our thinking had been enriched by the obvious great respect for plant life on Aerah and how it influences food production. Here on Earth we begin to realise how many food production errors we have—and these introduce toxins and toxic effects. In the light of recent Earthly adverse publicity, Aeran respect for plants interests us greatly.

~ "When you begin to see that all life forms are from the same source, you have more and more respect for them—as you would your own family. We are all from that same source. And on that note, I believe I should head back to my world."

The fond farewells left us much to think on. There have been clear, largely ignored presentations by Cleve Backster and others that plants are indeed SENSITIVE—respond to our thoughts, to music and to caring people, with their responses registering most clearly on a polygraph. These facts have been well documented [17, 18, 19], but sadly remain generally unheeded by agriculture and commercial practise on Earth. This must and will change.

Our next exchange with Bonniol was in the following year—16th May 2011. It began a little curiously. Eileen declared that she had the sensation of travelling backwards. Then a lady with distinctly Spanish accent spoke via Eileen, and looking towards Paul said:

~ "Why that man not speak?"

Paul replied: "Is there someone with me?"

~ "Try."

I explained that Paul is little used but is the chosen medium for Bonniol from another planet and he always speaks through him.

~ "Yes, I know—I know—they try now!"

There followed a short pause.

~ "Hello!"

Well, it had been an interval of nearly ten months and there was at first our hesitation—then overtly happy cries of welcome from all present. This was indeed another happy reunion.

~ "Yes, I've been trying to come for a while but it has not been easy. I am happy to finally make it back here."

I said: "We're delighted you've found us because we have very recently changed our meeting house."

After ten years of wonderful hosting by Lilian, we now meet in Eileen's home. Thick curtains were not yet in place, so that any facial expressions could be quite clearly seen. Now, a smiling Bonniol, with closed eyes, looked around:

~ "You have indeed—yes. I am enjoying having a little look at your new place."

And as we all laughed:

~ "I am sure it will be just as good as the other one."

Lilian inquired after Bonniol's family and friends.

~ "They are very well and send their love to you all."

She added: "We often think of you."

~ "Yes, they are happy to hear that. Thank you!"

And then she inquired of their mind travel activities.

~ "It is not *always* that we are travelling. We do have breaks as well as you, and yes, there are other activities—we have our gardens of course, as you know."

Lilian: "Yes—do you have the same problems as we do? At the moment we need some rain to water the plants. Do you have these problems (of drought) or maybe too much rain?"

~ "It is always one or the other isn't it? We have to sometimes be patient, but there is always a reason for it, and the plants are very good usually at coping with changes; but yes, we sometimes have to give them a little extra."

Next, I was able to give a piece of good news—that a good friend had given a talk to a spiritual group, in which 'Bonniol' and 'Planet Aerah' were mentioned and they were very interested.

~ "It is always fascinating to see where these things end up—what happens when we make contact, and what happens later on. It is all part of this wonderful journey that we are on."

I added: "I can also say that there is just one leading scientist on our planet who accepts our communications and agrees the little bit that we understand about the communications, and that is very nice and reassuring for us—so there are the first signs that the news is spreading."

~ "Well then I am sure that it is all happening as it should."

There followed a short pause.

There was some discussion about our practise efforts in sending mind-pictures to each other. Ann suggested that we are too easily distracted from this pursuit.

~ "I think it's allowed for you to be as you are—we cannot assume that you only have time for this in your busy, busy lives. You do have much around you which is distracting."

Rod spoke of a TV programme and how our scientists search for proof of life on other planets using totally material methods and material thinking—and how they *must* always have material proof. Hopefully, they will take the spiritual step and begin to seriously move forward soon.

Lilian added: "We have been told by Salumet that certainly the younger generation will be seeing people from other planets, arriving in their space-craft. I think our planet needs to grow up a bit before that happens—become a little more peaceful."

I had added: "Yes, there are signs that there are some very bright children coming along."

Rod: "But the one who is really bright is the lady—Jan—who is sitting next to the one who is channelling you. She can make drawings of what is going on in your planet. Do you remember that Bonniol?"

George: "Oh, Jan had very good clairvoyance—of scenes on your planet when you were through to us before!"

Jan: "And Richard!"

~ "Yes and hopefully she will have more over the next phase."

The clairvoyant scenes that Jan and Richard were able to compare during a previous session were just amazing. I suggested that perhaps Bonniol 'engineers' the clairvoyance.

~ "If any of you wish to get pictures of our world, then it is always possible for you. It is more your own capacity to link up or to see clearly with your mind's eye. It just needs to be open."

George: "Yes, I think one of the expressions that we have is 'opening the third eye'. Does that make sense?—that the 'mind's eye' would correspond to what is known here in some quarters as 'the third eye'?"

~ "Yes, or you could call it 'your REAL eye'".

Lilian: "Would I be right in saying that just before we go to sleep, that is when that third eye is used more—you're able to see?"

~ "I would say that it is not necessarily the case; but when you are going to sleep there is less distraction, and you are probably more relaxed to use it. So yes, it may well be that you are more receptive at that time."

I mentioned ability to 'astral travel' during sleep state—to awaken and sometimes half-remember as a dream. I wondered if this made sense to our friend.

~ "Yes of course—yes! It is part of your abilities that you can leave your body when you are asleep, and go on these journeys—so many journeys."

And we wondered how many were with Bonniol this evening:

~ "We are—um—sixty nine in my house tonight"

Rod: "Good gracious!"
Bonniol explained that his house was fairly full with a few new ones, but mostly the usual crowd. But this was the point at which Jan again began receiving clairvoyance:
Jan: "You have some fairly young ones with you this time though—there's one sat on your right knee!"

~ "There are two indeed, young ones with us—young in body"

Jan: "Very young! Would they be some of your children?"

~ "Yes, there are some—yes."

Jan: "They need to be rounded up just like our children. One is running away!"

~ "We often have these situations with our children. They can be very difficult to—"

Jan: "Control?"

~ "Yes."

And we had to laugh, while Jan declared she was pleased to see Aerans have that problem too. Then Rod had said how he was awed by the night sky, and does Bonniol think there is more than one God for the other universes?
George: "Well, we have to define what we mean by 'God'."
Lilian: "One Creator."
Ann: "Creative Force."
Lilian: "Is that how you would describe it?"

~ "Yes, we would prefer the term 'force'. It is a force. It is not like an individual consciousness. We would not think of it as a person."

I explained that we have the terms 'Great Creative Force' and 'Creative Principle', devised by those who think about such things, while Lilian declared she thought of it as 'energy'.
Ann: "Light and energy."
Lilian: "Force and energy."
Rod agreed; but then there was more clairvoyance. Jan began describing a natural but unusual fountain that had freshly emerged on Aerah.

~ "You—er—yes—the place that you are seeing is a new place for—it was recently discovered by one of our children. It is a recent 'fountain spring.'"

We mused between us that it is what we might call a 'volcanic geyser'.

Jan: "Yes, it's got something to do with warmth—there's a force underneath it."

~ "We would say it is a liquid like water, but it's—"

Jan: "Heavy! Dense!"

~ "Not the same as your water—"

Jan: "When it falls—I'm seeing it fall very dense and heavy—almost like mercury droplets. It takes a long time to find its way back into wherever it is coming from—strange!"

~ "It has the ability to—"

Jan: "Has the ability to form different things—"

~ "Yes, it maintains its shape for longer."

Jan and I discussed the way spilled mercury droplets run all over the place then join up together, but this liquid was clear.

~ "Yes, there is a bit of attraction that comes together forming larger—"

I asked: "So is this an ordinary occurrence, Bonniol, or is this something special on your planet?"

~ "It is ordinary for these springs to work like this, yes."

I explained that Bonniol had told us before how Aeran water is somehow 'thicker' than ours, so that even rain displays this thick tenacious property.

~ "Yes, it is um—it is like it has—it's difficult to put it into the right words, but I think you may understand from what has been said, that it behaves slightly differently from your water."

Rod: "You can wash in this water, can you Bonniol?"

~ "We would perhaps use different water for washing. It is coming from under the ground—it is not the pure water on its own. There are fragments of our earth mixed into it. It's a—"

Jan: "It's welcomed—"

~ "It's a natural phenomenon."

Jan: "It's welcomed because I think I'm right in believing that what I'm seeing only happens occasionally in this area, and it means there's a 'new-ness' to the planet. It shows rejuvenation—that's my understanding."

~ "Yes, they do not happen very often, so it is a pleasing event, and we hope it will keep going for a long time yet—but these things don't always last for that long. I—would like to come back again soon, now that we have found this link again."

Our farewells were fond indeed and Jan thanked Bonniol for the pictures received.

Eileen had remained silent throughout. Now another addressed us via Eileen, who as he was being welcomed, began to explain:

~ "I have waited patiently to speak with you. It has been a privilege to bring energy for you in order that the communication and mind projection has been able to take place this time. We did not intend to speak but the gentleman needs to have clarification—the gentleman who believes we need many Gods. Not so! Not so!"

He went on to make it unequivocally clear that there is just the one creation of which we are all mirror images.

~ "We all know that energy is ever-moving—ever-evolving; and that creative energy has many attributes to it. You must never allow words to keep you chained to some idea—some ideals. Creation will always change because energy is always changing. We know and we understand that it is difficult for you, and what we wish you to remember this time, is that the mind communication you have just experienced—those people, although not human in the sense you

81

recognise, are still non-spirit, and are still evolving, in the same way that you people on this planet are evolving. You must open your minds further. That is our message to you this time."

Rod declared that, as he looked up at the universe, it just seemed to go on forever, and our visitor explained that 'Gods', as we call them, do not exist in quite that way.
Rod: "So a proper word would be 'energy'."

~ "I would be inclined to use 'energy', yes—"

Rod: "—which is forever evolving."

~ "Yes, it is never static. I know that you will have been taught this many times—but it is good sometimes, is it not, to be reminded?"

We thanked this communicator for his participation and for his clarifying statement, and he made a point of thanking Jan for her clairvoyance, declaring it to have helped the conversation this evening. And then a parting gesture:

~ "Continue to watch the stars dear gentleman, because they will find some new ones soon."

Our Earthly history, language and sometimes lack of insight have all combined to cause confusion where the important matters of 'God' and the 'Creation' are concerned—so well illustrated by the Oxford Dictionary's definition of 'pantheon', that begins: 'Temple dedicated to all the gods...' If we assert that one God created all, it is clearly imperative that we have proper definition and understanding of what we mean by God. St John 1: 1 of the Christian Bible begins: 'In the beginning was the Word, and the Word was with God and the Word *was* God'. Well, God equals word, equals thought, equals energy, so to some degree these words are all well connected.

CHAPTER 9

AERAN SEWAGE, EDUCATION AND CLAIRVOYANCE

I t was now 18th July 2011 and our session began with some light chat. It seems that Bonniol, whilst remaining silent, is sometimes close by during our meetings. He and his colleagues now understand much about our world from information already gathered. We had made mention of the so many mistakes made during Earth's passage forward, and it was reassuring to hear:

> ~ "There will always be what you call 'mistakes'. We make them all the time too. BUT we do not have the same view of them. You, I am sure, also understand that they are always part of the process of growth. There is never the time when they are not around—because they are useful tools to help us to measure our growth."

I suggested it is important to *recognise* mistakes, and to look back on the mistakes of history—so that we can learn from them.

> ~ "Yes, you can always use them to help you move forward, as long as you don't become too downhearted by them. They are merely there to show you—point you in the right direction."

We felt happy with that, but now I wondered if I might ask Bonniol another technical question. This followed a journalist's sounding off about the silliness of supposed 'alien communications' and our not even knowing about sewage disposal arrangements on their planets!—such an outrageous senseless cynicism! So, I felt perhaps we should find out about Aeran sewage from our dear friend whilst we have the opportunity; so that the details are to hand should we wish to properly rebuff such cynicism in the future. I explained:

"On our planet, we have a way of dealing with our sewage and it goes from the bathroom through pipes, and it goes to a treatment centre, and *some* of the solid material gets ploughed back into the land for agricultural purpose. Would you have something along similar lines or have you got a different way of dealing with your sewage on Planet Aerah?"

~ "Yes, we like to recycle it also, but we have no need to process it like you do."

George: "Ah!—because you're vegetarian! Is that right?"

~ "It is very simple for us to store and use it on our plants—yes—but it is not treated. It is gathered in piles, left for a time, and then it is moved on to where it is needed most. There is some piping, yes. We like to drain it away from the houses in a similar way to you."

Graham referred to microbes and the need for hygiene.

~ "Yes, you have a set of problems that you are working through at the moment, and the answers are all there. The um—the simple solutions are often the best."

Perhaps there is more wisdom in that final statement than is immediately apparent. There was a little more talk of building houses using natural materials and mind power. Lilian indicated that in the past we made use of naturally occurring materials, but then it was once again time for our friend to depart.

On reflection, the processing of sewage is a *very* important matter. I was brought up on a small mixed farm in the 1930s and remember well the 'mucking out' of cowsheds, stables and henhouse. In appropriate season, the accumulated farmyard manure heap would be loaded onto a dung cart and spread on the fields prior to ploughing—a simple and effective fertiliser at no cost, and the yard was cleared for another year. The animals were vegetarian of course and no toxic chemicals found their way into the dung heap. Wonderfully simple!—just like that more progressed planet we know! Our *human* sewage is a very different matter. At the sewage works, it has to undergo a complicated and expensive process in separating tanks.

Upper and lower fractions are separated and water phase upgraded so that it can be discharged into rivers etc. Some toxic wastes, impossible to reclaim, go to landfill sites. All this is quite complex and as our dear friend says: simple solutions are often the best.

One month later (15ᵗʰ August 2011), Eileen was inquiring if one was with Paul, because there seemed to be an orange light. There was a short pause and then the familiar greeting:

~ "Hello!"

Following warm welcomes, Lilian got us going on the subject of child education, beginning: "I was thinking about your children—how do you go about their education? We have schools and colleges. Are they taught at home?"

~ "They are all—um—raised in our—"

I reminded that the Aeran kibbutz system had been referred to several years earlier.

~ "Yes, we have a place for all the young ones, and yes, they have a formal education. But of course, we feel it is quite different because the subjects are not the same. We train our children, of course, to use their mind power more effectively."

Jan: "Of course!"

~ "And they are usually very motivated—yes—and this is something that we do not always feel is the case with your children."

Lilian: "No, I think the education system here needs to be looked at a little bit more."

I asked if their children moved on to another teaching place as they progress.

~ "They learn what they need to learn, usually in the same place most of the time."

We now entered an interesting and different phase during which Jan felt a strong clairvoyant bonding with Bonniol's *group*, so that information now came to us from both Bonniol and via Jan.

Jan: "And often they are able to be on their own, because they're learning in a more telepathic way. I can see them learning as individuals rather than a group."

~ "They can learn like that—yes. We do encourage them to play and spend time together."

Jan: "That's mostly their social skills, isn't it?"

~ "Yes."

Lilian suggested they might learn more about nature than our children.

~ "They are often taught whilst outside in the fresh spaces, yes!"

Jan: "They have a vast interplanetary knowledge from a *very* young age."

~ "And of course, we tell them what we know about our explorations. So there is not the same treating-them-so-differently (from adults). We try to treat them like adults—they are spiritual beings like us."

Jan explained to Bonniol that she is not exactly butting in: "—but I obviously get clairvoyance from your side, so in our language: *their minds are much freer.* There do not seem to be the boundaries that we put on children. They're able to express and have that freedom because they can mind travel—that's their motivation. And when you gave us the parallel between your children and our children, it's so evident to me now, just how. This is quite exciting!"

~ "It is –um—"

Jan: "You *have* boundaries and discipline, but those are almost in-stinctual. It develops in a much more disciplined and natural way—that's how I describe it."

~ "Yes, it is not always easy to find the words, but that word 'natural' seems to cover a lot of ground here—yes."

Lilian: "Which means they're not so stressed as some of our children."
Jan: "You have conflict within families, but a much more structured conflict and the unit stays together—it tries to escape the boundaries of the family."

~ "I think the difference might be with the stress in your world, where there is so much confusion for the young people. Our young people usually can find the answers—which doesn't always make it easy for them. But they don't have that same 'stress.'"

Jan: "It's an inner conflict—the discipline and the guidance, enables them to deal with that much easier than our young people. They are not fighting establishment like ours."

~ "No!"

Lilian: "They have more spiritual knowledge."
Eileen: "Bonniol, when we name people here, they're often based on names from Christianity. Where do your names come from?"
George: "I think (from earlier data) your own name is a star, is it not?"

~ "We have—um—different types of—some names come from nature,"

Eileen: "Like the Indian races on the Earth—always chose names from nature. Do you mean you do the same?"

~ "Yes, many of our names are from nature—are the names of various parts of the natural world."

Eileen: "Are you able to name any?"

George: "Animals or birds?"

~ "I could tell you some of them. It is not always easy to give them the correct pronunciation."

Eileen: "Do you actually call them by name or do you just think of whom you are speaking? Is it important to you?"

~ "We still use the voice at times, yes. There are the two ways to communicate."

Bonniol then showed some hesitation.

~ "Yes, would you like to know the name of—?"

Eileen: "One of your children?"
Jan: "Who sounds like 'Saronga'? What in your language sounds similar to 'Saronga'? I might not be picking it up right."

~ "'Sheearonga'—um—it um—"

This line of inquiry progressed no further, Bonniol indicating that it is difficult, in this endeavour, to make one sound into another. We can well believe that! We referred back to the teaching of children in the countryside, asking if they are aware of other beings that are there—elementals—nature spirits.

~ "They would mostly be aware, yes."

I asked if becoming aware would be part of their education.

~ "Mostly they would (already) be aware of them."

Jan: "Be aware from birth."

~ "Be aware of them, yes."

George: "So would part of their education involve communicating with them?"

~ "Yes um—we would—"

Lilian: "That's interesting!"
Jan: "Instinct—they're born with the instinct."

~ "We would encourage them to communicate with them, yes."

Jan: "Something that maybe some choose to develop more than others."

~ "It is not obligatory. That would be counterproductive."

George: "So you are encouraging what is already there."
Jan: "It's a choice."

~ "If they are unaware of them then they are probably not ready to communicate with them. But most of them do."

George: "So your education is probably less formal and much more flexible than our system."

~ "It is, yes."

Jan: "It flourishes—it flourishes—it's ever evolving. It doesn't have the boundaries and limitations that *we* put there."

~ "Because the children are also the teachers to some degree; so yes, they are able to direct where the lesson may go at times."

Lilian: "To us sitting here, that sounds an ideal situation. But of course, they *do* understand mind and thoughts."

~ "It is a gradual process of course. There is always—there is so much. Each planet has so many differences and much in common too. But we just feel it's certainly not our business to consider that our system is in any way superior. There is much goodness in your world."

Lilian: "It's the stages that the planets are at, isn't it?"

~ "Yes, the stages—and the routes you take are different."

George: "Yes, it's probably true to say that there's no point in having every planet's evolution the same."

~ "Exactly—yes, it would make our visits so much less enjoyable!"

Eileen: "If you had a choice Bonniol, would you stay on your own planet or on one you have visited?"
A pause followed while Bonniol carefully considered.

~ "It's a very good question. There are several planets that I would love to go to for a holiday."

Amusement followed, as Eileen suggested: "But not Earth!"

~ "The planet that you are on is always the one you NEED to be on! But it is always nice to visit another world."

Jan: "You may not have the planet that you want, but you *have* the planet that you need!"

~ "Yes, and of course, none of these planets is our real home!"

Eileen: "No!"
I felt the need to quote Earth's shortest poem: "'East—West, home's best'; and as you have said, it's very nice to take a holiday break somewhere different."
Jan next sought clarification on the mode of transmission for her clairvoyance, which was very clearly not the regular arrangement.

~ "You are being sent pictures—thoughts."

Jan: "When you're here, I feel that around me—I almost turn to stone, because of how thick—I think I've said before: I pick up on an atmosphere that is not of here. And each time you work with us it gets stronger, and this time it's the strongest it's ever been!"

~ "We are—it is a way of—you are tuning into the—um—"

Lilian: "Would it be the thoughts of some of your colleagues?"

~ "Yes!"

Jan: "Because I don't pick up on *your* thoughts. But, as you're speaking, it's as if somebody explains what you are trying to portray—at lightning speed."

So, as we talked with Bonniol, Jan seemed to be receiving concurrent statements from his team members! There was a brief period of discussion amongst ourselves about this and how there is the language difference, but thought is not a language and can be downloaded by brain to *its* regular word language.

~ "Yes, it is the thought that is not a language at all."

Jan: "Ah yes, I see!"

~ "It is a good exercise to notice the differences between this and your usual clairvoyance."

Jan, addressing Bonniol: "When I sit next to Paul I don't notice Paul at all. When you come *through* Paul, there is almost a magnetic pull which I experience on my right side (towards Paul)."

Eileen declared that to be interesting and there followed a pause, while energy seemed to fade.

Lilian: "I think Bonniol's gone."

~ "It is time for me to go."

And there was just time for fond farewells. On reflection, this exchange might be seen as somewhat chatty and ragged, but it would I feel sure be wrong to always adhere to old standards; better to address the pathway that beckons. Apart from useful factual data, this session has significantly expanded our knowledge of mode of communication. We have now experienced two aspects:

(1) Bonniol's words: channelled via Paul—Bonniol's thoughts-behind-words being downloaded into English by Paul's brain (while Paul remains silent throughout).

(2) Jan's clairvoyance: Jan being impressed by thought/pictures from the Aeran team, which she then articulates in her own way with her own thinking. And as Bonniol says: *It is not always*

easy to find the words. And on other occasions he has indicated that it is useful to have things described in our Earthly way of thinking.

So, on reflection, we have taken a further step forward and are learning to cope with what that entails. Concerning child education, we should of course bear in mind that a major employment sector on Aerah is 'agriculture', involving very large numbers—and this is bound to influence what needs to be studied and would of course favour outdoor excursions.

Three weeks later (5th September 2011), we had been chatting delightedly about the Bonniol visits just prior to Salumet joining us, and he, it seems, was listening to our conversation:

~ "It gladdens us to hear you speak so openly about all manner of things. I have been listening, my dear friends, to your conversation, this time, and it is good that your hearts and your minds are open to all that exists, and although, you say you would wish to have contact with other beings, may I just say to you, my dear friends: it is important that you make contact and get to know your own fellow beings much better."

Well yes, clearly Earth still remains unsettled in a number of ways, so I feel sure that one valid deduction to be made is that we must get our house in rather better order before receiving guests! That would seem sensible. I added my own thoughts:

"Yes, these are very wise words, I know, but our brief taster of extra-terrestrial matters has nevertheless made it easier for some of us—for me at least—to endeavour to contact scientists who are often very material in their thinking—and I think there is a lightening of this condition. Some scientists are beginning to feel more that there's much beyond materialism—"

~ "Yes."

"And with our brief encounter with Bonniol, it makes it easier for us to talk to them about things that go beyond space-time, if I could put it like that."

~ "Yes, if you remember, the reason for Bonniol coming was to demonstrate to you all, 'mind projection'—which is part of your own being. It is to help you to continue to develop that—what you are here on this planet for, and when you adopt these attitudes to who and to what you are—then you become much better beings—spiritual beings, who would then be able to encourage many people in your world—by your words, by your actions, by your demonstration—that there is more to living than just this physical body."

So we have linked with Bonniol and his team on Aerah, and this has told us—demonstrated to us in no uncertain terms—so much about mind. Mind can clearly take us, not just beyond the physical body, but beyond this planet and far beyond this galaxy. Mind, as part of spirit is ever-ongoing. Mind has no set limits. The mind projection exercise helps us *indeed* to know who we are, and we can then become better beings; this through recognition of mind's fuller potential.

In exercising mind connection in this way, we have in so doing, become fully aware that our universe has many sentient life forms that already enjoy this kind of awareness. And of course, with that awareness of mind-potential there has followed mind-linkage, conversations between planets and the sharing of knowledge. Much more has then naturally followed in the wake of full realisation that mind and spirit—or should we say: mind as part of spirit—is a central factor of existence, within that all-pervading spirit. This has guided many in this universe beyond the restraint of materialism. 'Non-material' technologies for traversing universal distance have become possible, so that some sentient physical beings have been able to actually visit the planetary homes of others. At this point in time, there are many whom we might term *better beings* across this universe that recognise and have developed mind's potential. Does that affect us in any way? Well, it does raise questions for Earth dwellers, notably: have such advanced beings already visited *this* planet in times past? And is there evidence remaining of such visits—of *their* missions to *our* Earth?

PART 2

Pyramids: their Origins and Purpose

"If he is a stranger to the universe who does not know what is in it, no less is he a stranger who does not know what is going on in it"
– MARCUS AURELIUS, MEDITATIONS, BOOK IV.

CHAPTER 10

PYRAMIDS: DETAILS AND RAISON D'ÊTRE

The answers to those questions raised in the last chapter concerning possible visits to our planet are without any shadow of a doubt *affirmative*. It is clear from the huge amount of accumulated data that will be presented in due process, and from statements made by Salumet and others, that the earliest and largest pyramids on Earth are assuredly *not* by design of humankind. They have been built by visitors to our planet using methods of construction that were and still are unknown to present day humanity. Why pyramids? Why should visitors have need of pyramids? It is very clear from earlier statements that a pyramid with one pair of sides facing east-west, gathers or generates energy. The valuable work of Russian scientists has clearly demonstrated this. Visitors to Earth have had dire need of such energy both for their wellbeing whilst here and to assist their return passage home.

The Great Pyramid and Sphinx on the Giza Plateau, Egypt.

So the first task of those early expeditions to Earth has always been to build a pyramid to provide that energy. This necessity fits key facts that have become known to us and also presents acceptable logic.

Egyptian Pyramids: Volumes have been written on the 'Great Pyramid' that stands on the Giza Plateau, sadly much of it in error. Many have based dating on cartouches that adorn the walls within, but our information is that these were made very much later and by humans. The true age of the Great Pyramid is around 11,000 years and it is noteworthy that two early historic sources agree this date[21, 22]. The plateau area, on which pyramids and sphinx now stand, has been levelled to exceptional accuracy. Building blocks have been hewn, transported and fitted together, again with exceptional accuracy—well beyond the proficiency of humankind today; this because in today's world we are unfamiliar with 'dematerialisation' procedures. Salumet spoke on this during his visit of 10th July 2000:

> ~ "'Dematerialisation' as you call it, is an attribute of spirit; it is something that you all are capable of—many space-travellers have

95

used dematerialisation for their own good and their own benefit. To you human beings who have lost much of your natural capabilities, dematerialisation-and-materialisation seems to be an exception to the rule. It is not. It is just a matter of re-training yourselves, if I may put it so bluntly."

And more was said during the meeting of 5ᵗʰ May 2003:

~ "To you it seems such a strange and unusual happening. To those of us who know more, it is a *natural* happening. I told you when first I came that all of these great happenings, as you call them, were quite natural occurrences and that people of your past times had much more spiritual knowledge than many do now. The pyramids were built as points of travel for those who came from other worlds."

Who were those beings that came from other worlds? The beings: 'Osiris', 'Isis' and 'Horus', are much more than vague imaginary myth. They were visitors to Earth from a planet in the Sirius star system. Osiris had the title 'Lord of Rostau', Salumet acknowledging 'Rostau' to be the old name for the Giza pyramid complex. The meaning of Rostau is *the shaft to the Duat*, the Duat being the 'sky map of stars'. Furthermore, the Egyptian 'Great Pyramid' was never intended as a burial chamber for pharaohs. That was made crystal clear during the meeting of 7ᵗʰ August 2006:

~ "Within the structures that they built would be a chamber that would be used by all—for upliftment, for healing and to gain knowledge. Within these structures there would be one who would be willing to teach, who had come to this planet for that very purpose."

So this was in fact a wonderful mission to Earth 11,000 years ago from which Egyptians benefitted immensely; but there followed steady decline which our guide went on to explain:

~ "As time progressed, the pharaohs realised that they could amass great wealth, and it is shown on their drawings—the more cattle they could have, the wealthier and more outstanding they became. Materialism started to creep into their lives. Their downfall was that they began to think of themselves as infallible, and they themselves were godheads. And slowly, slowly this created many downfalls—many pharaohs came to no good."

It is clearly evident how Egyptian peoples had benefited from the magnificent mission that was mounted by extraterrestrial beings, and we may now in retrospect applaud. But following their departure and through subsequent millennia, the self interest of leaders and the dark shadow of materialism sadly took over. So much of what had been learned became lost, but the hard evidence of it all remains in the structures still standing on the Giza Plateau, in the cartouches on pyramid walls and in myth. These matters are accounted much more fully in chapter 38 of our earlier book[16]. It is appropriate that we now move on, devoting the pages that follow to a full account of the much older and only recently discovered pyramid complex at Visoko, near Sarajevo, Bosnia.

Bosnian Pyramids: Two of our group visited the pyramids in May 2012 and met with Dr Sam Semir Osmanagich who leads the excavation work. He has published a book[23] (2012) accounting that work. His detailed descriptions of the extensive excavations are accompanied by many photographs. Nature had long since overgrown the Bosnian pyramid structures, so that people had come to regard them as rather angular hills. But Dr Osmanagich, having visited many such archaeological sites around the world, suspected them for what they indeed are and arranged test drillings. And during the 1990s warfare, some had thought the thud of artillery shells hitting the *angular hills* sounded a little different from elsewhere. They were right! The larger pyramid (height 220 meters) has been named the 'Pyramid of the Sun' because of its similarity of form to the Pyramid of the Sun, Teotihuacan, Mexico. But it is larger—even higher than the Great Pyramid that stands on the Giza Plateau (147 meters). It is also much older than the Great Pyramid. Radio-carbon dating of a wood fragment found trapped in the base structure of this Bosnian pyramid indicates an age close to 30,000 years. Design details and materials of construction are very different from the Egyptian Pyramids. There has been early controversy as to authenticity of the Bosnian structures, and it is obvious that there has been logically unacceptable misguided criticism from uninformed sources; perhaps politically or mercenarily motivated—not uncommon where new endeavours are concerned! But there is no doubt whatsoever as to the truth of this discovery or of its immense value to the record of our planetary past. There are huge blocks made of a very hard concrete, sheathing the Pyramid of the Sun. Beneath pyramid and environs, there is a network of branching tunnels, ceramic

The Bosnian Pyramid of the Sun, Visoko, Bosnia.

The Bosnian Pyramid of the Sun, as viewed from a Visoko street.

artefacts at some tunnel locations and there is an energy beam that rises from the pyramid apex.

Excavations of a companion pyramid, named the 'Pyramid of the Moon', have revealed terraces made of shaped and double-layered sandstone slabs on its western face. They remain aligned and appear in very good order. Hundreds of volunteers have been and still are involved in exposing external ledges and stonework, and are also engaged in the clearing of the very extensive system of branching tunnels that have become filled with what is described as riverbed gravel. At some widened tunnel locations there are quite large ceramic artefacts—fired smooth clay artefacts—weighing as much as eight tons. Geo-radar examination of one ceramic block coded K-2 reveals that there is an object or device of some kind within —exactly in its centre. We understand that the various ceramic blocks are situated over underground water flows and they seem to have an effect on the energy charge of the water. On moving one such block a matter of one metre, water began rising through a previously dry floor area. It has now been returned to its favoured position!

There is clearly much more yet to be resolved but this is a truly fascinating project so far with a number of intriguing questions that remain unanswered. The overall construction pattern of the Bosnian Pyramid of the Sun would appear to be a stonework base surmounted by a pyramid shape of compact conglomerate, with its triangular sides faced with very large concrete blocks. Looking at photographs in the author's book, we estimated the blocks to be at least 40-times the volume (and weight) of one of our modern 18" concrete building blocks. Cement chemistry is surprisingly complex with composition normally given in terms of the element oxides that contribute to molecular structure. Such analysis is presented in the author's book with appropriate metal oxides listed. There is no doubt that the blocks are concrete and with strength rather better than our modern blocks in use today. Finally, there is the vertical energy beam, detected rising from the Bosnian Pyramid of the Sun. This seems to be a feature of all true orientated pyramids, and has also been reported rising from Alexander Golod's experimental glass fibre pyramids. The energy beam of the latter has been revealed by means of Russian military radar. We had spoken of these matters with Salumet (2nd April 2012)—his reply:

~ "Forgive me if I seem a little amused—I have said in past times that much more would be discovered in your world. There is much in your world still to be discovered, but it is very appropriate that the discovery is being utilised in this year that so many of you Earth people have decided is an important year. There is knowledge that is waiting to happen—nothing is by chance."

It is of course our *surprise at new discovery* on these occasions that amuses Salumet. He went on to confirm for us that these are indeed very ancient pyramids and were built by others of greater knowledge than is known to humanity today. It was following this unequivocal statement that Mark and Paul visited Bosnia, took photographs, learned much from Dr Osmanagich and returned with a copy of his fascinating and informative book[23]. We thus became equipped to ask further questions of Salumet during our meeting of 2nd July 2012. He informed us that the age figure previously mentioned, of 30,000 years, falls a little short and 35,000 years would be more accurate. Radiocarbon dating of debris in the tunnels indicates that *they* became filled with river bed material much more recently, around 5,000 years ago. Salumet informs us that the tunnels were in the first place made for moving and transporting materials in safety without being seen, the tunnel users being fearful of others who were less aware. There was a flooding problem with some tunnels and it seems that the ceramic devices were a means of controlling water flow. We mentioned the sheathing of pyramid sides with enormous concrete blocks; also revealing our surprise at their size and the superior quality of the concrete.

~ "Again, I have to say: the answer is simple. You have superior beings who were capable of much more than mankind today. That is the fact that you must *always* remember. You are dealing with a race of people much more advanced than humankind today. All their knowledge and skills would have become part of that creation. If you have a being who can travel space, who can create much that mankind knows nothing of, you should not be surprised that they can produce far superior 'goods' to what is available to man."

I added: "And I've no doubt, moved them through 'dematerialisation'—"

~ "Yes, all of these things are available to them. I hope it has helped you. There are many wonders yet to be discovered in your world. It is mounting evidence of other species of intelligence."

It has become clear that we must get used to the idea that Earth has received visits over many, many years from others of far greater intelligence and with far more capabilities than modern humans. Our history books need to be revised and re-written, and there is an urgent need for us to recognise Earth's place in a much wider universal scheme.

Towards the close of a later meeting (30th July 2012), we made it clear that transcripts are now being sent to Dr Osmanagich and that he has been most pleased with Salumet's answers concerning pyramid data. And he had asked if Salumet would accept further questions.

~ "I will—next time, I would be happy to answer questions."

So, on 6th August 2012 we were able to state more clearly that the tunnels extend far beyond the pyramids themselves and Salumet confirmed their purpose—so that beings could move in safety, and so that materials and food supplies could be transported. And our friend had asked if there are more pyramids yet to be discovered:

~ "I would say to him that one more may be found. I cannot guarantee that it will be in his lifetime."

We then asked about the possibility of rooms within, to which our guide gave reasoned response:

~ "If you have tunnels for transportation for people as well as goods, it becomes obvious that there has to be what today you call accommodation. I would suggest that is the way forward."

So that should be the direction of our thinking. And then, on the question of energy:

~ "It is still active but to a lesser degree—a much lesser degree. It (the energy) has not been depleted, it has been transmuted."

We next spoke of possible ley line connection, and it is clear that both humans and visitors would have been sensitive to and well aware of planetary energies in those days, and this would have its link to site selection. Sarah had then asked how long it would take to build a pyramid. Salumet's reply was subtle as if testing our view of what might be seen as credible:

~ "If you want a truthful answer—from extraterrestrials, it *could* be instantaneous. Again, we are speaking of the *power of thought,* as we do in our world of spirit—what you *think* becomes reality."

Some of us might have half anticipated such an answer although there were still exclamations of surprise from several. But of course, we already know of the thought-powered house-building practised by teams on Aerah.

I had replied: "Yes, we appreciate that the thought is instantaneous, and where pyramid construction is concerned, it may well be that things associated with that thought are also instantaneous."

Salumet affirmed this principle, and continued:

~ "(But) you have to remember that, not only are you speaking of other beings, but you are speaking of humankind. There would be slight alterations between the thought of the beings and the humans. There had to be collaboration."

So there *was* collaboration between the visitors and humans of the region, and our guide added that we should ponder on 'thought power' and its application here. I would deduce that in view of the collaboration with humans and use of tunnels, this had to be a project that was ongoing and not wholly instantaneous. Our final question of significance this time concerned the tunnels: were they filled deliberately or was there a cataclysmic event?

~ "Yes, it was a natural occurrence; that is the simple answer."

And we of course were most grateful to Salumet for extending further our knowledge of this past episode in Earth's history.

CHAPTER 11

BOSNIA: A FURTHER VISIT – OCTOBER 2013

As the pace of progress accelerates, we were becoming acutely aware that so much can happen in just eighteen months. There had been increasing correspondence with he who leads the excavations in Bosnia: Dr Sam Semir Osmanagich. And the area of the excavation activity is now described as 'The Bosnian Valley of the Pyramids'. So it had become appropriate that we pay a further visit to the site, this time three of us would go. It has now become very clear that the Bosnian Pyramid of the Sun is the *largest*—height 220 metres—as well as the *oldest* pyramid known to our world; and the associated tunnel labyrinth complex extends for more than ten miles. Thanks largely to unrestricted news coverage on the Internet word of this stupendous European discovery is at last reaching many countries. Significant numbers of individuals now realise the immense value to humanity of this discovery. During our visit we met individuals and parties from Germany, France, Spain, Italy, Switzerland, Bulgaria, South America, Canada, Japan, Vietnam, Hawaii and UK; and it was such a joy to see so much interest from afar.

Ceramic artefact K2, within the tunnel labyrinth.

Tunnel Labyrinth: Our tour would begin at the entrance to the tunnel labyrinth complex. This location is exactly due south of the major pyramid. Along the main tunnel that has been cleared we soon reached a place where it broadened, and where wooden seating has now been positioned around the eight ton ceramic artefact 'K-2'. Phase analysis confirms that K-2 is indeed ceramic (fired clay) material. It has two parts—a base 30 cm thick and a lid 10 cm thick, the join between base and lid being clearly visible. The artefact encloses quartz crystal at its centre, and is positioned on a support directly above the crossing of two subterranean streams. A poster depicts K-2 as a suitable place for meditation. The energy is certainly very good in this locality and some digital camera photos reveal energy orbs. A notice along the tunnel describes very interesting and quite exceptional atmospheric properties—continuous electromagnetic field: 28 KHz—ultrasound: 28-42 KHz—negative ions: 13,500 ions/cc—biophotonic measurements: 25,000 Bovis. And the air seems to stay fresh, with normal oxygen content— no pumping required.

On site K2 details.

[The ultrasound is beyond human hearing range, but we understand that a dog (audio range generally up to 60 KHz) will hear and become disorientated. Nicola Tesla had found that he could alter positive and negative ion content of air by changing radio frequency. So it is therefore likely that the electromagnetic field has a significant role in relation to the negative ions. Atmospheric ions are important. Positive ion concentrations instil tiredness while negative ions relate to feelings of energy and vitality. Normal fresh air should typically contain 1500 negative ions/cc, and would rise to perhaps 2500 ions/cc after a storm. So the tunnel atmosphere with its negative ion concentration of 13500 negative ions/cc is understandably most invigorating and has been designed that way—by highly intelligent beings. The Bovis scale of biophotonic measurement is a standardised dowsing procedure that compares spiritual energies. Numbers greater than 10,000 are considered 'ethereal' and 'places of power'. On this scale, the values in some tunnel locations would be high when compared, for example, to a Tibetan temple.]

Following our visit, Salumet was with us on 28th October 2013 and I was able to recount in some detail the wonderful atmosphere of the tunnel and how its energies have been measured by those involved in the work, and how it was felt by ourselves. I also made it clear that the object of our visit was to take photographs and to help spread the knowledge around the world:

~ "Wherever there is a gathering of spirit then you will find the purest of energies. You know of course that energy cannot be destroyed and where you have a great amount of spiritual energy, the forces will be more strongly felt; and this is what you have experienced. It happens in a number of places on your planet. Throughout time, mankind has felt this change of energy—this upliftment."

Our teacher was complimentary regarding the detail of our report, then added:

~ "but I will also say to you that there are many who wish this knowledge to be imparted all around your world. It will; but the time is not quite ready. But I will say to you: continue—continue to feel, and remember and to know of this spiritual work because it was indeed maintained to a great degree by spirit."

Paul referred to details such as the placement of artefacts in relation to water flows beneath the tunnels to achieve the wonderful atmospheric conditions:

~ "My dear friend, you could do whatever you wanted to, if your spiritual energy, was in the right place at the right *time*. All of you, I believe I have spoken before—all of you have that innate knowledge. All of you know all about the energy of all of the universes. But you have to *return* to that knowledge—it has been lost by so many."

It would be impossible for viruses and bacteria to live in the negative ion concentration of the tunnel atmosphere, and the subterranean sourced water is pure and drinkable. And as we continued along tunnels there were more ceramic artefacts. A number of side tunnels had been blocked off by dry-stone walling; this for some reason, by a later generation thousands of years after the original pyramid project. So, the exceptionally healthy invigorating atmosphere has its inbuilt control that still works today! There is sufficient accumulated evidence here in just the atmosphere alone, for us to see that this tunnel labyrinth was designed by beings of a truly advanced intelligence. They possessed remarkable abilities unknown to present humanity—unknown to us simply because, through many generations of neglect of that innate knowledge, we have forgotten.

Vratnica Tumulus: This is an artificially made hill of conical shape 5 Km southeast of the pyramid site. It is of layered construction rising to a height of 32 metres above the nearby road. Its rock layers are quite massive, with some slabs weighing as much as 20 tons; alternating with clay layers between. A curious feature is that the flat upper surfaces of layered rock appear to have 3-4 cm of a different rock fused onto it. One small patch has been chipped away making this clearly evident. A core drilling indicates two substantial concrete layers beneath the tumulus with 3 metres of air space between. A French laboratory has carried out a concrete analysis which confirms the presence of artificial geo-polymer cement binder. This likely chamber has not as yet been investigated. Croatian physicists report an electromagnetic energy beam of 28 KHz at the top of the tumulus.

Bosnian Pyramid of the Sun: Still feeling invigorated from that tunnel labyrinth experience, we next day walked through the town, out of town, along the winding single track road and finally up a stepped track to the pyramid apex. It was quite a trek for one getting on in years (fast approaching 83). But the input of all those negative ions the day before was magical! We did however stop for refreshment at Sanela's café a few hundred metres from our goal. Many might choose to take a taxi as far as the café! Looking to the south from the top, the structures named 'Pyramid of the Love' and 'The Temple of Mother Earth' are clearly evident. Looking to the north is the town of Visoko. The pyramid north face points accurately to 'cosmic north'—to within just 12 seconds of arc! The slope of the pyramid sides is 45°, and all four triangular elevations of the pyramid have been faced with quite substantial concrete blocks. This is not immediately obvious to the casual observer because nature has since taken over with soil deposition, scrub vegetation and pine forest. At a much lower level on the north face, areas of the block-work have now been exposed. I would estimate some blocks to be as much as 200-times the volume of one of our standard 18" building blocks, and all four triangular faces are, we understand, clad with this high grade concrete—a huge construction project by our modern standards! Organic material residue (leaf), sandwiched between concrete layers has been radiocarbon dated to 29,200 +/- 400 years. So the actual construction goes back at least that far. And then there is the quality of the concrete.

Samples of the concrete have been examined by scientific institutions in Bosnia, Italy and France. It is described as aggregate with an artificial geo-polymer cement binder, but it differs significantly from today's concrete made using conventional cement binder. Modern concrete is said to have an expected life span of 100 years but additions to the mix can very much enhance durability, it is thought up to around 16,000 years is possible. The pyramid facing has clearly lasted much longer than this and remains in excellent condition. The hardness of concrete is described in terms of its MPa value. The *compressive strength* of the product of commerce is generally 17 – 34 MPa (2500 – 5000 psi). Values greater than 41 MPa are considered 'high strength'. Higher values are possible with special additions to the mix and concrete of 70 MPa is made for special applications. The compressive strength of the pyramid concrete is 133 MPa. It is therefore superior to its various modern counterparts and is a most remarkable product. At around 1 %, its low water absorption value also differs from today's concrete which is generally in the range 4 – 9 %.

German geophysicists have examined the structure using geo-radar and confirm that there are inner passageways. Croatian physicists have detected an energy beam at the pyramid apex having a diameter of 9.0 metres. Italian, Finnish and Serbian experts have measured electromagnetic field, ultrasound and infrasound at the pyramid apex. (Human audio range is generally 20 Hz – 20 KHz. While ultrasound refers to higher frequencies, infrasound refers to lower frequencies.) So the energy beam that rises vertically appears to be of a composite nature. This is all most intriguing and much has been learned at this site during just eight years of study and excavation, with clearly much more to follow.

Vratnica Tumulus – Dr Osmanagich conducts a guided tour.

Vratnica Tumulus – Exposed rock layers.

Bosnian Pyramid of the Sun, north face – Concrete cladding.

The 45° sloping concrete, now clearly overgrown by
vegetation and pine forest.

CHAPTER 12

CAHUACHI:
NAZCA RIVER VALLEY

Referring back to Salumet's informative visit of 6th August 2012, we might ask ourselves: "What next?" Well, I have to say: there are times when we are quite bowled over by surprise at what follows next. On 20th August 2012, Salumet devoted time to encouraging us in self-development. There followed a 'rescue'; then one spoke via Sarah who very clearly had quite a full knowledge of our previous meetings. He began:

> ~ "You have shown much interest in the last few sessions about pyramids, and I would like to tell you that I was one of those working with the pyramids at that time."

I replied with understandable surprise: "Wonderful!" and quickly inquired which ones.

> ~ "The pyramids were in the south of what you call America; I was much involved with the comings and goings of those who were brought in to help us."

George: "Wonderful! I see, so you were of the Earth—you were humankind, and extraterrestrial beings were coming in to help. Is that correct?"

~ "That is quite correct—it was a time of much discovery for both our worlds, and I was greatly influenced by those you call 'extraterrestrials.'"

Well, Salumet during his early visits to us had spoken of a well-progressed ancient civilisation in South America—it was all beginning to knit together very nicely.

George: "Would it be true to say: you were learning from each other?"

~ "It was—yes, quite true. But I have to say that I think us Earth people were learning more from the extraterrestrials than the other way around."

I asked if the region in South America might be the Nazca Plateau, but that name was not known to our communicator. I explained the reason for asking was that we are aware of many lines crossing the area and there are animal representations. This immediately fired renewed interest:

~ "I *can* tell you yes, that we became very much more aware of animals and we were most keen to put this down on whatever surface we could, so that others could learn from it. So, if you are talking about art form and animals, this could well be the place where we were."

I responded: "Yes, we are aware of very large animal designs and lines which may have related to space travel vehicles."

~ "Some of those animals were influenced by the extraterrestrials—they were not just our Earth animals."

And then followed further clarification:

~ "The extraterrestrials influenced us in their design—but I cannot say if they were exactly how the extraterrestrials view them on their own planet. But they DID influence the drawings that you I understand can see today."

Paul: "Can I ask if the extraterrestrials appeared in human form or different?"

Nazca Plateau Lines.

Nazca Landscape Images – contrast enhanced photo.

~ "They were in a solid form but they were different—although solid, they took on a *slightly* opaque appearance. They did have arms and legs—not quite so wide as us and they were much shorter, but they did have quite large heads."

Having details of others who had visited Earth in past times, I asked how many fingers per hand:

~ "There were three."

Further conversation established that heads were wide, and although much of the time they walked with humans to better facilitate cooperation, they could also teleport. They would teleport when wanting to get somewhere quickly. Humans of that time were able to communicate with them by mind-link, but on occasions needed to resort to sign language. Rod asked how many visitors would be present at one time.

~ "I would say, at one time there would possibly be fifty."

Now this was getting to be really exciting! And I was able to say:
"We have been privileged to speak with beings that answer your description, and they referred to an earlier teleported visit when their pictures were drawn on what is known as the 'Atlatl Rock' in the Nevada Desert. So we have actually been able to speak with beings that answer your description."

On the occasion when we spoke with them, Jan had clairvoyance. She could see clairvoyantly a group that she described at the time as consisting of around fifty. And she was able to make a sketch immediately following, illustrating their wide heads and three-fingered hands. Our first joy of discovery came when we found that Jan's sketch compared so very closely with the Atlatl Rock inscriptions (of which none of us in the group had previously heard). The name we have for their planetary home is 'Crogaria'. Now we had matching description of these same beings as extraterrestrials who build pyramids! Our friend declared this to be very good news, and in response to a further question from Paul:

~ "They were there for the last part of my lifetime. When I said there were about fifty, they were not necessarily the same fifty all the time, because they could come and go as they pleased—travel was most easy for them."

So as with Jan's previous observation, they even seem to favour the fifty grouping! Our friend then made the statement:

~ "Well, I think we are all in agreement, and IT IS THIS AGREEMENT THAT I WOULD WISH FOR THE WHOLE OF THIS PLANET, because it is a peaceful living amongst all—not just Earth beings but extraterrestrials—so harmonious, and if we could all work towards this, it would be a most wonderful drift."

Rod then inquired about the overseeing of the project which produced an interesting reply:

~ "They made our lives so easy. They were able to do so many things that we were not able, and we tried very hard to learn from them. It was hoped that what we learnt we would be able to pass on; but I can see from life today on this planet, we did not do a very good job in passing this information on."

Well, where passing on is concerned, acceptance also has to be taken into account!
Mark: "Would you be able to speak now about any of the things you wanted passed on?"

~ "Well, I can say to you that all heavy work need not be heavy."

I suggested this would involve dematerialisation and power-of-thought.

~ "Yes, that is correct."

Paul: "Did you gain some ability to move heavy stones and objects?"

~ "I was able to do some, but it was not normally by myself. It would take a group of us Earth people together to be able to do what one extraterrestrial could do."

Paul: "Was it a simple case of imagining these heavy rocks to be lightweight?"

~ "I would say it was more a case of putting yourself into a mindset where you were actually being helped to do it. So you would wish for something to happen, and then put yourself into that—I would not say meditation—but getting towards that way where you are not quite in your body and not quite out of it."

Sara: "A sort of light trance?"

~ "Yes, perhaps you could say that. So yes, you do not need to concentrate too hard, but you do need to get yourself away from total Earth thinking. To dig a hole in the rock—as long as we had focussed on that before we went into this trance, we were then just able to do it. If we could do it as Earth people, then there is no reason why YOU cannot do it."

Sara: "And so, the power came from spirit to you?"

~ "Yes, it is really a concentration of energy and this is what produces the actual movement. It is a state of mind and it is the use of energy."

We asked for a name to know our friend by. It seems that exact translation is difficult but 'Theodore' is close enough. And Paul wished to have a name for the extraterrestrials:

~ "We called them 'The Greens' because they had a slight green tinge, but once we got to know them better, we had individual names for them."

Theodore could not remember a name for their planet, but it was usually referred to as 'The Green Planet'.

George: "And were you aware of pyramid energies? Were the pyramids built in order to produce energy?"

~ "It was something that the extraterrestrials taught us, and yes we were aware of the extra energy inside; and this energy was also used to boost the energy of their return journey to their planet."

Atlatl Rock petroglyphs – the beings have arms, legs, wide heads and three-fingered hands.

In reply to a question about a craft for their interplanetary journeys:

~ "Yes, they had a small craft that was to us, not solid enough to take anybody without collapsing. But it was very strong and it needed just a little extra energy to be able to take off from the heavy Earth pull. And this energy from the pyramid was enough to set them back on homeward course."

Rod: "We've noticed the great accuracy of these pyramids. Did they have instrumentation to create that accuracy?"

~ "They were able to do it without instruments. They knew how, and they told us what we should do, and they informed us of what they were doing. It was very much a combined effort of learning for both parties."

Rod: "You must have been very proud—"

~ "I have to say 'yes', we were proud of the finished article. But we were also quite in awe of what had been achieved. It was I have to say, a very good time."

We inquired of Theodore's further Earth lives since then:

~ "I have had other lives, but they have not been in the same vein as this one, so long ago."

As to the period of the pyramid work, our friend could only say that it was an extremely long time ago and before what we would now call 'general education'.

~ "So all of those (humans) working with these extraterrestrials were very spiritual people and those who were not quite so spiritual were not involved in the pyramid construction. There was not any bad feeling between the two sets of Earth people. It was peaceful, but it was a time of lack of understanding. So I would say that so long as the two groups did not come into contact with one another, each group led peaceful lives. But lack of understanding can create many problems."

Rod said how wonderful it is that Theodore has such clear memory of it all, and Paul asked about his recollection of local topography:

~ "This particular pyramid—it was in a valley. There was water and there was plenty of food. There were lots of trees on the slopes. It was a fertile part."

We learned that their food consisted of vegetables and fish from the river. Our friend had lived initially with family as part of a small group. They were very spiritual and we understand it had been known through several generations that extraterrestrials would one day be coming to join them. When the extraterrestrials came, some organisation occurred, such that they were able to live as a larger group with a more structured sharing of tasks.

~ "We were able to lead what you might call a more sophisticated life. But the spiritual side did not change."

Finally, we asked if he was saddened at the lesser understanding of spirit that in general exists on the Earth today and does he feel there is hope for us. His reply produced hearty laughter:

~ "I do feel somewhat sad that so many have grown away from spirit, but when you reach the bottom, you cannot go further down—you can only go up. So I would say to you that you are on the way up!"

When it was time for Theodore to depart he was of course enthusiastically thanked for such an enlightening exchange and the door was left open for him to come again should he find that he has the opportunity. The Nazca Plateau region is generally rated by modern peoples as an area of great mystery, with the numerous lines running across the plateau and many, slightly odd as depicted, large animal designs. We now have some small measure of explanation for these, and know that they are *not* just heavily stylised art form. I think from the information given, Theodore's pyramid would be in the Nazca river valley—at Cahuachi. And we would think it to have been the original of several that now stand upon the site.

CHAPTER 13

PYRAMID BUILDERS
FROM PLANET SIMKAH

Just three weeks later (10ᵗʰ September 2012) and it was another memorable meeting. Three guests had travelled 200-miles from Norfolk to join us and we were so pleased that it became such a wonderfully eventful evening for all who were present. Firstly Salumet came through and spoke of the eagerness that he sensed with everyone. One question placed to him concerned the different races on Earth and how these might have come about, with speculation from a purely material stance. Our guide saw fit to deflect from that material view:

> ~ "Yes, too much in your histories, of not only this planet but others, are concerned about this. I would say: rather concentrate on the spirit. Whether you came from another planet and met with another here—the spirit would be the same. Therefore, does it really matter what the outer structure becomes?"

Indeed, as to *material* forms on a planet and how each has evolved, what does it matter when the same spirit is the essential essence *of all life* that runs throughout the universe? This has to be seen as an intrinsic logic—a wise adherence to the principle of Ockham's razor, with no needless multiplication of assumptions when explaining something. In response to another question, Salumet spoke on the intrinsic nature of 'truth', firstly reiterating:

~ "When first I came I wanted to bring to this world some truth. Mankind has always elaborated and contorted truth. My purpose was to tell the truth of *all of creation* which has always existed. So much is constructed in your world which does not have the basis of truth, but is elaborated to suit mankind. Mankind has in a sense the most active physical brain, but what mankind lacks is the equation of the quiet spirit. To find complete and utter truth—you will only find it when you go within quietly and find your own self. That is the only *true* pathway, then all these happenings around you begin to fall into place and you either accept or do not accept. That is why you have been given free will."

So we now have guidance on the very essence of life and on the pathway to truth.

~ "That spiritual being that you are, *knows* the fuller truth—that is where the questioning begins—because you have that inner knowledge."

So truth comes from that small voice within. Further questions had concerned openness as opposed to secrecy; the expanding Internet— Julian Assange finding political sanctuary in the Ecuadorian Embassy in London, and how one might possibly see him as a 'Champion of Openness'. Salumet had responded by firstly declaring that he does indeed advocate openness and truth—as we well know! Then he followed with the statement:

~ "I would say only that I champion 'truth' and 'love'—your world has to find these things for itself. Without 'love' you would be as well not to exist. There are too many people in your world, who seek only for themselves—who have no thought for others. But the time must come when they face themselves, whether it be in this world or in our world, and it is much better to deal with these things whilst on the Earth planet."

Having thus enjoyed a session of Salumet's alpha plus enlightenment, a further treat then came via Sarah—a pyramid builder who visited Earth and who had actually worked on the *Bosnian pyramid project*; he now of course in, and addressing us from, the spirit realm of his own planet. He began:

~ "I know that you are all with knowledge of spirit and therefore I do not need to tell you that I have come with much love from your friends. Your friends are those who you were talking with last time. They wished me to come back just one more time, because these friends of yours who are from other planets—they were the ones from South of America. But there is a group here (in spirit) who have asked me to tell you they are aware of your knowledge of the visit made to the *other* pyramids that you were so interested in last time. So this is a message from them to tell you: they are aware of your interest and what you have discovered about them. They are most happy that you are on the right track!"

I replied: "Oh thank you for that! Yes we feel we are beginning to understand now. There's obviously much that we don't know but we have *some* knowledge of these pyramids that were built by our extraterrestrial friends many, many years ago and we do respect all this work. And I think we are *beginning* to understand that one of the first things that visitors to our planet have done in the past has been to build a pyramid which will provide energy to assist in their return journey."

~ "Yes, and not only for the return journey but also to give energy to those who are on this planet visiting; because although they are able to travel in such a way that they can arrive on your planet Earth, they still need extra, what you might call 'boost,' in order to be able to function here."

Paul asked for confirmation that we are talking about the builders of the Bosnian pyramids?

~ "Yes—because these friends were very much aware of the conversation last time and they wished you to know they are ALL able to communicate."

We checked that this is indeed mind-link communication that we speak of, and affirmed that we on Earth are rather backward in our ability to do this.

~ "Yes—in many parts, but I will tell you: not in all. Yes, although you are as you would say, a little backward in your knowledge, or should I say the USE of it. There are indeed other planets who are in perhaps not quite so less a degree of knowledge, but still they are struggling. So do not feel too down trodden."

So we are not alone in being backward!

~ "No, but you will get there I am sure. I would say also: we are pleased that you are interested in us, so it is a good thing for us both."

Paul: "Well we'd love you to come back and build some more, or show us how, when the time is right."

~ "Well maybe we can arrange something, let us work together and see what we can do."

Paul: "Mm!"
I asked if the pyramid building to produce energy is something of the past or does it still go on? Perhaps there is now a better method to produce the energy?

~ "I would say that if we were to come back to this planet Earth, we would still build something similar, but it could be that we could make them perhaps a little smaller now."

Paul: "And I guess you could only come back if your guides directed you as to when the appropriate time would be to re-visit?"

~ "Yes, the problem we have now with your planet Earth is that there are so few places where we would be left alone to work with you, and it would be most difficult if we were to be interrupted in the middle of a session."

George: "I would imagine it could be quite damaging to be interrupted?"

~ "It might well be that we could get trapped here."

Ray: "How long would it take to build one of these pyramids, would you say?"
Now this was a good question that produced an intriguing answer. It *could* it seems be fairly instantaneous—and this is consistent with other statements that we have received.

~ "But it would depend on those we are working together with."

It would of course depend upon the mind potential of those others cooperating, and a purely mind-powered construct *could* indeed be fairly instantaneous. But of course, with the mind development of Earthlings being what it is, one can envisage the need for a more lengthy project. Trish then sought further details of energy in relation to using a smaller pyramid size:

~ "Let me start like this: your planet has evolved and so have ours—knowledge is ever-growing. So we would also be able to condense things. Let me take as an example, your computers. In the beginning (they) were so large—they can now do so much and they are small."

All agreed—and what a splendid Earthly example, coming from an extraterrestrial in spirit! He is aware of key details of *our* development!

~ "We too can achieve more with less. So we would be able to make some smaller structures, but there again, we have not done this before with the smaller structures. So it would be a trial to start with; but let us not push this completely away, because all is possible, and we are as keen to work with you as with other planets. So maybe this is something that can be achieved if it is felt it would benefit your planet at this time."

I responded that as far as those in this room are concerned, that would be absolutely wonderful; then asked if their planet is in the same galaxy as ours. It is not. Olive requested clarification at this point for the mode of transmission being used. It was confirmed that our friend is in spirit and can relay messages to and from others in spirit; also to and from those living physical lives on their planet today. (And of course, those who built the Bosnian pyramids lived physical lives 35,000 years ago!) We asked about relative size of their physical being compared to humans and it seems they were smaller.

Paul: "That makes sense. We walked some of the passageways in the Bosnian pyramids—and we had to bend a bit sometimes."

Paul then inquired—if returning to Earth, could you with your spaceships land without our satellites detecting?

~ "Yes, we could—and do not forget they are already coming here and giving you messages with the crop circles."

Paul: "Well it would be lovely as far as *we* are concerned, to have you back on the Earth."

Trish: "It would also be very, very nice if we could understand the messages sent with those crop circles—"

~ "Yes, I think you will find that part of these messages is to help you to focus on your inner self and to work them out for yourselves, because if this knowledge is just GIVEN to you, it will not be accepted as well as when it has been worked out, and suddenly the light dawns. So I am of the understanding that it is something for you to work on and not just to be given."

I ventured: "Yes, so it is up to us to go within and discover within ourselves the meaning. There are I believe residual energies with the crop circles. Is there some factor in the crop circles that might *help* us to go within?"

~ "Yes of course. That energy that has been left behind, was used by those visitors and yes, I would say that any extra energy that your bodies can be given can only be of good. But I would also say that it is up to you to focus—you cannot allow others to do all the work for you. But yes, I would say if you were to put yourself on this area that has been left energized, you would find your thoughts much easier to come to the fore."

Trish inquired as to the permanence of the energy:

~ "Yes, not for all (time), but it does stay there for a while and then like other energies it gets absorbed into other, in this case areas, and you will have other crops growing on there that each time they grow, they take a little of the energy away from the soil."

George: "So there would be an advantage to visit these crop designs and imbibe that energy?"

~ "Yes, if you are interested in getting to know what messages are being sent then I would say yes, this would be a good idea."

Paul asked about the possibility of finding remaining artefacts during pyramid excavations:

~ "We would not have brought any with us, but I can tell you that much work was done in the pyramids, and as gifts to each other, small artefacts were indeed exchanged. So it is possible that you might find, let us say a small tablet or perhaps—and I don't know if this would still exist, but carving into wood was always most popular. So I would say there could be some small tokens, but if you are looking for something from our planet, then I would say you won't find that."

I declared that to be interesting, and this I felt was a good time to mention the large ceramic artefacts: "There are large ceramic objects which weigh several tons. I believe they were used—I think they were enclosing devices that have an effect on the ground waters of that area. But I know there are large fired clay objects in some of the tunnels—"

~ "Yes, they were used to fill with water and then you could take water from them without the water coming up into the passageways."

George: "Ah yes, so that would be water for your use — for drinking?"

~ "Yes—and for whatever other reason."

George: "One of those other reasons might well have been for making what we call large concrete blocks, for constructing the outer faces of the pyramid. Is that a term that you would understand?"

~ "Yes I do understand what you are saying, and yes, some was done by the population and indeed they would have needed water. I would also say quite a bit of it was done by the visitors, and this was not needed when the visitors did it."

Paul: "Using Power of Thought—"

~ "Yes."

Olive sought clarification as regards thought-power and use of levitation, referring to a time when she herself had once been levitated—a wonderful experience to have had!

~ "We were able to create and place in one—movement. But yes, you can levitate and levitation of those things that have been made by man (was necessary), but those that are made with the mind—they do not need to be levitated, because they are placed directly in the right position, once created."

And we all appreciated that to be very clearly stated. Trish then inquired as to the origin of the drawn water:

~ "Yes I can tell you: It was underground and it was used within the pyramid itself. So all was able to be achieved within one place and for us visitors that was not so important; but for the people from Earth, they needed shelter and would not have found it so easy if each time they needed water they had to go on long journeys. It was all very well planned."

George: "Wonderful! Can you tell me: was there any element of teaching involved once the pyramid was there? Did you have gatherings where the Earth people were instructed in any way?"

~ "I would say that the main teaching that was done was during the construction. Much was learned in this time and because the knowledge and the actual physical building was being constructed at the same time, there was no doubt in the minds of those who were there, that what was happening and what was being taught, was real."

I suggested that we might call it 'teaching by example'.

~ "Yes that would be a good way of saying it. I am afraid I am being called—I must go now."

George: "Yes — just finally—this was a happy occasion for you, you were all good friends?"

~ "Oh yes, it was a most useful and cordial time."

Well, that was good and much appreciation was voiced by all of us, including one cry of:
"You must come again!"

~ "Yes, I am beginning to smile because maybe I come again—for real!"

Even more enthusiasm was expressed at that thought, and we asked if we might have a name:

~ "I do not remember my name—"

Paul: "Or possibly just the name of the planet that your people were from?"

~ "Yes I can tell you that—it was Simkah."

Paul: "Simkah—right!"

~ "So now I am returning."

And so much gratitude and LOVE was expressed for our new-found friend, or should we say 'old friend', from just across the Cosmos. Perhaps I could be forgiven for imagining this unnamed dear one from Simkah as J M Barrie's 'Peter Pan' traversing the heavens—*'Second star to the right and straight on till morning'*—a phrase also echoed by Captain Kirk of Star Trek!

When Salumet was again with us on 24th September 2012, I suggested that the knowledge we receive from more advanced peoples of this universe, helps us to see what would be good for us in the way of further evolution:

~ "Yes, we all come to you with a mission—for some it is to give further evidence or advice about your world. We choose those who come, carefully; and always I have told you: I like to keep to the simple word, because truth is simple. You need no extensive words—complicated language, to tell you that what you are about is 'love'. It is a small and simple word, but it has a meaning that enfolds ALL of your Universes. And I would like to think and feel that that small word called 'love', comes from within each one of you, much more easily than at one time it did — I'm sure you all feel this."

It is exactly so; and the 'love' extended to our new friend has very quickly been highlighted by Salumet as enfolding *all* universes—*all* creation; and that is one big statement! On 15th October 2012, there had in discussion, been mention of 'fear', and I had made known my feeling that it is so important for this planet to conquer its silly fear of others from across the universe. That there are sentient beings out there, far in advance of humanity, should not be seen as reason to be fearful. Their advancement and greater knowledge equate to a more fully developed spirituality and a more advanced awareness of love, so why be fearful? We have been extremely fortunate as a group in hearing from the spirit realms of other planets, about various pyramids that are here on *this* planet, and the purpose for which they were built. And we have been able to cross-reference this information—which *should* result in all such data becoming acceptable to those on Earth. This should help everyone to conquer any *fear of the unknown*; and that which is currently unknown *must* eventually of course become known.

~ "Yes, you can only give out the information that is available to you. It is then the responsibility of those people receiving, to decide whether or not they also accept this information. You cannot rush the process of acceptance, but as time continues and we all do our best to influence your world, then more and more people are beginning to think for themselves; to question also, what they read and hear. This is healthy and we would not discourage people feeling that way, and if it means that their own emotions at times override their own common sense, then so be it. But it is important that we continue to strive for the truth and the knowledge which is available to you all. Your world will become a much better place, but it is slowly, slowly."

On pointing out that an axiom of one of our institutions is 'knowledge dispels fear', I was corrected, and had to agree that it is truth that dispels fear. The knowledge has to be *truthful* knowledge!

~ "Yes, not all knowledge is truthful."

Sarah had had Internet correspondence with one who had taken digital photographs inside the Bosnian pyramids. They showed in addition to the expected subject, coloured light effects and white orbs. Sarah sought an explanation that she might relay back to the one who had taken the photos; so on 26th November 2012, an explanation was requested:

~ "We have already discussed that spirit has been involved—and what is being seen are spiritual lights, which of course you would understand to be different from your everyday colours and light. So there is really no mystery for those who have knowledge. But of course it is more difficult in trying to explain to those without spiritual knowledge what is happening there."

So, as ever, a succinct statement—a phenomenon easily understood once the spiritual homework has been done. Some effects showing up in general photography will of course be due to light scatter—that is not in dispute. But there is also sufficient evidence for a spiritual energy basis for certain orbs, especially within pyramids where such energy factor is known to be present. It should also be stated that some people are more sensitive than others and will have a direct awareness of the spiritual light phenomena that digital cameras operating in low-light conditions can be quite good at revealing.

Orbs of spiritual light within the Bosnian tunnel labyrinth.

CHAPTER 14

MORE FROM BONNIOL THROUGH 2013

It was now 4th March and Bonniol was once again with us; this after a break of 18 months, and we were just so delighted! All this time, I had so much wanted to report to our dear friend the discovery that Earth's one kilo weight standard had lost 50 micrograms through a period of 122 years, in-keeping with that universal law—'as spirituality on a planet increases, densities <u>de</u>crease'. Well, I got carried away and voiced the news rather too early. Our friend had replied:

~ "Well!—that's quite a welcome isn't it!"

And everyone fell about laughing. I had made a booboo, but at least this serves to illustrate Bonniol's mastery of wonderful witty repartee. He was next apologetic for the lengthy break, pointing out that the connections are not always as easy as some might think. He continued:

~ "There are always changes aren't there? But that is what part of life is about—these changes. It is part of our journey—nothing stays the same, not even your weight measurements!"

More chuckles followed then Sarah inquired: "So how are your meetings going? Are your friends all around you while you are talking with us?"

~ "We have had many more of our meetings and we have continued to — I was going to say WORK with other peoples from other planets. It doesn't *feel* like work, but we regard it as work, to build these bridges to other worlds."

George: "I think when we last spoke there were ten planets—"

~ "We are continuing with that number, it has not changed."

I explained about our communication from Planet Simkah spirit realms and how we now recognise the value to space-travellers of pyramids to provide their energy requirement.

~ "And you have become more aware of the importance then, of these pyramids."

George: "Yes, absolutely. This is not information that the major part of the population is familiar with yet — it takes time for people on Earth to be accepting of new information, but yes, we here in this group and those that we are in contact with, are familiar now with the importance of pyramids and how they relate to visits in the past from others, to our planet. So this I feel is quite a big step forward that is being taken."

~ "Yes, there are so many ways in which we take these steps forward and your past friendships with these pyramid builders must give you a lot of inspiration."

George: "Yes, inspiration, joy—it's so wonderful to know that all this has happened, and the bonds, the links—are still there!"

~ "And they will only get stronger. The hardest thing is to start, and once you've started, then you have the momentum that builds up and pulls you along."

Sarah spoke of our feeble efforts at mind-linking to send each other simple pictures, which led our friend into expression of his philosophical views:

~ "We can only focus on so much in one lifetime. There is always enough time to achieve what you NEED to achieve."

Rod: "Do you have many people who are negative on your planet Bonniol—negative attitudes?"

~ "This is something that takes me a little time to answer, because I feel there are DEGREES of negativity, which may not even be noticeable to some, but we would not suffer the depths of negativity which occur on your planet quite often. When we lose our focus, we consider that to be a little negative and we then need to look at ourselves to discover the reason for that. But I wonder if that's the same as you are referring to?"

Rod: "Yes, very much so — very good answer."
George: "Yes unfortunately we have a few people that get rather fixed in negative attitudes at times, but I think at the present time we are moving into better attitudes generally; but we still have quite a lot of work to do on the planet. I'm sorry you had difficulty in getting to us. Is the difficulty a matter of spiritual connections?"

~ "Yes, there are several factors and it's not always the same issue that causes the reason why I cannot always come. There always will be breaks in communication."

George: "Yes of course—have there been times when you've been *around*, but not been able to speak?"

~ "I have sometimes been around yes."

George: "Ah, that figures, yes — I've felt that at times."
Sarah was encouraging that Bonniol should speak and not wait to be spoken to, if that was a problem, and this led to further comment on communication:

~ "Thank you, I will make the efforts when we can and we feel there is the opportunity. Of course there are other things happening within your group which also need time. But we wish to keep this friendship alive, even if it means sometimes not always speaking. There are other ways to communicate of course. We don't have to be masters of mind projection, to be aware of each other and send each other thoughts. So we don't always have to have this physical method of contact. We understand that it is necessary sometimes. And remember yes—your thoughts can always reach us. Thank you for this time together."

That is indeed so. The session was concluded with the fondest of farewells, and our dear friend managed to get back with us again just three weeks later.

Sarah: "Good evening Bonniol—I *thought* you were coming this evening—nice to have you back!"

Sarah had sensed his presence, and our friend explained that it was sometimes difficult making the final *push* to complete the connection. I now crossed the room to be closer, the conversation being muted this time, so as not to disturb Salumet who was silently working with Eileen.

~ "It's not always clear even for us what the problem is sometimes, but once we've come through we are through!"

Sarah: "Yes, anyway you've done it—that's the main thing. Jolly good!"

~ "Thank you. Um, yes it's always lovely to reconnect with you people."

George: "It's wonderful to have you through again, Bonniol."

~ "I've been thinking of you, even though we don't always speak. I think it's good to have these thoughts because—it's becoming a smaller place, isn't it!—this universe."

The expanding universe becoming smaller! But yes, in a manner of speaking it indeed is. Our conversation moved into comparative lifestyles and how Aerans love to be close to nature.

George: "Yes, I think this is perhaps one of our faults on this planet. We've moved a little away from that; and I would like to see everyone going back to a simpler life, much more involved with nature than we are at the moment."

Sarah: "There is a bit of change beginning. There are people with allotments to grow their own vegetables. These things take time, when you've moved so far away from it."

George: "Yes, there is home-gardening and organic agriculture; this is beginning to come in. We use far too much mechanisation and chemicals in our farming. I feel it will be much nicer if we can do things on a smaller scale, so that more people are involved in that work."

~ "Yes, it's um—it's so nice to share nature with others. We are all individuals, and yet, when we share our thoughts and feelings, there is a new awareness that begins. And in nature, we can share this—these feelings."

I said we are beginning to realise just how fundamental to life 'thought' is.

~ "Well, even for us, who work with it in ways which you are not yet able to do—we still wonder at the potential there is. It is truly the most important thing in Creation—from what we know."

George: "It's nice to hear those words. Perhaps, connected with that—we are only really just beginning to realise what the large pyramids mean, on our planet. When other visitors have been here, the first thing they have done is to build a pyramid—to capture or create the energy for their wellbeing while they're here and to provide power for their return journey. I don't know how widespread in the universe pyramid-building is, but it seems to have been a favourite thing to construct pyramids in the past on our planet."

~ "Yes, it is um, certainly not something that is unique to Earth. We also have pyramids on our planet, also used to gather the energy."

George: "Well, that's interesting."

~ "We have um, developed um—there is um—we have um—"

A pause followed—we were beginning to get some difficulty with the word flow.

~ "The shape of the pyramid is of course um, a perfect shape for collecting and steering or pointing this particular energy in the direction and when we are sitting inside the pyramids—it can be of great help to use this to focus."

George: "Would you describe this as an aid to help meditation?"

~ "The meditation um, comes from within the person I would say but the pyramid shape helps to build the power that is generated."

Sarah: "I was wondering how you built your pyramids, because you are able to use your thought much better than us. Our pyramids are made up of big blocks. Are yours similarly made?"

~ "Yes, the rocks of the earth, we find are the best for—um—capturing if you like, the energy—um—the shape itself is important."

George: "Yes, and it must be aligned to planetary spin; and I would think the energy arises from sweeping through the aether in accord with planetary spin."

~ "Yes—the position has to be at the right angle for intercepting the flow of energy that is being collected."

George: "Yes, I imagine the energy within the pyramid adds to mind energy, or helps in some way, when meditating?"

~ "The mind is not helped as such, I would say: there is power to be used, and it is put to use for whatever purpose. There are ways to use it but it is energy not of our selves."

I replied that we know pyramid energy causes seeds to produce greater crop yield.

~ "Yes, they have been used to help with the storing and protection of seeds."

George: "Do you use pyramid-storage to assist your agriculture on your planet?"

~ "We have experimented with this. We find we do not actually need to use them in that way—the seed can be stored in other ways but the pyramids can be used to improve areas which—um—which have conditions which cause problems for plants."

George: "Of course, the area surrounding pyramids is influenced by the energy, I believe."

~ "Yes, and if they are located in the right places, this can improve the fertility, if you like, of the area."

Lilian: "So, do you build them just to help a particular area?"

~ "That is our main interest—we are people who spend a great deal of time working with nature; and where pyramids are used it is usually with—um—in connection to improving the nature in some way—whether it's for our crops—"

Another pause occurred, and I inquired if there was interaction with wildlife.

~ "There is always interaction—when you build pyramids, they have an effect on the area."

Lilian: "Do lots of other planets have these pyramids?"

~ "Yes, they are a shape—a structure which has a definite affect on the energy flows, and so they can be of use for that."

Rod: "Are the dimensions of the base and the height of the pyramid a common feature throughout the universe? Are ours similar to your sizes?"

~ "I would say the size is not important. It's the positioning and what they are built with."

George: "I think the proportions—height in relation to base, vary considerably. But I think you are saying that the position is more important than the precise proportions—"

~ "They should be positioned precisely. The size of them varies, depending on the nature of the area and the requirements of the area."

Lilian: "So would it be that energy-lines (ley lines) are used—to put them on?"

~ "Yes, they are used, always with the energy lines, yes."

Mark: "Are they used for healing and purification?"

~ "They can certainly be used for healing, yes. Yes, and um, when you say purification—"

Mark: "I understood that you can purify water and even give it healing quality—"

~ "I would say in the sense that the water would be energised—it would be—um—improved in that way."

I pointed out that our water normally freezes to solid ice at low temperature, but this is not so within a pyramid.

~ "Yes, I would imagine that is due to the greater energy in the water."

George: "The bonding between the atoms of the water just doesn't seem to happen, when the energy is there—"

At this point, Salumet had completed his work with Eileen, so that she was now herself and able to participate in the discussion.

Eileen: "Could I say: you are so much more advanced than we are on Earth—is it still necessary to use pyramids to change energy? Have you not reached that stage yet? Can you not transmute energy with your mind, without use of pyramids?"

~ "There is—um—we have abilities to transmute energy, yes. The pyramids are permanent features, which require no additional thought or attention. So, in areas where we may wish for nature to create— um—a different energy situation; where plants and nature can begin to grow and benefit from more constant environment—"

George: "So we can think of a pyramid as an ongoing permanent energy transmutation device that does not have to be fed or up-kept in any way."

~ "Yes, we could of course still grow our crops but we feel they are a natural—um—tool to use, much like other tools for growing crops. They can be placed and—"

George: "Do they alter your climate at all? Do they have any effect on climate?"

~ "Yes, they affect the area around them, and yes, they will have an influence on the climate."

We were surprised at this point, as another began speaking with quite a throaty voice via Jan, from across the room:

~~ "They are regulators! They act as regulators!"

~ "Yes, they can—um—"

~~ "The weather—it is much more regulated, because of the energy that it transmutes."

A few questions and it became clear that this was one from spirit wanting to assist. He now addressed Bonniol:

~~ "May I help you sir?"

~ "Yes please."

~~ "You are struggling with language are you not?"

~ "It is sometimes difficult."

~~ "Of course it is! We understand entirely. You are doing magnificently well!"

This was a new development! After a short pause the spiritual helper continued:

~~ "The older the base of the pyramid that you speak of, it will hold the greater amount of energy—the *older* the base of the pyramid, the greater the amount of energy that will be released from the top."

Mark: "So they use older materials for the base—"

~~ "—Older rocks, yes."

George: "Is it that the energy builds up over time?"

~~ "Yes, the OLDER the pyramid, the greater is the energy released. So hence, when they are growing their crops, the older energies are the ones that regenerate quicker, better—so their crops are grown nearer to those energies. And the younger crop does not need it quite so much. Do you understand?"

George: "So the longer the pyramid has been there, the better will be the crops."

~~ "Yes, so the older the pyramid base—that's what holds the energy of that plant completely. That's the origin of that plant and foodstuff. Do you understand? That's the energy that that plant came from. As the seedlings—as they reproduce these things, of course, they don't need so much energy, because their life force always belongs to that OLDER pyramid."

We expressed our continued interest.

~~ "I know it's difficult to understand because you can't see exactly what I can see."

So he sees a clearer picture of the pyramid energy from spirit! That figures. The speaker preferred not to give a name, but we established that he has no connection with Bonniol's planet—he is simply a spirit helper, assisting with language.

Mark: "So if I understand correctly, the older rocks which are used for the base of the pyramid will have a higher concentration of energy which is utilised by the plants for their initial growth."

~~ "Correct! You have it."

Eileen: "So as you reach the top of the pyramid, is the energy much more refined?"

There was a pause—then our helper resumed:

~~ "'Refined' is quite a good word for it. I was trying to find a better word. In actual fact I think 'refined' is quite good. As the energy rises above, to the pinnacle of the pyramid—where you are using the word 'refined', I would use the word 'resourceful'; because that energy—it goes to where it is needed. As it travels upward, it knows exactly where to go—it's 'resourceful'. It becomes a lighter vibration, so it's able to travel exactly where it's needed.

Mark: "So would people use that for healing?"

~~ "Absolutely, it's used for everything."

Mark: "So how do people harness the healing energy?"
It was a single word answer to that—'thought'.
Mark: "With thought, right."
Our helper then apologised for taking up so much of our time and withdrew. He was of course duly thanked for his assistance.
Lilian: Are you still there Bonniol?

~ "I—"

George: "Ah, you're still with us!"

~ "I've been having a little break!"

And we all had to laugh—with relief to find Bonniol still with us and that he was happy to have been helped.

~ "It is most welcomed, to have someone more familiar with the words to help explain."

George: "Regarding the assistance from spirit, I thought at first it might be from your team—then I realised and understood from the one who came through, that it was coming through from spirit."

~ "Yes, that is absolutely right. My team are with me in a sense, as I speak. I speak with the team very much in the background."

George: "Yes. On certain previous occasions, I know that Jan, over there, was picking up from your team. That's why I thought it might have been like that in this instance. That was wrong thinking on my part. I understand now."

~ "It is easy to be confused, I would imagine."

George: "But it's a wonderful evening for us, to have all this input."

~ "But you have so much in this group. I have been around long enough now to know the wonderful evenings that you have."

Jan then began describing a clairvoyant image that she had received—seven rows of pyramids with larger plants growing near the biggest pyramid. But the connection with Bonniol was now lost. Well, it *had* been a lengthy session, and with so much accomplished.

PART 3

Prophecy, Thought and Historic Voices

"The really valuable thing in the pageant of human life seems to me not the state but the creative sentient individual..."

ALBERT EINSTEIN, THE WORLD AS I SEE IT[20].

CHAPTER 15

YEAR 2012: DOOM PROPHECY DELUSIONS

Exchanges with others of this universe have brought to us explanations, understandings, wonder and excitement. We share with those friends out there the same spiritual basis of existence. By opening our minds we can have the awareness that we are part of one big evolving family—wonderful! So where does that leave the *prophets of doom* that have periodically plagued Earthly populations; and so very recently too, throughout the year 2012? They have used the printed word and have swamped the Internet with their ill-founded fatuous diatribe. Now that 2012 is past, perhaps this would be the perfect time for a little analysis of their out of order and altogether wayward behaviour. Through publication of distorted data in books and on the Internet there have been attempts to mislead public which is quite unacceptable. It would be fair, I feel, to criticise offenders on two fundamental counts:

(1): Their failure to address the spiritual basis of existence.

(2): Their failure to comprehend the publications of *real and successful* prophets who have been conversant with, and who have paid due respect to, that spiritual basis of existence.

Long ago, the Mayan peoples addressed their spiritual source; they also made amazing in depth study of motions in the heavens spanning huge periods of time. Based on intricate observations, they calculated that a Fourth Great Cycle of Existence began (using the mode of expression of our present day calendar) on 13th August 3114 BC; and this cycle would last exactly 1,872,000 days. I would stress that this prophetic number of days has been derived of the cosmic patterns themselves, and notwithstanding overriding spiritual intervention, remains immutable. The Fourth Great Cycle as thus defined would come to an end on 22nd December 2012. *Immediately,* an ongoing Fifth Great Cycle of Existence would then begin. New Earthly conditions would prevail in the new cycle. There has never been any suggestion in any of this that our world would end! That is an entirely false idea fabricated by modern doom prophets in their gross ignorance and error.

You may know of the 'crystal skulls'—these are *pre*-Mayan. Spirituality was well developed prior to emergence of the Maya, and the crystal skulls have been honed by purely mind-power as of a single crystal. Today's world has no technology that could even come close to producing such perfection; and the function of the skulls was to aid mind-focus for between-worlds communication. So we can view these artefacts as existing *material evidence* for spiritual input to Mayan constructs, which modern mankind would today be incapable of devising. What I am saying is that the skulls are prime evidence for *pre*-Mayan and Mayan expertise, and it would be impossible for mankind to falsify such evidence today. Salumet had spoken of this matter on 10th November 1997:

~ "The Mayans were indeed a much developed race—aware of all things spiritual—they knew and understood the workings of all energy forms on this Earth. These skulls you speak of were used in the way that many of your psychics and mediums of this age, use glass balls—crystal gazing—to build up energy between our worlds. It was a form of communication, to which the Mayans developed their use, in developing their own consciousness. They (the crystal skulls) are older than has been said."

So we should take good care not to undervalue the legacy of this once-great nation that inhabited our planet; and we should consider the Great Cycles of Existence as calculated, with due respect. We had requested our guide's advice concerning the year 2012 as early as 25th February 2008:

> ~ "What is happening in the year you call 2012 is an accumulation of those changes which *have* taken many, many hundreds of your years to evolve, but by that year, there will be a wave of understanding. That is the great change—it is an *understanding* that will take place. It is a realization. But always, too, you must remember that the consciousness of mankind can alter these, what you term, predictions. So always keep that to the fore of your thinking."

So free will may possibly influence prediction slightly. We had voiced our feelings that the then current material system of things on our planet has to change—it can't continue in its present (2008) direction and by about that time (2012), there should be a realization about this.

> ~ "Yes, those changes, as I have said, have gradually been taking place; but that is why there is this *excitement* about this one year—but I would say there are many, many more exciting dates in your calendar."

I felt at the time that Salumet's statement had very nicely placed the matter firmly into a proper perspective; and yet the notion that 2012 was to be a doom year still loomed large both in the Press and on Internet—and these authorities can be so persuasive, even when presenting nonsense. So on 29th March 2010, we passed on a question that had been sent in about expected havoc to be caused by the approach to Earth of 'Planet X', sometimes called 'Nibiru'. When placing the question I had added:

"It is just part, I am sure, of this 'doom malaise' and I only mention it so that we can talk of it and firmly knock the idea on the head."

> ~ "Let me say only this to you, my dear friend: You can never be responsible for others' thoughts, and unfortunately, as human beings, there does seem to be an element of impending disaster—not only in this day and age but in times gone by. How often have you heard that 'the end is nigh'? I believe those are the words used?"

We agreed this to be so, midst a few titters.

~ "Yes—and still you are here with feet on the Earth Plane."

I explained that the new development seemed to be the rogue planet and people were being deluged with enormous publicity about it:

~ "Yes, in the same way as you have mass-hysteria—thoughts travel and people are brought into this way of thinking. Instead of standing back and being rational, they are gathered up in the sea of disaster. And I will say to you: Give out thoughts for those people—to help these negative thoughts to dissipate quietly. The best that you can do, is not to discuss these negative aspects that go around, but always to think positive, not only for yourselves but for your planet. But, as I have said, it has happened so many times before, and for some time to come there always will be those people who seek disasters. Send out love—that is my only expression to you—give love."

Indeed, I have come to regard love as the all-purpose salve that always works to good effect. A little before 2012 arrived (3rd October 2011), the much revered and spiritually progressed philosopher Rudolph Steiner, spoke with us from spirit via Gary—Gary has a group in Bournemouth, but he has occasionally sat with us. Rudolph Steiner clearly has full knowledge of all the Earthly hoo-ha and gave us his slightly more esoteric view of things:

~ "A planet evolves on the basis of how much light it holds—how much light it can absorb. But this is changing as the end of the Mayan calendar comes in what you call '2012'. Ultimately, it's a phase of more light. It is a phase where darkness cannot overshadow so much. The deception will begin to lift, like a mist."

The *deception*, we take to mean the doom prophecy in its entirety. We sought clarification that it is the 'spiritual light' that our planet holds:

~ "Yes, more light—spiritual light of the sun really—and the solar energy. The sun is the nearest emanation of light in this part of the universe. It is our spiritual battery."

He went on to say how many in the past had worshipped the sun and it was the light, of course, that they worshipped. We replied that we were aware of both spiritual and physical light emanations of the sun and asked if he saw them as blended:

~ "It is one. On the lower realms separation is always seen—the higher you go, the less—separation ceases to exist. Everything becomes one, and ultimately, you reach the Godhead—the Source."

He went on to say how everything is created from Source to which we are ultimately drawn. A bit of Source is always within us, so that we are drawn individually; also as a greater collective. And by going within, we discover our Source connection. These are the philosophical teachings of a great thinker and his words came over rather like a lecture. On Earth, he always enjoyed delivering his fluent lectures from the platform—except for just that one time when Hitler Youth in their misguided ignorance intervened.

One to seriously address the *spiritual basis of existence* was born in France as Michel de Nostredame (1503-1566), whose name became Latinized and more widely known as Nostradamus. He was an apothecary, having studied at Montpelier University, where he gained a degree and licence to practice medicine. So Nostradamus was a healer as well as a successful seer. It is often the case that spirit realm connection runs hand in hand with the healing profession and a caring nature. This was certainly true of this one. Many of his prophecies are seen to be succinct and accurate, whilst others have not yet come to fruition since in total they extend through more than two millennia. He gives a number of precise year dates and sometimes statements from which year dates may easily be deduced. Examples are:

1666 – Great fire of London.

1792 – The French Revolution with installation of the new revolutionary calendar.

1917 – The Russian Revolution.

1991 – Conclusion of the Russian Communist regime.

He named significant people from history—Louis Pasteur, who discovered bacteria—Montgolfier, who flew a hot air balloon—Adolf Hitler (whom he spells 'Hister' and describes as *child of Germany who observes no law*) and he gives several World War II key dates. A full discussion of these matters is given in 'A Smudge in Time'[1], chapters

11 and 12. There are two conclusions to be drawn from the Nostradamus prophecies. Firstly, there is no doubt whatsoever as to the accuracy of many of his predictions. They lie well beyond any accidental correspondence, and his description of trance procedures adds further reassurance. His expressions are sometimes quaint and spellings not quite 21st century, but that is to be expected of a 16th century author! Secondly, he states quite clearly in the preface to the first edition of his great book 'The Centuries' that his quatrains of prophecy continue until the year 3797[24]. Having made this statement that acknowledges Earth's continued existence, it might be interesting to see how Salumet regards the successful seer. A question had been placed during our meeting of 18th July 1994:

~ "Nostradamus, as you call him, was indeed a man of vision, a great scholar of his time; but a man reared with religion."

'Reared with religion' was to explain his use of the term 'Antichrist' in reference to Adolf Hitler.

~ "He was influenced by the religions of his time. He was a great visionary and of course, with his extended views and knowledge, he could predict events to come."

Several years later (10th December 2007), one of the predictions had been on my mind. It concerns a prophet who chooses Monday for his holyday, and who travels far and delivers a great many people. Well, since our group always meets on Monday evenings and Salumet comes to us from Angelic realms, I could not resist asking if it was he to whom Nostradamus refers:

~ "I have to say to you: no, it is not the one known as Salumet—but thank you for those thoughts."

Salumet went on to remind that many spiritual beings come on missions to help mankind, whether we give them the name of 'prophet' or not; but then added as if by afterthought:

~ "But I will tell you that that prophecy has yet to come."

In some surprise I reacted: "Oh! Oh!"

~ "I need not say more but it will be made known amongst those who know and understand that there is one who will indeed travel far in his mission—in the physical sense."

So we have Salumet's assurance of the Nostradamus truth; also a re-minder that our angelic guide has all-knowledge—which includes that prediction of Nostradamus that has not yet come into fruition.

Four hundred years before Nostradamus there had been another noteworthy mystic and healer. Saint Malachy was Archbishop of Ar-magh, Ireland for a period of five years. He made accurate prophecy of the time and place of his own death—that was to be All Soul's Day, November 1148, Clairvaux, France. Perfectly correct—but his major prophetic work[25] was to provide a 'Pope List'. It was eight years before his death, that he and a party of Irish monks approached Rome on pil-grimage. They stopped and spent the night on Janiculum Hill at the city's edge. A scribe moved close with candle as he became entranced, 'received' and spoke 111 short phrases, each depicting a pope, from the then current Innocent II to the end of papacy; no names, just descrip-tive phrases pertaining to each pope—many being most clearly fitting. Looking at the final four that he listed, they are:

John Paul I (1978): described as *'From the half moon'*. He was ordained priest in Belluno (meaning 'good moon'); that was in 1935. He became pope in 1978, but died after only thirty three days, whilst there was a half moon in the heavens.

John Paul II (1978-2005): described as *'From the sun's labour'*. He was in fact from Krakow, Poland—the town where Copernicus had laboured on his theory of the sun being at the centre of the solar system with Earth as an orbiting planet. Copernicus had laboured midst huge con-troversy between his science and the church. It was a highly signifi-cant time for both.

Benedict XVI (2005-2013): described as *'From the glory of the Olive'*. The Mount of Olives is central to Christian tradition and Benedict XVI has been very much a traditionalist. He also has been a pope dedicated to peace of which the olive branch is a symbol. His resignation came as a big surprise to the world, it being the first since the Middle Ages. Pope resignations have indeed been rare; and within hours of it, in the

Vatican, lightning bolts twice struck the top of St Peter's Basilica! It is not unusual for lightning to strike this tall building during storms, but it happened twice on this occasion and was well photographed for the world! This might be seen as fitting punctuation, prior to introduction of he who is to follow, and is described by Saint Malachy as— 'Peter the Roman'.

Francis: (2013-): described as: *'Peter the Roman, who will pasture his sheep in many tribulations, and when these things are finished, the city of seven hills (Rome) will be destroyed, and the dreadful judge will judge his people.'* At this time of unprecedented changes (2013) there are already to be seen, tribulations within the church. But why Francis and why Peter the Roman? Francis—after Francis of Assisi, who in 1205, had made pilgrimage to Rome and joined the beggars at St Peter's. Pope Francis is now very much committed to Rome—principle city and centre of what was the Roman Empire; also of what has become the Roman Catholic Religion. Rome is now very much his home. And Peter because Jesus addressed Peter when he said *'on this rock I will build my church'*. Peter identifies with church foundation, as it was envisaged at that time. The final destruction referred to is probably not meant to be seen as a physical destruction of the city, but as the far more consequential end to Vatican controlled Roman version of Christian ethic. Since its formation in the fourth century, one must accept there has been a lengthy and alarmingly chequered history. This has included mass exterminations, the bloody Crusades, the Inquisition, inadequate affirmation of Mary's visions and messages through the twentieth century, irrational confrontations with advancing science and non-recognition of spiritual communications via mediumship. The *dreadful judge* of course will be none other than our own self-judgement on passing to spirit, which might well be a time dreaded by some. But we must remember, and this is important: there are many good, kindly and selfless people who follow the Roman version of faith. These are the *sheep* whom *Peter the Roman will pasture—in many tribulations.* This is a righteous task for a loving and caring leader. Truth will prevail; and the words relayed by Saint Malachy during that night as he overlooked the city, are in no way to be seen as doom prophecy, but a prophecy of inevitable change towards a greater perfection.

Salumet had been with us on 4th April 2005, following the death of Pope John Paul II:

~ "I would like to speak with you a little about the outpouring of the grief that is on your planet at this time. I would like to say to you how this grief affects those also in our world because you see, there are a great many who still hold fast to the same beliefs as they held upon your Earth—they all feel the grief that comes from your Earthly plane."

I suggested that Pope John Paul II is hailed as one of the more outstanding popes to have held office and Salumet responded:

~ "In as much as he has done his job well."

Then he went on to refer to omissions that will be recognised once in spirit. But Salumet, on this occasion, merely wished to remind us that Earthly events have rebound effect in spirit. Our guide then invited questions on the matter and this gave opportunity to draw attention to St Malachy's prophecy and how this seemed in accord with Salumet's earlier words to us about the papacy being in decline and how it will not go on forever:

~ "Yes, I remember my words to you all—I said that your Earthly religions cannot last forever, because so many of us, including myself—we come to bring truth, and truth and love cannot fail this time. Therefore Earthly religions will have their day; when people realise that there is but one truth, one creator, one who loves and nurtures all things, all experiences, all planets, all universes, all of life—

YES, THIS RELIGION HAS LIMITED TIME.

The people within your world are now able to think and to feel and to see for themselves. This I gave to you previously when I told you that each successive generation will not take any form of religion at its face value. Each *individual* will decide as time continues, what is right for them."

I mentioned to Salumet *the sun's labour* and the amazing Copernicus connection:

~ "Thank you. It always surprises me, my dear friends, when you seem so amazed by all of these happenings, when indeed I feel by now your understanding of all creation and how it works—it should not surprise you as much as it does!"

I made a case for our emotion being not wholly 'surprise', but in part 'joy'—at seeing the revealed truth of prophecy'.

~ "Yes, if only more human beings could find that joy within their lives, how their lives would change! Each one of you needs love, needs joy, in daily living. But yes, to answer your question more fully—

THE END IS NEARING FOR MANY, MANY EARTHLY RELIGIONS

Unfortunately, in many of your Earthly religions the greed of power has taken the lead, where the *chaining* of the populations and the fear has remained—it must be broken in order for people to be free-thinking; and that is what, my dear friends, those in our world are trying to do this day."

Paul suggested a way of putting it might be: to do away with the middle man:

~ "Yes—what a wonderful way to describe it!—'middle man'. Yes, I like that! Each individual is responsible for their life on this planet—each one will recognise that it is so; that you cannot put blame to another, or to a church, or to a religion. But you must take individual responsibility for your lives and your deeds upon this planet."

In further discussion, our guide agreed that religions have achieved *some* good, and I suggested that since there is divine teaching at the central core of each, this has to be the reason for a modicum of success.

~ "Let me say that divine teaching is at the very core of every *individual*. That is the way you should describe—it is an innermost thought, an innermost knowing. It is an all-knowing from within, and only when this is available and the understanding is available to all people on your Earth, will things truly begin to change."

Perhaps then, formal religions with their material constructs, might be seen as 'bridges' leading towards an awareness of that inner knowing; but they are temporary bridges—as floating pontoons that will in due course be swept down the river of time, to their place in history. Some individuals will have seen them as springboards, and will have long since leapt to wider cosmic enlightenment. There are many pathways used as we evolve, and the above messages are consistent except for one small point—timing. Saint Malachy fixes this while Salumet does not. Our teacher has often made reference to the free-will factor and how it may influence prophecy. A rule-of-thumb in relation to this will mean I understand that the timing of prophecies as sensed by a seer will approximate to 98% accuracy. We shall see! So, a huge task now confronts Pope Francis, and he will, I feel sure, have awareness of the pressing need for change, as with gentleness and great care he pastures his sheep through 2013 and beyond.

CHAPTER 16

POWER OF
THOUGHT

Thought is of mind and mind is of spirit, and spirit is that essential essence that underpins all material existence. Each belongs to the non-material and hence to that less easily understood part of this universe. It is mind that has connection to the biological computer that we call 'brain'. In these pages, we have already seen how 'thought' of the developed mind can create material form, can replace the light industry of a planet, can make and move massive stone-works; and then through mind-link, can communicate across the countless light-years of this universe—instantaneously, with total disregard to space and time. 'Thought' is not subject to the laws of the material space-time creation. And in the very early days of Salumet's mission (4th July 1994) he articulated the statement:

~ "Thought—thought is the most powerful thing that you have."

And this phrase has since been repeated a number of times across the years of his teaching. Thought is a fundamental gift to humanity of immense value, not to be overlooked—never to be disregarded. It was just six weeks later (15 August 1994), when the subject of moving colossal stonework during pyramid construction had first come up, Salumet had on that occasion confirmed 'levitation' as the modus operandi—then he had asked:

~ "What is levitation?"

Leslie had replied: "Just the power of thought", and Salumet responded:

> ~ "I must stress to you all again—the power of thought. It really—it really is an *incredible* thing. I wish I could express to you in words, *just* how powerful it is."

One from higher spirit realms had once referred to purely-thought-communication and being able to identify friends by their thought patterns—no need for names, the thought pattern being sufficient in itself. So Leslie had asked for clarification of this from our guide:

> ~ "I have told you that thought is energy—all is energy—as you progress in the spirit world, physical speech no longer exists, it becomes extinct, if you like; because the higher spiritual nature takes over. So the power of thought is all that is needed. As you see and feel so many energies around you, the thought patterns used vary greatly, within the spirit world. It depends on the expertise of the spirit involved—as in all matters, it must be practised to perfect. You understand? But I do not understand what you tell me about it being a language between *some*—it is a language for *all*. There would be no separate groups of peoples, who would understand; it would be an understanding for *all*, because it is of the one energy."

Well, this is looking far ahead, to a time in spirit when communication based on physical speech no longer exists such that thought energy alone suffices. I think this well demonstrates how thought is the central part of our existence—how it continues after we have evolved beyond the old physical attributes. But these were the early days of our meetings, before it became possible to amplify further.

There was a remarkable episode during the Salumet exchange of 1st February 1999. Leslie was saying: "We are forgetting I think, and I'm guilty of it sometimes also, that the power of thought is not only a power for good, it is an everlasting, ongoing power. And as Salumet has said, thoughts go into the aether; and he's said in the past also: there are those, whose duty it is—" at which point, Leslie's voice shut down and another of entirely different tone and character spoke through him—continuing the sentence he had begun:

155

~ "—to direct those thoughts, where they are most beneficial, for those who are in need of that help. You do not accept always, that thought is an everlasting, living power. You treat it like a page of words, to be examined and ingested, a little at a time, and (the) book then closed. Thought is not one volume. Thought is the complete and utter knowledge of the Universe. Thought is everlasting, all-creating, all-pervading, and what you do not realise—all-knowing. You do not necessarily have to issue the correct words, physically, for your thoughts to be understood—if your thoughts are directed in the right way, to those who may need the benefit of them. Do you understand that?"

The statement had been made to clarify the thinking of one of our sitters, after which, the one who had spoken thus, of the pervasive nature and the utter grandeur of thought said:

~ "Now, with apologies to the Master, I will withdraw."

In Leslie's latter years, this kind of interjection from spirit sometimes happened—there would suddenly be the heavy breathing, Leslie became a medium, and another took over with continued commentary. This understandably left us in a state of wonderment, but on this occasion, Leslie was quick to continue as self again, looking around and saying:

"Does anyone else have a question for Salumet?" And so that evening had then continued as was customary, with a further clutch of questions. But it is now clear that there is very much more to 'thought' than just our thinking, our prayers and the universal mind-link capability—much, much more!

Another three years on—it was now 22nd April 2002—and Salumet took us a little further along this road. He began in a practical way, by energising the room and asking each how we felt. Some felt 'heady', some 'lifted', some had a feeling that was plainly difficult to describe. He explained following this, that 'thought' is an *energy* that we utilise, and it is so important that we take full control of our thinking. But we are bound to slip sometimes because, at this point in Earth's evolution, humankind cannot be perfect. He further explained: that is why he and others are here to help—not to help just these small gatherings, but also endeavouring to influence world leaders; and indeed elsewhere also, not just this one world. And as spirit continues, so does thought—you cannot have one without the other. At this point we began to struggle a little, and Paul had queried the difference between thought and spirit—the same energy perhaps? Good observation!

~ "Yes, you are correct but remember that the spirit is evolving at all times. Thought has *always* existed as energy. We are coming to complicated matters now but I will try to explain it simply for you. The problem is—you have a human brain and the human brain perceives thought to be separate from the spirit; but all 'energy' which exists is but *one* energy but on different and various levels."

It slowly became clearer that what is seen by Salumet and others as 'true thought' is that collective which exists in spirit and not the output of physical brain. It was necessary to differentiate. I suggested the brain output to be more of a mechanical output while the spiritual thought is an ongoing evolving collective.

~ "Imagine the human brain as a series of mechanical instances that work automatically within the human frame—I use these words only to simplify it for you. But 'thought' is the all-existing energy that belongs to the spirit. Thought cannot be destroyed *because* it is spirit. I would say to you: try to perceive it on a spiritual level and then and only then will it become just a little clearer."

So 'spiritual thought' is a living, growing, ever-evolving, fluidic, indestructible prevalence; while brain output is in comparative terms, an infinitesimal mechanistic feed into that prevalence. Lilian had brought 'intuition' into the earlier discussion and Salumet was now able to give useful comment on this:

~ "When the lady speaks of intuition, of course that is the human brain picking up the spiritual thought, the spiritual energy. But it has to be transmuted in some way and because of the humankind having freewill it is often placed to one side. But my purpose in speaking about thought is to help you understand the wider issue of energy, and until you can leave behind the human thinking and allow yourself *to be* that spiritual energy—which you are—then we will always have some difficulties. But my dear gentleman friend has explained it quite simply I feel, for your understanding. It is a difficult subject but I felt perhaps it was time to introduce you to wider thinking."

I felt it might be useful following this, to mention relatively recent experiments with 'random number generators' (RNGs). Examples of primitive RNGs are dice, coin flipping and I Ching yarrow stalks. These had their various uses for the selection of randomised numbers in times past. There are now computer-based RNGs that can create randomised numbers many, many times more efficiently; and it is found that the power of thought from some individuals can induce a bias—can make the numbers go slightly non-random. So RNGs respond to human brain output! Evidence of the brain-generated thought power! Furthermore, a linked series of RNGs appears to respond to the collective-consciousness-thought-energy that results from people's reaction to major world events—an example event for which this was observed being the horror of 9/11. Looking for further clarification, I asked if the response would relate to just spiritual thought energy or would it include brain output:

~ "I would say to you my dear friend that anything which tries to capture energy cannot always be pure, therefore I would say to you that not only would spiritual energy but also negative energy would be picked up."

George: "And the negative energy would connect with the human brain?"

~ "Yes."

Graham then brought meditation into the discussion:

~ "True meditation, my dear friend, excludes the human brain—if you are in what you call meditation in the proper sense, then all human thinking should be quiet."

Graham then observed that meditation must therefore be a valuable practise for us:

~ "Of course, because then comes forth the spirit, that true part of you. That is why we always encourage you to have quiet times, not only for *your* benefit but so that those in our world can come closer; because what happens to you is that *your* energy is quickened and *ours* lowered in order that the two can communicate. But that is where you will find your true self—in the state of deep, deep meditation—not the meditation of the light kind because the human thinking is still rather close. The meditation I speak of is the one where you do not exist in the sense of feeling—where the human form no longer belongs to you but only that energy is left which we call spirit. That is true meditation my dear friend. If you are in what you call meditation in the proper sense, then all human thinking should be quiet."

During our 28th July 2003 meeting Salumet observed that it is sad when from his world, so many are seen to be engulfed in human emotions and do not know what to do—they cannot control their thinking:

~ "I have told you: the power of your thinking is indeed the most powerful thing that you possess. Therefore it speaks loudly in all of your best interests that mastery of your thinking be something that is foremost in your life. When you can achieve this, your lives will feel complete, even with the situations of trouble, heartache, whatever comes to you—it will not matter, because you have full understanding of who you truly are."

At our meeting of 23rd August 2004 Salumet took the thought theme a little further:

~ "Thought is the most powerful thing that you possess; not only in this world, but in ours and all of existence. Those small everyday thoughts, they do not make a mark; they come and they go although the energy will remain as residue within all of the energy of all things."

We should therefore take great care with our thinking. It seems that thoughts given out in love will always reach their target and present no problem. Let us all therefore endeavour to be forthcoming with our thoughts of love—love for friends, love for others, love for planet and all nature. Thoughts that are negative, weak or undirected may get reflected, may harshly influence innocent people, or may form a 'residue' of unwanted energy. In spirit, thoughts can be transmuted. Thought residues can, we understand, be picked up; and if people lack that inner strength and knowing, then it is possible that they become disadvantaged in some way—*life seems to treat them unfairly for no particular reason.* Perhaps we should leave it there for now, but these brief statements may be sufficient to show that 'thought' has a very complicated nature such that there is good reason for us to take great care with our thinking. When thoughts are sent out into the aether, the process does not end there. As stated, any thoughts of love present no problem; it's the other kind that can give rise to so many difficulties—that our world and spirit can well do without.

A book by Dr Masaru Emoto, accounting his inspirational water experiments had been published in Japanese in 2001. An English version became available in 2004²⁶. We made reference during our meeting of 25ᵗʰ October 2004, explaining that several of us had read about the experiments of this Japanese gentleman—that highlight the fact that good thoughts can change the energy within water. The good thought and word and good music all seem to have an effect on water such that when moisture films are frozen, then the little snowflake ice crystal patterns have extreme beauty but the reverse happens if water is subjected to bad thoughts and bad conditions; there is then no beauty in the crystallization, it is just a mess. We sought Salumet's commentary:

~ "Let me say this to you. I have listened to your words quietly and what I wish to say to you is this: this has begun to reinforce all that I have told you!"

I declared that to be precisely my own feeling:

~ "Have I not told you my dear friends that the power of thought is the most powerful thing that you will ever possess in this human form? That power of thought is crucial for all of mankind to survive this physical being. So the simple answer to you my dear friend, (is) that the gentleman you have named is only reinforcing what I have already told you."

I suggested that he seems to be *proving scientifically* what has been stated.

~ "He is being influenced. He is being given help in that direction. His word, because of his standing, will be accepted by many who would otherwise deny such a thing."

It is a fact that denial was running rife at the start of the 21st century where such matters are concerned. Dr Emoto's standing should certainly help in breaking that mould. His work is consistent with other reported phenomena—the priest, for example, who watered one canna house plant with holy/blessed water and found that it grew to four times the size of others. And plants respond with faster growth when melodic music is played—but they do not like 'Heavy Metal' style!

~ "Why do you not my dear friends take this information and also what I have told you and use it for yourselves for the betterment of your own health? Use the thought for the water that you drink, for the food that you eat. We have spoken of the plants in the fields—in the gardens; all these things respond to thought in the same way that healing thoughts are given to those in need. Now you are seeing examples of my words. I did say when first I came to you that there would be other sources of information and this is what is now happening."

It became clear on 6th February 2006 that one particular time for those good and loving thoughts is when we enter sleep state:

~ "The point of connection is made easier for you—that is why it is most important that the time before your sleep state, places your mind, *which of course belongs to spirit*, into a frame of thinking, which would then make it much easier to connect; because again, as you think, it then becomes your reality. Remember this always. That has been the point of these many months of demonstrating to you the power of the mind."

Paul had observed that we should practise going to sleep in a higher state of thinking, with the intention of improving links with spirit friends and guides:

~ "Firstly you must pay attention to your everyday thinking—all thinking. You must become masters of your own thinking. That is the pathway—to being in command of what you think; and then to make sure as you enter your sleep state that the purity of your thoughts is much greater, and then you truly can move forward. And as you say, the gifts of the spirit will indeed unfold before your very eyes. It is entirely within your grasp but I do not want you to think that these things can happen in a blink of an eye—it has to be worked for."

Thought is indeed complex, with still more complexity coming to light at our 5th March 2007 meeting. Our teacher had referred to the raising of humankind's consciousness; this in part due to good Earth-dwellers who show their love and knowledge and set good example. But then there are also projects being mounted from spirit:

~ "What we in my world, are trying to achieve now, is to alter all of the 'stuck' knowledge that is within your DNA. This is little known at this time, but there are those upon your Earth who are gaining knowledge of this particular aspect of change."

He went on to make comparison between 'stuck' DNA pattern and reincarnating with a past life problem. I had ventured:

"So, I think you are saying that there is a spiritual connection to the DNA helix."

~ "Of course, of course, although it has the physical connotations, all of spirit has to be involved in these things. That is the way forward to release people from past thoughts and actions—changing your lives and (your) thinking, to become that more spiritual being. It is something for you to think about."

Sara: "Re-programming the mind with better thoughts—more positive thoughts."

~ "That is exactly what it would achieve. Again it demonstrates the power of the mind. Do you see how thinking joins in all aspects of your lives and how powerful it is? It is that part of you which will always exist."

I added that it is probably true to say that we had just not thought about a DNA link.

~ "No, it is something that is very new to your knowledge I know, but of course in our world it has been known for ever; so it is not new. So, I hope my dear friends it has given you a little more to consider."

Just three days later, an article was posted on the Internet by Fotopoulou Sophia, beginning: *The human DNA is a biological Internet and superior in many aspects to the artificial one—*. Research on the planet has progressed much since the discovery of the double helix structure of **d**eoxyribo**n**ucleic **a**cid in 1953; but of course, Salumet in spirit knows all! There will be further discussion of this in chapter 24.

The above Internet article, also another—each related to thought modifying DNA, and I was able to mention this to Salumet the following week:

~ "Yes, that energy, whether going in or out is transmuted. But it is not new, as I have told you; it is only that it is beginning to enter the consciousness of man—it is now becoming more available to human thinking."

I added that certainly there is the evidence appearing on the Internet, to which he responded:

~ "Yes, that is the purpose of it; and of course, that mankind might have better control of his own spiritual being."

I suggested that the influential, thought-that-modifies might come from the individual himself, from a healer, from those in spirit or from that *deeper* spirit; and Salumet agreed this to be correct. So perhaps we might think of the DNA of the cell nucleus as a spiritual interface that may receive modification from spirit if deemed necessary.

Moving on to 11th May 2009, Paul had queried the connection between 'thinking' and 'unhappiness'. Salumet was quick to respond with:

~ "Your thought my dear friend, creates your reality, it is so powerful— do you not feel, my dear friend that negativity of your thought creates the feelings? It is a two-way mirror, where one affects the other. All negativity of thoughts should be dispersed as soon as possible, because of the power that lies behind them."

Paul had then suggested that instead of focussing selfishly on material things, if we focus on what we really want to do in life—that would put us in touch with our guides?

~ "Of course, one thought my dear friend, can place you before your guides and helpers. The power of the thought is all-essential in creating your reality."

Paul: "I think sometimes we feel that we are being selfish if we focus on things that we really *want* in life, but—"

~ "If your desire is spiritually based, if it is to help you attain greater spirituality, growth, understanding, love—then that cannot be selfish."

The principle of thought-initiation was then made crystal clear in a further statement:

~ "You can only feel bad, my dear friend, if the negative thought is already in existence. So, I would suggest the negative thought comes first, then the negative feelings. But, if you are not aware of the negative thought, then your feelings will help you to understand and to change that thought pattern."

Paul: "Right, and are these feelings sometimes coming from our guides who are nudging us to change our thinking?"

~ "Of course—they would be there to help, to uplift you in any way that they can. You, my dear friends, are never alone. There is always someone there to help to pick you up and to help you to recognise all this negativity in everyday living. And of course, the more you are in tune with those guides and helpers, the better and the easier your life can be."

Later that year, 7th September 2009, our teacher brought 'forgiveness of our past' into the equation; suggesting that in the group, we had not yet attained this:

~ "Another important point—is forgiveness of the past—because it is past. How can you be open to truth or going within, without first having that forgiveness of past things?"

We had responded that as we were all part of that past, then it is like forgiving ourselves:

~ "Of course, you *are* the past, but it is gone. Until you forgive all past issues, you cannot go forward. And again, we enter into this conversation the word 'fear', which is so much part of your human makeup—part of the condition of being human. But you must let all fear go, because whilst you have fear, you do not have that purity of love, which is your right, which is your spirit. Do you understand what I am saying to you?"

We tried to differentiate between ordinary fears that we should be able to control and 'intense' fears, thrust upon us, which do not seem to be within our control:

~ "Let me stop you there. *All* fear is within your control—whether it is fear that is outside of yourselves, or fear that is deep within—you have that control."

I made reference to those rare occasions when memory is actually *blanked out* as a result of the sheer intensity of a fearful situation:

~ "Yes, I understand all the queries and questions about fear. I am speaking in a simplified way, but we move *then* to what we call 'mind'— that all-powerful thing that you all possess. The mind has the ability to reject all fear. You are not putting it behind you. You are saying it does not exist, but it is still there."

I referred to a personal experience—a first parachute descent as part of conscripted military training. It began with free-fall of 100 feet or so through dense cloud. I have no memory of that part, but 40 years later during a psychic reading a *'military situation fear'* was detected by she who did the reading and I was utterly amazed! It had to be that one time.

[In fact, on 10th February 1994, it had been a spectacular reading from Patricia whom I had not previously met. She channelled accurate details of my childhood, facts about our old house, details of the book I was writing, introduced me to one in spirit who was assisting with the chapter in progress and quite unexpectedly healed a condition of bursitis (extensive leg swelling), the result of twisting a knee.]

Salumet spoke of my fear that mind had rejected:

~ "Yes, it is a human condition of course—in the same way as those who are in danger for their lives allow the fear to build. It is part of the human condition, but you still can control any fear that you experience—and in allowing the fear to dissipate, then we can come close to help. Whilst you grip fiercely this feeling of fear, what you are doing my dear friends, is blocking us from helping you. Does that make sense to you?"

I think we can see that 'thought' and 'mind' have their connections to the conditions of 'forgiveness' and 'fear', and indeed it all makes so much sense.

On 5th November 2012 we had been discussing that state of mind we call 'depression' and how music can uplift. This had led to a reference to that Beijing hospital, mentioned earlier, where doctors chant to induce the feeling of I have been healed in their patient—with amazing results. Salumet had commented:

~ "Yes, you are not fully aware yet, of the many vibrations that exist. In fact it is something that is being worked upon in our world at this very time."

So we might see this as a striking *practical demonstration* of the power of thought, recorded on film. But especially in view of Salumet's comment, this might well be an oversimplification. There is still so much that we do not know.

CHAPTER 17

PROPHETIC STATEMENTS: PROOF OF SPIRIT

It is probably clear to all that, whilst Salumet is of all-knowledge, he does not use that knowledge for the purpose of prophecy—that is not his mission. There have been occasions, however, when he has responded to widespread planetary fears, much talked-about problems or to questions that have been placed. And his commentary has sometimes included indication of what will happen in the future. One particular evening that was prophetic in this way was 28th July 1997. He spoke about adversity:

NATURAL DISASTERS:

~ "Much has been spoken in your world of devastation, and I have to say to you: it *will not* happen to the degree that you can imagine. But I will tell you that the planet *will* continue in its evolution, and in so doing, there will be for many of your years to come, natural disasters. But we would not consider them all to be man-made."

He went on to explain that the planet has a plan of its own—it evolves, and:

~ "I do not always think that you humans fully understand the workings of your own planet. What I tell you now is what is to come—what has been foreseen."

We already had at this time, the affliction on the Earth called AIDS, which Salumet saw as a problem for which most people had some concern:

HIV/AIDS:

~ "I feel that your Earthly planet, has at this moment in time, become a little complacent, but I will tell you dear friends, you have not seen this disease at its height yet. It will spread to all parts of your world, but what I want to tell you is that there *will* be a cure; but not before it has reached all corners of your world. The cure will come, I am sure you will be most interested, in work that is being done on what you call 'outer space'. It will come from work that is being done, in connection with this."

In 1997, the number of those affected amounted to around 22 million. By 2010, the number with the AIDS virus seemed to have peaked at around 34 million and the disease had indeed spread worldwide. But late in 2013 came news of a much better understanding of genome therapy through what is known by the acronym 'Crispr'; and this step might well help us on our way towards an AIDS cure. But following this, our guide then looked much further into the future:

CHANGE IN THINKING:

~ "There are areas in your world (where)—and I do have to say: not within any of your lifetimes here, I speak of many years to come. Within the next thousand years, there will be a change in the way of thinking of mankind — there will be a spiritual brotherhood of man. So for that to happen, there has to be many changes; I am sure you can reason with this and accept that fact."

Leslie had declared: "I was going to ask if we would be right in presuming, that the devastation to come, will be the trigger for moral regeneration?"

~ "Yes—yes, there will come—"

NUCLEAR ACCIDENT:

~"—And I will tell you, not to make you afraid, but to enlighten you, that there will be a nuclear accident, but it will not extinguish this planet—it will not have the repercussions that mankind expects."

One should observe that, at this time there were many who feared the possibility of a severe nuclear devastation through default, so it was good to hear Salumet's reassurance. But the nuclear accident referred to, followed fourteen years later. That, of course, was the Fukushima Daiichi disaster, with equipment failure, nuclear meltdown and release of radioactivity; following the Tōhoku earthquake and tsunami of 11th March 2011. It was rated 'Level 7' on the International Nuclear Event Scale, on a par with the earlier Chernobyl disaster of 1986; although thankfully, much less radioactivity was released to atmosphere.

Salumet then moved on to speak of space and those who live on other planets:

EXTRATERRESTRIAL VISITORS:

~ "I want you to know dear friends, that in your next century, there will be space people come to this Earth and (they) will make themselves known to *all*. The time is coming and it is not too far distant in your time."

Leslie: "I'm sorry we shan't be here to see it happen, except from your world."

~ "It has been building, in the last 200 years of your Earth time that these communicators are interested in your living, in your way of life—in human beings in general. There is much dispute I know in your world, about these matters. But you cannot deny that there exists other life forms—many, many life forms and the time is nigh, when there will be one particular race, of what you call 'aliens', who will present themselves to the world—who will stagger you with their knowledge and their spirituality."

Leslie: "We can only hope that whoever is alive in those years is going to be sensible enough to welcome them properly."

~ "They *will* be welcomed dear friend. It is coming that your political spheres throughout your world — they have been influenced for many years. We have spoken that they have been denying the knowledge, but the time must come, when all will come together and it will be accepted. This is your destiny that this life form *must* come to you. There will always be fear, but once your political leaders accept, then the common people will also accept."

Leslie: "Good. I think the common people are ready to accept them now. They are well aware that a lot has been hidden and denied."

In the years since 1997, we have of course been privileged with in excess of 80 most informative conversations with our dear Aeran friend Bonniol; also conversations with beings from other planets and from the spirit realms of other planets. And the possibility of their visiting Earth has actually entered into some of those discussions. It is of course heart-warming to know that mankind will be *staggered* by their spirituality—which of course must always underpin the truly progressive technological advancement that leads to and is necessary for space-travel. Space-travellers will always have that developed spirituality. But we have a problem. What about all the misunderstandings and confusion in our world concerning religions and the seemingly senseless associated violence?

RELIGIONS AND MIDDLE EAST UNREST:

~ "I want to go now onto your world religions. I would like to tell you also, that as you enter into a new century, that some of your most powerful church leaders will fall. I speak in particular of one religion which has held power over many for too long and that is the one ruled by the papal institution."

On hearing this, Leslie explained that we would be glad to hear this news in one sense, but would feel sorry for those people, in another.

~ "Of course you must keep your hearts open, but you must also realise that all peoples *must* be free to know and gather own-thinking. There is coming new religions, mainly in the countries that you term Middle Eastern countries, where much discord, much strife to this day, still continues. There will continue for much time, discord in these lands.

But also there, the time is coming when a new religion will show itself. I have to tell you also, that the nation that you know as the 'Arab people' will pay for their injustices; they will reap their own rewards, for the harm they have caused, throughout those countries."

[Seven years on, 3rd May 2004, Salumet elaborated on the significance of TERRORISM. His words included:

~ "There is no nation upon this planet—free from that accusation."

He made it clear that when such seeds are sown we must take the consequences; and looking to the fuller picture:

~ "Mankind is now awakening to the realization, that 'fear' creates many things—and to balance fear, there has to be 'love'! It is a time of adjustment for all of mankind. It is an important time in your Earthly evolution; not only (for) those nations in disharmony with one another. Counteract all this negativity by sending out your love, by helping others to understand what it is they need in order to live peaceful lives, lives without fear, lives without harm. It is achievable but it will not come tomorrow."

This statement, although condensed, is profound. There are deeply karmic issues here that must be resolved; and this statement is surely the only logical view—the only rational sense, to be made of the bombings, the bloodshed and the mindless sectarian violence.

Leslie, in 1997, had expressed his pleasure in hearing that people will at last be freed, from dogmatic shackles that have been holding them, to which Salumet replied:

~ "It has already happened. We have seen, have we not, the freedom of the peoples who have been bound by (Russian) communism? It is only a name, but it is that people have been held back in being allowed to know themselves, to know their inner God, to know that they have freedom to search for what they truly believe."

Leslie: "Good. So it would seem that the work that all of you have gathered to do, is going to come to fruition."

~ "There is much to come for this planet. It is still in its growing stages. But mankind is coming to the realisation that he has some power, he has the power of his mind, he has the power of his love—he must allow himself to be open to all men, to all situations, to be open to those cosmic forces which surround your planet. Once you can strive to achieve these things, there would be no fear in your world."

This then, had been a rather special evening during which our teacher revealed a little about Earth's future—this perhaps to give some idea of where his mission is heading. If mankind is to become a spiritual brotherhood within the next thousand years, and if Planet Earth is to take her rightful place in the cosmic order of things; then we *must* experience significant milestones along the way. Salumet has given us an inkling of the path that we must take as we grow up and shed childish inadequacies. And the sprinkling of accurate prophecy, some of which has already come to fruition since 1997, might be seen as a form of proof of our spirit connection.

To all who meet in séance groups or who read attendant literature, there is of course the ongoing immediate evidence of spirit connection—*they* need no convincing. Where a presentation of proof is concerned, it is really just for those having no such inclination or for those whose minds, for whatever reason, are closed to recognising the ways of spirit. These are often termed 'sceptics'. Scepticism may be the result of a physically cluttered lifestyle or to a total adherence to scientific or intellectual thinking. Either way, the mind becomes preoccupied in physical matters or in physical intellectual thought. A problem of society through the 20th century has been that those devoted solely to physical brain-work have held much sway—have very heavily influenced institutions, governments, finance houses and news media. This blinkered view has to change and the Internet is helping in this regard. We should also observe that, as young children, we all begin with open minds and 'feel' that spirit connection. That is the way of childhood. But as the result of education, upbringing, and societal input, this is too often lost, so that a wholly physical lifestyle becomes the norm. So for thoughtful consideration by the latter and possibly for the entertainment of those who are already aware, a brief list of meaningful or accurately prophetic séance details is now presented:

- Early in 1994, we received word from a spirit communicator that there would be a 'happening' when the roses bloom. That was the time when Salumet first joined us.
- On 11th October 2010 word was received from a communicator that Eileen's role would be changing, and she would receive guidance ~ *"In the direction of this new challenge."* It transpired that on 9th May 2011, Lilian, after ten years of wonderful hosting of the Kingsclere Group meetings, felt the need to retire from that responsibility and Eileen took over hosting of the meetings; so we all now meet in Eileen's home in nearby Whitchurch.
- On 28th November 2011, some of us had arrived a little early, to find Eileen listening to last week's recording. I read to those who were gathering, a quotation from Chairman Mao Tse-Tung's *Little Red Book: 'We are advocates of the abolition of war, we do not want war; but war can only be abolished through war, and in order to get rid of the gun it is necessary to take up the gun.'* I suggested that we ask for Salumet's comments on this self contradicting statement. We then moved into the séance room. There was no need for me to read Chairman Mao's statement—Salumet declared he had been listening to our earlier conversation! It seems that his attention had been aroused by his own spoken words on the recording!
- We had learned whilst speaking with our dear friend Bonniol of Planet Aerah that *as the spirituality of a planet increases, densities decrease.* Following that, it became evident that Earth's 1 kilo weight standard set up in 1889 has mysteriously lost 50 micrograms—seemingly proving the point. On 14th November 2011 Salumet confirmed that this was indeed in accord with that universal law:

~ "It is always welcome news when your scientists have some proof of what is happening."

- But in scientific circles, as I write (2013), the penny has not yet dropped and they still remain unaware of the reason for the weight loss.
- We receive many different visitors from spirit. On 1st August 2011 it was a Chinese acrobat who had been with a travelling circus—originally from Shanghai but he became much travelled. He had enjoyed touring the United States, Toronto and Mexico

City in the '50s and 60's. He spoke of Tibet, and why the Chinese should respect the Tibetan people. We mentioned that several of us had read books by the Tibetan Lama Lobsang Rampa. Our visitor remembered this author and whilst on the Earth he had actually read his first book; published 1956.

- During the meeting of 15th March 2010, Eileen was relaying personal messages from ones in spirit, and the question was asked:

~ "Who has been reading a heavy book today?"

That was me. I had been checking a point, by reference to a John Brown illustrated bible with brass clasps—they don't come much heavier than that! This book had been handed down to me via my grandmother and I was aware that it had once belonged to her daughter Dorothy who had sadly died early in life (1908-1926). The lady in spirit went on to explain that she had given the book to her granddaughter on either her 5th or 6th birthday. On returning home I read the faded handwritten inscription inside the cover: 'Dorothy Moss – From Grandmother Moss, January 25th 1914, her birthday.' So it would indeed have been Dorothy's 6th birthday. Needless to say, I had met neither Dorothy nor my great grandmother. As a child, I recall going with my mother to tend Dorothy's grave. No one in the group had awareness of my early family history. I should however, mention that my father had visited our group seven years earlier. Wonderfully, he remains close, watching the progress of his grandchildren and he had expressed a fondness for what he described as Paul's 'wanderlust'! Paul has indeed travelled much.

- When Rudolf Steiner, speaking via Gary, visited on 3rd October 2011, I asked if it had given him pleasure from spirit, to see his teaching establishment situated just inside the Swiss border, being rebuilt—a fire had destroyed the earlier building. His reply began:

~ "The Goetheanum, yes—it was a great joy!"

The point about this response is that I did not know of his admiration for Wolfgang Goethe or that he had named the cultural centre at Dornach after him—he gave us the name from spirit. Rudolf Steiner

(1861-1925), rebuilding completed 1928—one of seventeen buildings for which he was the designing architect.

- Another who spoke via Gary led to some most interesting name-dropping. He felt comfortable with our group because, as he explained, his mother had been a trance medium who did platform work. Perhaps we would know the name?

~ "My mother was a friend of the one charged with the witchcraft act."

Eileen: "Helen Duncan!"
[The most bizarre episode of World War II was when the UK battleship HMS Barham, was sunk with loss of 861 lives and the Admiralty, fearing decline of morale, at first withheld the news from public. But Helen Duncan revealed to parents, during séance, the drowning of their son and the loss of the ship. She was seen by Admiralty as a security risk! Helen Duncan was imprisoned under the Witchcraft Act. Winston Churchill described this episode as *obsolete tomfoolery* and visited the lady in prison. The Witchcraft Act was finally repealed in 1951.]

~ "They knew each other and they were close—Florence."

Eileen: "Your mother was Florence!"
Further questions revealed 'Florence Kiers', formerly Smith—who performed many spirit rescues through the war years—soldier deaths from battlefield situations. Our guest had himself been a sailor—injured but survived when HMS Exeter sustained heavy damage during the Battle of the River Plate.

~ "Death has a way of awakening you—when one sees much death, one can become enlightened by it, in a strange way."

It is true that there has been enhanced interest in spirit world and messages from loved ones during those hard-pressed periods of warfare.

- Leslie—Leslie Bone—our group founder, made his journey to spirit in 1999. He has visited on several occasions since. At the conclusion of his 25th August 2003 visit, he left us with typical Leslie-style humour, saying:

~ "—and I don't like what they've done to my bungalow!"

It was a reference to the attic conversion job by the new residents! So there was hearty laughter as our dear friend, host of so many interesting evenings, made his exit that evening.

- My dear wife Ann made her journey to spirit in the summer of 2012. She returned and spoke with us via Jan during our 9th December 2013 meeting, sending everyone her love. And she giggled, which was very typical.
- During our meeting of 9th March 2009, we pointed out that print-on-demand publishing and Salumet's mission each began in the same year, 1994. This new publishing facility plus the expanding Internet with its websites, make the spreading of Salumet's mission message so much easier. And we invited his comments on this observation:

~ "Yes, my dear friend—as a human being, I would be feeling my head was swelling!"

The laughter that followed was unrestrained. He then went on to say that the timing was planned very well and confirmed:

~ "There are no accidents."

It is so easy to feel on such occasions as these that there is a between-worlds orchestration at work. There is—there can be no doubt about that!

CHAPTER 18

RECENT NOTARIES NOW IN SPIRIT

It can be exciting to hear from notaries now in spirit; especially if facts are made known that have not formed part of recorded history. And sometimes unrecorded facts are mentioned that make the known history fall more satisfactorily into place. We do have errors in historic record and these occasions present opportunity for revision. There have been a number of revelations when such notaries as Rudolf Steiner, queens and political figures have visited. On the evening of 8th December 2003 a communicator was with us who had herself promoted the truth of spirit world during her Earth life. This one spoke with a wonderful self assurance and had what might be described as a 'public speaking voice'. We asked for a name, and she gave: 'Emma'. Later, a little research revealed that this might possibly be Emma Hardinge-Britten, an early pioneer of the movement who had given public lectures and who had published the books 'Modern American Spiritualism' (1870) and 'Nineteenth Century Miracles' (1884). She also founded 'Two Worlds' magazine—still available on the bookstalls today. So, when Salumet was with us on 12th January 2004, we asked if he could confirm identity for us. Our teacher felt obliged to say that naming names was not really a part of his mission. He did however, reflect on the matter:

> ~ "But on this occasion I will tell you that indeed you are correct. The dear lady works tirelessly still for what you call spirit. She is always

attracted by dedication to the work and that is possibly why she was attracted to speak with you here. She speaks many eloquent words does she not?"

I replied that she spoke extremely well and gave the impression of being a public speaker.

~ "And she still is."

Emma Hardinge-Britten (1833-1899): was with us again on 13th June 2005, this time to help Eileen's return to full consciousness following Salumet's withdrawal. And during that process, she became aware of my mother's cousins, Winnie and Tom Wilson, who wished to send their regards. It was a joy to be able to exchange fond hellos with these dear ones from past times. I then pointed out to Emma that her full name is in our history books and we are impressed by her Earthly deeds. Her reply carried modesty:

~ "Well, I've been humbled that you should remember a name that is hardly for remembering, but of course, I know that when you are on the Earth plane, that names sometimes have some kind of meaning and seem important."

The dear lady went on to say that she always just gives the name 'Emma' when people ask. Emma has since become a valued friend and a regular visitor, bringing news from time to time of her latest wonderful project. World consciousness is changing and Emma 'influences' the downtrodden women of our world, beginning with those in India who need to take control of their lives—and there are those who are obliged to cover themselves with the burka in public. That is all changing. Emma's work aims to encourage women to feel their equality with men-folk—an important part of current world change.

We have got to know some of this dear lady's ways over the years. She has an unquenchable love of Victorian era hats—large and adorned with feathers and flowers; and continues to wear them! Our more clairvoyant ones can often discern their colour and a little of their decoration. I have got to know when Emma arrives because she sits with a very upright (Eileen's) back, and straightening the back causes Eileen's wicker chair to creak. So when Eileen sits up and the chair creaks we know who it is and I can say: "Welcome to you Emma!" But her arrival on 8th

October 2012 was different. The wicker chair had needed a small repair job, and so Eileen was seated in a chair without the creaking facility.

Sarah, observing a presence: "Good evening."

~ "Good evening to everybody!"

George: "And welcome!"

~ "I can always expect a good welcome."

Sarah: "Have you been before?"

~ "It is I—Emma!"

—Whereupon we all spoke at once and the recorder went into a state of confusion. Then Emma was pleased to give us an update on her project:

~ "The work is progressing beautifully—I am sure you must be aware of the change in the women of your world, even in those places of disruption and war. You know well my work took me to those places where women were downtrodden. And that is slowly, slowly changing—I am so pleased to report."

George: "Your work centred on India, or does it go wider?"

~ "It goes wider now, but mainly India—that is my mission. But I am so pleased that it is happening at last!"

Paul ventured that it is clear from TV documentaries that some Middle East women are now able to do jobs previously denied them. Emma concurred; then received a message to pass on to us, that Eileen had this time forgotten to switch out the phone line for the period of our meeting. There are occasions when those in spirit can be just so on-the-ball and helpful! We moved onto the subject of 'hats':

~ "Many are amused by my headwear—as you know this is one of my great joys, to wear these hats. I don't surrender them too easily, but that is not important. I am unimportant. The work *is* important."

We discussed the significance of the hats worn by western ladies:

~ "Yes, it was a form of recognition, but of course, that is not why I wore those hats. I have a particular love for them, and I still retain that, even to this day."

Rod inquired if she drops by at the Ascot race meetings to see the hats:

~ "I have seen, and I am quite amused I have to say. Some of them— could you possibly call them hats?—I don't think so do you?"

Sarah: "Not only could you not call some of the hats, hats; you couldn't call some of the dresses, dresses!"

~ "Well! They look more like *underwear* to me!"

Hearty laughter followed, as we all saw the funny side of how Ascot attire must appear to a lady in love with Victorian standards. Rod felt he was perhaps missing something because he did not see a connection between fancy hats and downtrodden women, but Emma explained:

~ "—Because that is just who I am—or was."

Exactly so! Some of us fly a flag of identity, as did or does the gentleman who visited on 7th July 2008.

Sir Winston Churchill (1874-1965): We were first asked by a communicator to voice any impressions sensed, and in conclusion, one described as a 'great spokesman' would then join us. Paul sensed 'the writing of diaries' and Sarah named: 'Churchill'. This acted as a trigger:

~ "That is I—I have refrained from speaking too soon."

The voice that came via Eileen was rich, powerful and very closely typical of Sir Winston in Earth life—even with that element that might be described as 'a forced lisp' as the word 'speaking' began. This was, as I recall from his speeches, a strongly reminiscent characteristic. But its powerful vibrancy made Eileen cough a little at first:

~ "Dratted voices—causing nothing but trouble!"

We laughed, but then clear speech followed:

~ "This I have to say to you: not all that is said is true—about spirit and those who come to speak with you. It has been said that those well known in the world, only return to those they love—not true! There are those, as myself, who still need to communicate, and will take any opportunity that is available to us."

George: "Wonderful! And I am old enough to remember your speeches whilst you were on the Earth, and I note your voice is still strong and has that kind of intonation—"

Rod: "—and the inspiration you gave us all. Thank you very much for that!"

~ "I was amazed by the attention I received when I passed. I suffered many disappointments in my life, unknown to many. But I have to say that my heart was touched to see so many who had good thoughts for me."

Lilian: "I think the country and everyone in it needed a figure that was giving us hope."

~ "One thing I will say: to give up any habits that you may retain—"

Sarah: "Are you referring to smoking?"

~ "Indeed I am."

This was another occasion for a little good humoured laughter, as Lilian added: "We've been told that."

~ "I assure you that this is so, and I did for some time suffer—I use the word guardedly."

Jan appreciated that he missed his cigar and asked if he had the emphysema:

~ "Slightly, but not widely known."

George: "But we realise it was more than just a cigar, was it not? It was a symbol that went with you."

~ "It was a presentation of myself. Yes, even now I feel my hand go to clasp one."

And Eileen's hand was raised a little in clasping gesture.

George: "And whatever one's feelings about war today—it's strange having lived through that period in the '40s—it seems to me both then and on reflection, to have been a very special period in our history when we were getting things sorted. On reflection I cannot see any different solution or outcome for that period. But hopefully, *world*-warfare has now ended and there will be no more of that. Have you any such thoughts?"

~ "I do. I follow all that takes place in your world, even today. I wish I could rewrite history, but that is not possible. My part I played was to the best of my ability, and although many errors were made, I feel justified in saying that I travelled the right road as far as war was concerned."

Sarah: "You were probably being influenced from spirit anyway, weren't you?"

~ "I now know that—at the time I hoped, but did not fully know."

Jan: "Mr Churchill—I can remember you being prime minister when I was a little girl. I cannot let this opportunity go by without asking you if yourself and Mr Hitler have met in spirit and spoken—shook hands and made friends?"

~ "I cannot say that to you. For some time my goodness was not strong enough to do so; and still, although I am aware of this gentleman, I have no desire to meet with him—but of course, all forgiveness is there."

Lilian: "I think we've been told that he will be in darkness—for eons of time. So possibly he is not even ready."

~ "He is not ready, because he feels he was justified in making a new world. But there is no resentment, no malice; and I have to tell you:

182

I admired his earlier strategies of war, as a man who knew where he was going—not the actions that were committed, but in the earlier part—"

Jan: "—As a strategist—"

~ "Yes, that part of him I can congratulate him for—as being a person myself of great detail."

Jan hoped that he had no objection to the question being asked.

~ "Many people have made and written judgement—I am happy."

George: "Well, we all realise this is a learning planet. We are all learning, and where you are now, I think I am right in saying: *you* are still learning."

~ "We are all learning."

Jan: "Has your viewpoint on warfare, now that you have passed over, changed?"

~ "Slowly I am changing."

Jan suggested that Sir Winston had been in spirit but a short time, relatively speaking.

~ "Yes, it doesn't happen in a moment."

Rod: "So what about your wife? Have you got a happier time meeting with your wife again?"

~ "Families are always different—and acquaintances. There is always a love bond which isn't severed on passing. That still stays strong."

Rod: "That's lovely."

~ "But I have to say: I am still interested in my family of the present day, and I am sure at times they feel my presence. My family has extended greatly, as all here know."

Jan: "Are you a public speaker in spirit?"

~ "Every opportunity I can, I will speak. I do not now command such attention, but the oratory still takes place."

Jan: "That's nice."
George: "You said that you had the desire to rewrite history. I would add to that, that while you were on the Earth, you did a very good job of actually writing the history!"
(That work amounted originally to six volumes—and various abridgments were to follow.)

~ "Yes, I have to say: my pride took a place to the forefront of those writings, but I speak not only of the time when I was with you, but previous history."

Jan: "I believe you used to meditate—I read about you in a book. You used to sit quietly and meditate—"

~ "Yes, I had connection with spirit. I suffered many black days when the knowing and feeling spirit was my salvation."

George: "Yes, I can feel and imagine that."

~ "Yes."

George: "And you painted—"

~ "I suppose you would say I was an artistic person."

I suggested that also helped with relaxation.

~ "It helps me—you must forgive me—my voice is going, because my energy is leaving. Before I found expression in my writing—my paintings—many forms of art—"

As the power faded, there was just time to voice our farewells and heartfelt appreciation. We were so privileged to have been able to exchange a few words with this talented and respected gentleman from our recent past. And the powerful voice was so close to that which delivered those wartime speeches, still vividly in the memory of several present.

Adolf Hitler Note: A film had been made and shown on TV, concerning the last days of Adolf Hitler. In that film, one was interviewed who had been a personal secretary, who had survived the war and who still lived. The statement was made, that he who led the Third Reich—*regarded 'compassion' as a weakness to be trodden underfoot*—a key to his wrong thinking perhaps? Bearing in mind that compassion has its spirit connection, I queried the point with Salumet—that was on 6th March 2006:

> ~ "Firstly let me say: this is again a very good example of why you cannot judge your fellow human, because you do not have the full picture at any time. The gentleman in question was indeed *a confused human being*. He was not of sound mind much of the time at the end of his Earthly life. But what I say to you is this: of course, compassion belongs to spirit—to the mind, but you also know that the physical being is activated by the mind. And the mind is controlled by the physical action. There always is interaction between the two. Therefore, when there is some kind of discontent within the human being, whether there be fear, whether there be confusion; of course this has to have some effect upon the whole structure of being. The physical and the spiritual are intertwined, but whilst you remain upon this Earth, oft times is the physical reasoning the more powerful, which then creates all of these situations."

I suggested physical intellect would then control input from spirit or would in effect shut out the spiritual mind.

> ~ "Of course, remember I have told you: there are so many in your world who are spiritually inadequate, and this is the reason why they do not allow those spiritual attributes to shine forth. Remember always the balance of light and darkness. Perhaps a better word than 'control' would be 'influence'. But always there has to be interaction between the two. It explains, does it not my dear friends, why so many in your world create what you have termed 'atrocities'. It is a lack of light within their spirit whilst, and *only* whilst, they inhabit these bodies."

Graham had then queried of the atrocities committed: are they then really their own fault if the spiritual influence is disconnected:

~ "I do not like to use the word 'fault'. They of course must be *responsible* whilst in these physical garbs for every deed and action that they take against their fellow man, and they will become aware of these things when they return home to us. But what would be much better is if they could begin—and I will use a saying within your own world that is used frequently: if only they could see the light! If only they would allow their true selves to step forward then all the negativity and hatred and fear within them would dissolve."

Graham: "And presumably they live such a life for learning not only for themselves, but also for others around them."

~ "Remember that like attracts like and in so doing it makes a greater picture of all that is dark. I am sure you are aware in your own world of many who are like this."

George: "And with Adolf Hitler, it was quite amazing the way those close to him seemed to be swept along by his—I could call it 'wayward philosophy'."

~ "Yes, of course."

So we would do well to, when reviewing past events or when formulating opinions from reading history, not to judge individuals when we just do not have the wider picture. We know details of the single lifetime—what about the soul in spirit and what about the learning that ensues for all? Was that a part of some ongoing master plan? I would think these thoughts should apply with particular relevance to Sir Winston Churchill's World War II adversary.

Rudolf Steiner (1861-1925): Gary Samdaliri has a meditation and channelling group in Bournemouth and he has sat with us several times. The Chinese acrobat mentioned in the previous chapter came via Gary; also several Rudolf Steiner visits. But also, I had previously asked Salumet about Rudolf Steiner; that had been on 25th June 2007. That inquiry had referred to 'biodynamic agriculture', a means of reviving arid or worn out agricultural soils and kick-starting them back into activity. His recipe, or part of it, was to fill cow horns with manure and bury them in the ground for several months, then stir the resulting material into water, carefully stirring to right and to left and using this, prepared as an extremely dilute solution on a very large area of soil. Perhaps he was developing the right bacteria in the soil to initiate humus production. But that is just conjecture. Anyway, his method works, that is the important factor. So, I had asked for Salumet's comments:

~ "Yes. Names matter not as you know, but of course he would have been influenced in some way and the simple answer is: when you speak of burying the horns deep within the earth - we have spoken of earth energies and those who work *with* the earth (elementals). So you see, although there is a simple explanation, he has elaborated in his own mind, what has been given to him, and made use of that information. But of course he would have been influenced, as all people on this Earth are influenced in some way: your chemists, your doctors, your scientists; name any of them who create new ideas, or (what) you *think* is a new idea—"

We had laughed, because *'new' being in fact 'recycled old'* has been an oft repeated phrase.

~ "So always my dear friend when you read of these things or see these 'new' inventions, think spiritually."

I suggested our teacher had implied that the elementals were involved in this work.

~ "Of course!—that is their task, but we need to influence some human beings to start the process off."

Gary sat with us on 5th September 2011, and although more than four years later, it was almost as if he continued where Salumet had left off!

~ "Good evening—it's Rudolf Steiner from the higher dimensional plane. We have to be like yourselves; very patient in spirit to develop the channel—the medium. We, in a sense, have to be tested with more patience because we have all the knowledge and want to share this with humanity. We become excited to share this, but the difficulty is, what is termed: 'grounding this knowledge in its purity without it becoming tarnished by the lower dimensional influences'. Throughout history, it has always been a challenge for us in spirit to achieve this. It is our spiritual development to master this—to create a high quality communication that gives you a pure source of knowledge that humanity has built up throughout history, from the past—so much knowledge to share—not just the future."

George: "Certainly, we all have this feeling of wanting to share knowledge *here*, and in this modern world, there is the Internet, and websites which are, perhaps, an aid in this. Are you aware of these things?"

~ "Very much so—we even try to influence it! It can be used for sharing higher knowledge and wisdom—what is called 'spiritual information' can be passed on through computer/Internet, yes. Much is being shared on sites. Much of it can be considered 'conspiracy sites'; but there is an extension of that where it is more 'higher knowledge inter-dimensional' communications—channelled sites, where there is information from spirit being passed on, through this powerful, global medium—so we support that. But unfortunately, it can also be manipulated by the lower levels. It is an open channel really, the Internet—it is very open to influence, and so much information, so much thought. Being on the fifth dimension, we can see how this intense energy of the Internet is growing bigger all the time—expanding—like an ocean, a bit like the Akasha—it's become its own Akashic record.

George: "Akashic record?"

~ "Yes, it is a source of holding information—storing knowledge."

George: "Yes, so are you saying there's a comparison here?"

~ "Yes, I believe there is, yes. There is a natural, higher dimensional record—library; and now there is (also) on the Earth level, through the Internet. It holds everything, good and bad—purity, impurity—yes."

Following this brilliant observation concerning the Internet, we referred to his work with the buried dung-filled cow horns that could restore failed agricultural areas:

~ "Biodynamic!—and I suppose it was ahead of its time."

I pointed out that it seemed to be much more effective than one would expect from the small amount of material used.

~ "Yes, in places like Israel and Egypt, the concept is being used, and Australia and South Brazil. I keep an eye out on the various communities, but it is quite spread out—Japan, yes."

He added later:

~ "It is an ancient knowledge that I tapped—the Egyptians used similar methods. They mastered these techniques, and I managed to access this in the Akashic records—a vision of old Egypt, and their methods of farming, and that's the basis of my biodynamic inspiration. It goes back to the Ancient Egyptians. They were true masters of growing food. They had to be."

Paul observed that it is a shame that more of the planet does not use the biodynamic agricultural method. Our philosophical guest then moved on to the new energies that will bathe our planet:

~ "All to do with the sun—it will instigate higher wisdom—the trigger. The sun is going through a huge shift at the present. Your scientists know this, yes."

George: "Changes in the sun will benefit the planet?"

~ "It will benefit the planet very much so. It will spiritualise it—purify it."

George: "Yes, I think it is realised amongst scientists that changes are about to take place in the sun, but I don't think it is understood terribly well about what those changes will accomplish."

~ "The sun is a spiritual entity ultimately—the ancients knew this. It has a spiritual dimension. Once science recognises the spirit of the Sun—the Logos—then transformation is guaranteed—the beginning of an advanced society can be realised."

We declared our interest—this we were finding interesting in the extreme!

~ "—what we also can term 'Ascension'—the raising of the planet."

Jan: "So we should turn our attention more spiritually to the Sun, then, should we?"

~ "You can worship it, if you wish. There's no sin in that."

Jan: "But surely, that would have a positive effect on the Sun if it is a spiritual entity?"

~ "It will recognise your calling. Part of it has a consciousness, as does the planet."

Jan: "Ancient civilisations worshipped the Sun."

~ "It is worship in the 'physical' sense, in creating and beautifying the body—see it as being alive. I will finish on that note."

Graham declared: "You've given us a lot to think about."
Now that was a gross understatement if ever there was! The physical solar activity, we knew was involving magnetic field reversal and powerful solar flares directly facing Earth—solar flares do not usually face Earth directly. These things are known to our scientists, but at this stage, spiritual considerations were sadly either non-existent or unaccounted.

A further visit from this interesting one the following month began:

~ "Rudolf Steiner here—coming through again. It interests me that you do 'rescues' here. 'Rescue' is not so common nowadays, but they need it—they need mediums to come through."

Our evening this time had in fact begun with several rescues—a remorseful lady who had taken her own life—another lady all het up because her pig had got out of its pen. Situations vary enormously. And the gentleman who had died sitting in a pub comes to mind. His parting question had been: 'Can I take my pint of beer with me?'!

~ "In a sense they're still asleep. The lower levels of the astral are in a deeper sleep—the ability to reflect clearly is limited. But I'm beyond that, on the ascended level. Once you ascend, then you see things totally differently, and clarity comes. All the lives fit in, history begins to make sense and confusion goes."

We agreed there have been periods through history that seemingly make no sense at all.

~ "There's progress—setbacks—progress—setbacks. Humanity goes forward a bit, then it has periods like the 'Dark Ages' when it seems to revert backwards, and the lower annihilistic ways of the Earth come back. Then you have a 'Renaissance' with a push forward towards the realm of spirit. This is an age of being drawn back into spirit realm again—dropping the lower physicality—the material domination—not to be trapped by the 'illusion of materialism'. I tried to convey this in my short time on the Earth."

Yes, materialism lacks love, logic and outlook—ultimately there's no tomorrow; hence the illusion. Looking to 'tomorrow', Sara placed a question about child upbringing, and this led straight into our friend's condemnation of violence in computer games:

~ "They play these games that express—encourage an aggressive streak, which I see as unhealthy for their minds."

George: "Yes, 'aggressive streak'—that's a good term in relation to computer games."

~ "War games—war games really, aren't they?—which are allowed to be played—yeah."

Sara pointed out how difficult it is for parents today, because all the boys at school are playing these games and there's that feeling of comradeship.

~ "They become psyched into the games so much, they develop certain traits of the characters of the game—being a Ninja or a soldier, and they lose their own personality within it. That upsets me a great deal. I do not like these games at all. They are poison to their minds. There's an addiction issue with them—what I would call 'satanic games'. I have to use such a term because that is applicable."

We suggested these to be wise words that should be set down and circulated.

~ "I'm quite happy to express my views on that in the strongest terms. They are dangerous and unhealthy in society, basically. And those in power should know this, but they're so weak."

Finally, this progressive and authoritative one from the higher realms left us a gift:

~ "What I wish to do before I go, is to put down the Christos—the Christ Golden Light for you—to assist you in your lives—that of the sun, the divine love of the solar Logos."

Thus ended a truly amazing evening! Clearly, this 'ascended philosopher' has much understanding. He sees from his high level how Earth is bathed in new energies and is poised to move forward—all aligning to the Salumet teaching of course. And he understands the import in our lives of Internet, making the comparison with Akasha. How very apt!

CHAPTER 19

ROYALTY NOW
IN SPIRIT

Royalty have significant places within recorded history and there are four royal ladies that have spoken with us, imparting much helpful and often fascinating information. Our historians have done their best with facts from the Earthly record, but of course they cannot know inner feelings. There are with certainty errors of detail in the record, and some of these are pointed out in this chapter. We begin with a royal who preferred I think, for reasons of etiquette, not to give precise identity—just the family name.

Romanov Family (→17ᵗʰ July 1918): Whilst this lady, understandably preferred not to reveal precise identity, it seems highly likely from her statements, that she would have been the Tsarina Alexandra. When Nicholas became Tsar in 1894, he became free to marry Alexandra; that event followed in just twenty-six days. There had, prior to that, been resistance to the proposed union with *Princess Alix Victoria Helena Luise Beatrice*, from a grand duchy within the German Empire. Following the marriage, it is said that whilst in the Russian Court, she had an air of cold superiority and she became a reclusive figure. There were four daughters in the marriage and finally a son and heir Alexei, who sadly suffered incurable haemophilia. During World War I, Tsar Nicholas spent time at the front while the Mystic Grigory Rasputin treated Alexei's condition. There was talk of a relationship with Alexandra. Later, during Russia's civil war, and while the Romanovs were under house arrest, Rasputin's tomb was raided and his body remains burned. Then, on 17th July 1918, the Romanov family together with close associates were summarily executed by the Bolsheviks. That, very briefly, is the background history to what follows.

It quickly became clear that this lady who now visited has since progressed extremely well in her spiritual life; speaking via Sue on the evening of 17th August 1998—her salient statements being:

~ "I will say to you that since I have been on this side of life, I have learnt a great lesson in humility, but I cannot change my carriage or the way I sit or stand or move around. But I have learnt humility and that surely is one of the greatest lessons mankind could possibly learn. I came to the new life, very full of self-importance, very sure that people, many people, were way, way beneath me on the ladder. Can you understand this?"

Leslie: "Well that's how you were brought up, wasn't it?"

~ "Indeed, and that possibly was the undoing of my family. But that is enough of that. It was a very hard and painful journey; but I gradually had my haughty exterior broken down piece by piece and I can say to you quite truthfully, that when the final piece came down, I could see light and love, as it should be for the very first time. I was led into light and love, by some wonderful and caring souls and I am honoured to say that since I have become more human, and less of a glass ornament, I have been permitted myself, to give the kind of help I received, to others of a similar nature."

Leslie: "Good—and you're giving that help in your world, are you?"

~ "Indeed I am and let me tell you, I am so ashamed of how I behaved, because now as you say, the boot is on the other foot and I am having to deal with people I so closely resembled. It is not easy, in fact if I could, I would tear my hair out!"

Leslie sympathised and could well understand those feelings.

~ "I'm sure at times when you've been doing your rescue work, you have thought to yourself: how on Earth can I get through to these people? Well as you know, eventually you do get through—I am a living proof of that, but goodness me, I feel deep remorse for all the problems I caused my beloved carers, and I can only continue in my life, helping others in recompense for my past ways."

Leslie, at this point, reiterated that her upbringing had contributed so much.

~ "Yes, yes. My one concession, when I feel the need to have four walls and a roof around me—and of course I can if I wish—I do have rather beautiful and luxurious accommodation! But gone are the sycophants that surrounded me. I have to cope alone and I thoroughly enjoy it; and when I am replete of the luxurious life, I remove myself from the trappings of wealth and go on my way. It is a little indulgence that I feel I have earned."

Leslie: "Yes I would agree with you, we would all feel the same I think. I don't think anybody would have any objection to that, would they?" All present agreed and well understood!

~ "Thank you. Next time I feel the need to surround myself with fine furniture and velvet, I will think to myself that my new found friends would not object to a little decadence for a short time."

Leslie: "No we wouldn't. We'd love to share it with you!" And as the laughter subsided, the lady added:

~ "Perhaps in time my friends—perhaps I will welcome you all to my little palace! And if I had another luxury to go with my beautiful little palace, then it would be fresh fruit—and fine wine, which perhaps I should bow my head in shame for—"

Well, we all like our little indulgences, and as Leslie explained: this helps one to feel more comfortable.

~ "Does that mean I have permission to go and indulge myself, with some wine and not feel guilty?—because my new found friends have told me that it is quite in order? Goodness me!—that's all I needed to know! I think I shall presently leave you and see if I can find someone who will join me in a small indulgence!"

And that was a further occasion for much hearty laughter.

~ "Of course, you know it is all in the mind. I do not anticipate taking a glass of wine and putting it to my lips, but I will *think* I am putting a glass of wine to my lips and that will be just as intoxicating to me. As you know, it IS the mind, when you come through the curtain. It is thought that takes me into my beautiful palace, it is thought that removes me from my beautiful palace and puts me in the real world."

As our visitor departed, she made it clear that she was leaving the door open for possibly another to sometime come through with more detailed family history. She left with expressions that well demonstrate her hard-learned humility:

~ "I am honoured to have been accepted into your private quarters and thank you for taking the time and having the patience, to listen to the ramblings of someone like myself."

Leslie: "Well they certainly weren't ramblings and we've all been most interested. I don't think anybody would deny that, would they?"
There was general agreement, and I added that it had been a delightful experience for us all.

~ "Then I offer you farewell, and my final words to you are: always have a little humility. Do not plump yourselves up, with unwarranted self-importance."

And that we all felt to be a wonderful message for humanity. But our visitor had then popped back again very briefly, having realised she had not yet given her family name:

~ "I do not wish to give my first names, because—and I jest here—you would be here all night, I had so many. My surname was 'Romanov'. I will leave you now."

Further to that, another spoke via Leslie, endorsing the fact that self-importance is simply of no value in the spiritual life:

~ "That applies to all, irrespective of birth, of previous experience on this Earth, or what you call: the higher echelons of society. It is absolutely of no importance whatsoever! The only thing that concerns us when you come to us is your degree of spiritual development—not the trappings of so-called civilised life."

So this dear lady, who once lived on Earth as a Romanov, has left us with a most powerful message.

Lady Margaret Beaufort (1443-1509): The visit of this one was very brief, came as a great surprise and the few facts that identify her seemed to come about by accident. It was during our meeting of 15th November 2010 and Sarah's youthful daughter Emily sat with us. Firstly, our visitor stated through Eileen, that she wished to speak via the young lady (Emily) to give her experience. She then transferred to Emily and was welcomed by us. I asked if she wanted to discuss anything in particular, or just have a cosy chat—just a chat it seemed:

~ "I spend a lot of time in the Halls of Learning. When I lived here (on Earth), I enjoyed reading."

George: "You enjoyed reading when you were here?"

~ "Yes."

Sarah: "Do you remember how long ago that was when you were here?"
There followed a pause, then a most surprising answer:

~ "I was here in the year 1501."

How very precise! She then went on to say more about the Halls of Learning. This lady was clearly an avid reader both here and in spirit, but 1501 was an early time for book availability on the Earth.
Sarah: "If you were here in 1501 and you enjoyed reading, you probably came from quite a rich family. Is that right?"

~ "I was part of a royal family."

Ann: "Oh! What was your name?"

~ "My name was 'Margaret'."

Lilian: "Can you remember who was king or queen at that time?"

~ It was a king—Henry."

George: "And there would not have been so many books available at that time—"

At this point the conversation ended, with Emily saying: I'm back! So the facts are few but in combination, they are highly significant: an avid reader—Margaret—a royal—1501—and she knew right away that the king of that date was Henry. It was indeed Henry VII and Margaret Beaufort was his mother! Thank you so much for wanting to help with Emily's development!

This lady was from changing times. Just as the Internet spreads knowledge today, printing and books were the new influence then. William Caxton (1415-1492) had brought book printing to England. He was our first retailer of printed books and established the Westminster Press in 1476. Lady Margaret Beaufort had married Edmund Tudor at 12 and gave birth at age 13, to he who became Henry VII, and she was grandmother to Henry VIII. She has been described as the richest woman in English Medieval history, educationalist, scholar and philanthropist—and was a founder of teaching institutions. Lady Margaret Beaufort was a sponsor of Caxton and supporter of the new media of her day—books and printing. She remembered particularly the year 1501. She had been entitled to sign herself 'Margaret R' from 1499, and her granddaughter Margaret became Queen of Scotland through marriage to James IV in 1502. So perhaps the year 1501, leading to that, had been a very, very good year in the memory of 'Margaret R'!

Soon after the Salumet mission began, he arranged visits by two queens from Earth's history. This was a bold and admirable move— a teaching through demonstration; to reveal just a little of how spirit world is organised. It is made wonderfully clear how an Earthly life becomes a part of ongoing soul, yet may be returned from soul to speak its truth—the memories of chosen parts of that Earth life becoming as real on presentation to us as on the day of their happening.

Mary Queen of Scots (1542-1587): The evening of 20th November 1995 remains so sharp in memory—heart warming—emotionally charged—historic. The visit had been attempted several months earlier, but conditions had been less than favourable and after a few minutes was terminated. No name was given then, but one present had sensed an identity, wrote it down, sealed it in an envelope and handed it to Leslie for safe keeping. But now, this time the link was strong:

~ "I am here now."

The voice was elegant with clear pronunciation. Leslie welcomed, explaining that Salumet had indicated that our visitor would be with us.

~ "I come to you, to show you all that the Spirit of one long gone can indeed return. I speak to you on the last memory of my time and perhaps I will become a little more accustomed to speaking with you."

Leslie: "Thank you, we look forward to hearing what you have to say."

~ "I would like to tell you that some points raised about my death are not so accurate as they may seem."

Leslie: "That doesn't surprise me."

~ "Now — as I return to these vibrations, the memory returns. I must tell you that I have attempted to return before to you, some while ago, when I mentioned about your seating and I would need more room, do you recall?"

Leslie: "Yes and you did ask for a hard seat, didn't you?"

~ "Since that time, I have discovered that it is unnecessary. So let me say how I feel to come back to speak to you."

Leslie: "That would be wonderful if you can—I remember you also asking me to stand back from you, because you were not used to people being so close."

Mary Queen of Scots.

~ "I indeed did say this to you."

Leslie: "We've been waiting for your return."

~ "I am most grateful for those words. But of course you know it is always for a very good reason."

Leslie: "Yes—and your instrument was very aware of the clothing you used to wear too."

~ "She will be this time too, but I have tried to modify it for her, to make it a little more comfortable."

Leslie: "Good. And you yourself are quite comfortable now with us?"

~ "I am indeed."

Leslie: "Thank you very much. We shan't interrupt you again. We'll now wait for you to talk as you wish."

~ "I want to say to you, that my last day upon this Earth, is still very vivid in my memory, as I return to you. It was a beautiful bright February day. The sun shone and to all intent and purpose, you could feel that spring was around the corner. I awoke that morning, after a very sleepless night, because you see, there was much noise throughout the previous night. I was ready to meet—how I would have termed then, 'my maker'. I truly believed myself, that I was completely composed. I promised not to shed a tear—I had to be strong for those who had cared for me, in those long, dark days. Dear Jane and Elizabeth, to them I owed so much, in those last dark days. I will have to ask you to be patient, because memory torments me even now."

Leslie, quietly: "Of course, we do understand."

~ "I truly believed that I left this plane of existence, with goodness in my heart, even for Paulet!"

Sir Amyas Paulet was appointed by Queen Elizabeth as Mary's jailor. These words were spoken with emotion and a deep sensitivity:

~ "How wrong I was—how wrong I was; that when I met my maker, as I would have said in those days, did I discover how much I had loathed that gentleman. He was a jailer of hatred! I am sorry to display these emotions. I did not feel I would, but you have to realise that on returning, how painful these memories become."

Leslie: "I can quite understand, they must be a great burden to you."

~ "What I want to say is this: much has been written about the words I uttered on my last breath. It is said that dear Jane and Elizabeth thought I uttered the words, 'Sweet Jesus'. I tell you now, that I had been praying as my head lowered to the cushion, I prayed earnestly to be taken quickly."

She continued tearfully and with deep emotion:

~ "As it struck my neck, I was saying the words 'Je suis!' 'Je suis!'—'I am!' 'I am!' And so I left behind the Earthly torment, which had me jailed for so long. No one knew, no one knew, that my sweet dear little dog was gathered amongst my underskirts. How could they know, how could they know? And this is something else I want you to know, that only those close to me, would have known that my dear animal was known to me as 'Piers'—dear sweet animal. And I know it has been written, that when I was disrobed, by those sweet dear, Jane and Elizabeth, that those who watched — and can you, *can you* imagine, the humiliation to be disrobed in front of so many others?"

Leslie: "Of course."

~ "I was dressed intentionally, I must say, in red undergarments, not, *not* to hide the blood, as it has been written, but being a devout Catholic, I wore the colours, of the blood of Christ. So I was preparing myself to meet our saviour. But on going there, I was shocked at my stifled deep dislike and hatred for some of those who treated me so badly. I have to tell you also, that whatever has been written about Elizabeth, she really did not mean to sign my life away."

Leslie: "No, so I understand."

~ "This has to be made clear to you; she also was unaware of the treachery of Paulet. He was indeed an evil man."

Leslie: "Yes, have you met him since?"

~ "I have not. I would not wish to, but I have come to terms and forgive them all. But I did not meet him face-to-face, I think you would say—is that the words? I did not wish to. I have much in memories of those last hours and now they have been spoken, they must be forgotten."

Leslie: "Now you can go at peace."

~ "But now I have to tell you why I have come, because — thank you for your help, I am so appreciative of it, and I know you will be rewarded for it. I want to tell you now, why this has been important, not the words I have spoken to you, but to tell you that the person that I was then, has subsequently returned in another form, to your Earthly plane."

Leslie: "Is that so?"

~ "Salumet has told me, that he wanted you to realise what he has taught you, that you are more than one. And whilst I retain the memories, of those painful times within that lifetime, that part of me returned for the betterment of others. And so he hopes we all can share this time, to know that we are not just ONE."

Leslie: "Quite. We can only hope that this visit of yours, will now enable you to forget those memories completely, they can be removed from you."

~ "Yes, for me this has been most welcome."

Leslie: "You have been here during the day I believe today, haven't you?"

~ "Yes and I want you to tell the one I use, that she too has been aware today, that I have been around, preparing for these words."

Leslie: "Thank you."

203

~ "Now, I want to say just a few words more before I go—I feel much stronger now."

Leslie: "Good, we're delighted to hear that and do hope that our combined love and presence has been of assistance to you."

~ "It has indeed, and I want to let you know of the time difference from which I come. We are speaking, can I give the year? To let the others know how long ago I existed here?"

Leslie: "Yes please do."

~ "I am speaking of the year 1587."

Leslie: "1587? And would you care to tell my colleagues your name?"

~ "It's unimportant but —I was known as Mary Stuart."

Leslie, quietly: "Yes, Queen of Scots."

~ "But I have to be honest and say that truly, my heart belonged in France."

Leslie: "In France?"

~ "Yes. But it matters not now—these facts are well dispatched. I hope that all of you in this time find your world religions much more humble, that people no longer suffer for their religious beliefs, because truly that is why I was put to death."

Later, the sealed envelope was opened. The name sensed previously had been correct—'Mary Queen of Scots'. The first blow of the big axe was not straight—it was the second that severed. Immediately following execution, the Skye terrier Piers took up position between the head and blooded shoulders of his mistress and would not move, causing deserved embarrassment to those responsible. *'Dear Jane and Elizabeth'* were Jane Kennedy and Elizabeth Curle. They had been close ladies-in-waiting, sharing Mary's bedchamber. Elizabeth's brother Gilbert had been secretary. Following the execution, the Curle's left England to live in Antwerp. They commissioned a portrait, possibly together with Jane, of Mary—she holding a crucifix. In the background is the execution scene with Jane and Elizabeth in attendance. It is appropriate that Mary's last words should have been *'Je suis! Je suis!'* She was born of a French mother, Marie de Guise, on Scottish soil and then crowned Queen of Scots as a 9-month babe. Mary was educated in France (age 6-19) and those were happy years for her. So it is small wonder this monarch's final words should have been in French.

Catherine the Great (1729-1796): Born as the German Princess Sophia Augusta Fredericka, this lady became Empress of an expanding Russia, through rapidly changing times that would launch Russia as a major world power. It was therefore a huge privilege when this one addressed us on the evening of 29th April 1996 via Eileen—an instructive visit arranged by Salumet for our further education. A control firstly advised:

~ "Now we are ready to bring forward the one who awaits."

There followed several minutes of silence, then our guest spoke:

~ "Your silence and expectation is commendable—I am so pleased to be here with you."

Leslie officiated, welcoming our royal guest, discussing the temporary confusion of thought that sometimes happens on these occasions and asked if there was anything we might do to assist.

~ "I ask only for your love please."

Leslie: "Right, well we can certainly give you that."

~ "It is strange to be touching such rough material."

Leslie: "Yes I suppose it must be rough to you now."

~ "Yes, it is not unpleasant, but strange. I was not prepared for it, so please bear with me and we will begin our conversations shortly."

A few further preliminaries and our visitor asked:

Catherine the Great.

~ "Do you know why I have been sent to you?"

Leslie: "No we don't. Salumet said that we would have somebody coming, who we would find to be very interesting. That's all he did say."

~ "I am deeply touched that those words should have been used about me. But of course the reason behind my returning is the teaching that you have received—that I am in fact a cut of—of the personality of the whole, which is returning in different time and different body. It is not that we wish to impress (but) that we wish to give details. We do not need to give you evidence, of life after your so-called death. That is not why we return, because you have gone further than that. So the reason behind this return visit is to show you that the personality can cut itself off from the whole, and make a return."

So in the first place, this visit demonstrates how a single Earth life can be split off from ongoing soul to speak its truth to much later generations. Small wonder there is an initial confusion of thought as part of the process!

~ "I will try to bring forward some facts, as you may bring to memory, and help you to recognise who I am."

Leslie explained that all was being recorded for the benefit of many.

~ "I am not familiar with your recording machines, but I have been told of this. Let me say to you all: it is good to be amongst an audience once again. This happened many times, in the lifetime, which I have come to speak to you about. It was quite normal for me and I accepted it too easily, as being the norm. So once again to be amongst a group of people, does indeed seem strange, because of course, as I have gone on in this side of life, I know how unnecessary this was. But of course, it was my life's plan, at that particular time and I do accept it now."

Leslie declared our understanding of this.

~ "Firstly, I would like to give you my name, although I do realise that you probably will not recognise it. I was known as Sophia Augusta Fredericka."

In fact Leslie was able to declare his recognition.

~ "But of course to others throughout the world, I would have been better known as 'Catherine'. But I have to say here and now, I always objected to changing my name. And always I was known as Sophia, when I came to this side of life. I rather resented the intrusion on my birth name, but being a young woman, I had no say in these matters of state."

Leslie: "No, unfortunately in your time that was so wasn't it?"

~ "Indeed it was—and of course I was a young slip-of-a-girl, and I did not dare to speak out."

Leslie suggested that it is very different for her now.

~ "This is what I come to tell you. All of your life's troubles—everything comes into perspective; you see your life's plan, you see the pitfalls and you see the good points of it all, and of course you learn from your many lives. You understand this of course. I have been instructed that you have been told much. So an evening of this kind I believe, is light-hearted for you?"

Leslie assured that this was nevertheless most interesting, especially from one such as she.

~ "I had much to regret when I left this life—the life I am speaking of. In your yearly terms, many years have gone by. But I speak only of this time, in order that you can make recognition, for yourselves and to understand that time is of the least importance, when it comes to the continuity of your lives."

Further reference was made to the initial period of confused thought.

~ "It is strange how these things become misty. You would assume that all would be natural in memory, but it is not so. I am recalling just a few times, of this lifetime, which I can tell you about. They obviously made a great impact in my life, when I lived here. So may I tell you a little?"

Leslie: "Please do! You undoubtedly are aware of the intense silence—everybody's anxious to hear you."

~ "My childhood was mainly uneventful; I believe I was a loved child, but my mother had great promises made for me. Her ideal was to see me married well. So this is how my name came to be changed, much to my annoyance at the time. The decision in my life was made firstly in 1744—this is the time we go back to, because this is my first strong memory. When I was taken from my homeland, a small duchy from Germany, influenced I might say, by Frederic, who was a strong powerful man at the time—I was transported by my mother to Russia. I have to tell you, I was terrified at the prospect. I was a petite young woman, aged only 15. Can you imagine what it must have felt like, to be transported from one's homeland and bosom of your family, to be confronted by a woman so strong, so powerful, that not one word was uttered in her presence?"

That would be the Empress Elizabeth, and the powerful Frederic would have been King Frederic II of Prussia, who had made the arrangement.

~ "The Empress, I have to tell you, she was not unkind to me, but also she did not show affection either. To one so young, it was indeed disturbing, and distressing."

Leslie: "I can imagine. Why did they take you there?"

~ "I was to become betrothed to the empress's nephew. I was instructed in Russian language, which I have to say at that time distressed me. I was instructed in the orthodox religion, I was instructed in the court ways — in so many things in such a short space of time. Also my name was changed to Catherine and I was betrothed to Peter. He was a thin gangly pock-marked young boy, only one year older than I, but I would happily have joined him with love, if only he could have shown me some affection, but that was never to be. The memory now distresses me, when I think back to the love I left behind, within my own family background."

Leslie: "Were you never able to visit your family?"

~ "My mother stayed with me and frequently wrote back to my father all progress made, but I was so unhappy. But I could never show it, because of course I was constantly told how great an honour was being bestowed upon me, that one day I would become a great lady. I never wanted that, but fate and circumstances were due to bring me just that. I am speaking to you now, about the human element of this woman; I am speaking to you about the feelings within her heart that were never spoken aloud at the time—because she was a woman so young in age, she was terrified to say one word out of place. The next memory that comes to me is of the marriage ceremony. I was taken to the empress's home, where she took charge to dress me, to bejewel me, to instruct me. And so both Peter and I were transported to the great cathedral, The Virgin of Kassam. I remember thinking how appropriate that name was and how terrified I was to become the wife of this 17 year old boy."

Leslie voiced his understanding of our visitor's inner feelings.

~ "The cathedral was beautiful, and will always be imprinted on my memory. It took several hours—I don't know how much you know of the Russian courts in those days, but such a wedding, was indeed spectacular. We returned to banquet and feast. Can you imagine so much food! But the worst part for me was the obligation to dance with so many old noblemen. I was horrified! Even now I can feel myself quake from this old memory."

This was just a temporary memory long since lost, but revived only for this one evening.

~ "I fully accepted when I came to this side of life, I knew what I had done, what I had done wrong and I knew what had to be done. There are many memories within a lifetime, which have to be faced up to. And I will tell you now, because it took me many, many of your years, to fully accept what I had done. Although I did not actually raise my own hand, I was responsible for Peter's death."

Les: "Were you?"

~ "Of course, those in court circles saw me distressed when the news came, but I knew in my heart that is what his fate would be. You see by then, I had become a worshipped lady throughout the lands. The people wanted me to rule, because Peter was a weak and infantile man and I have to say his mind was not fully there. He was subject to many stormy outbursts and he did not please the people, because he was in favour of Frederic, who was a powerful — in Peter's mind, 'ally.' And all the Russian people, they could see that he could not be a good and strong ruler. Do you see?—the power came to me, without even my soul wishing or desiring it to begin with? But once, ONCE you have the adrenaline flowing through your veins, once you have the feel of the power and the adoration of your peoples, then your life can take a turn for the worse. This I had to face up to. I had much to face up to. *He* was an unfeeling and unloving young man, but *I* was a warm-hearted, pretty young woman, who desired the love of a man. I do not deny this, neither do I feel grief about it, because circumstance you see, dictated always that I find love. I have to say and I must say to you, that it is not well known or understood, that Peter fully accepted our child as his own. In fact, my three children belonged to different men, this I am not sorry for, because I loved each and every one of them. But I have to say, if life could have been different, I would have chosen another pathway."

Leslie: "Yes, you didn't wish for the power that was thrust on you."

~ "I did not—and when I looked back over that lifetime, I could see I had done much good. For the people close by, I had fond memories and not least my own son. And that was my parting memory and one which caused me continuous grief for a long time; because although my peoples called me, 'Catherine the Great,' to my own son I was neither a good mother, nor heroine. He despised me, because you see he always believed Peter to be his true father. So on my death, he instructed that Peter's remains be dug up and that both of us would go together. And he instructed—"

Sophia now spoke most tearfully:

~ "—Alexis' father to carry both of us also — if only he had known that Alexis was the father of my loved one he would indeed have been shocked. You cannot imagine what it was like to watch this from this side of life and to be unable to comfort him! But it opened my eyes to what I had to accept."

Leslie: "But I believe I am right in saying that though you didn't wish to have the power that you did have, in the main you used it for the benefit of your people?"

~ "My peoples were so glad because as I have said, Peter would have sided with Frederic of Prussia and he (Frederic) would have eventually turned against us, but he could not see this. He was a simple man, with little strength, little true knowledge, and so I had to take control, not only for the peoples, but for the future of Russia. I have since spoken with Peter, who has told me he also was afraid and we were both so young. He also was like a little boy. All he wanted to do was to play with his soldiers, in his gardens—with his toys. He was not ready for manhood, to rule a great country, or to take a wife. These things also came to him — you have to understand that in those times, you had no say in what your fate was to be."

Leslie: "No, but it would seem it was necessary for you to take the part you did in that life, because of Peter's short-comings."

~ "I understand that now, it is the one thing I have accepted. I reigned for 34 years, of your time and I do say to you, most of them were good. I developed from a petite soft young woman, into a woman of strength, of knowledge, capable of great love. And to say I truly loved the first man, I had my first child with — there was no one to match him, but he was sent away, for diplomatic purposes, because of the rumours it caused."

Leslie: "I see, so that happiness was taken from you also?"

~ "I know now, it was this that made me strong. I then looked to guiding my son and to trying to influence Peter, who ignored me and had no love for me at all. And he also could see that he too was at fault, but he was simple in his mind and at times very destructive with his words, though all was forgiven at the time. And I have to say that since that lifetime, my heart has been heavy, not only for what has happened in Russia, but in my homeland of Germany. But I think I would be right in telling you that the nations of your world are becoming much more sensible, that they are beginning to recognise that love for all mankind."

Leslie: "Yes they are beginning to realise that, it's a slow process, but it's beginning, and for that we must be grateful."

~ "I do believe I must depart now. I thank you for allowing this time, I thank you for the opportunity of memory, I thank you and I say to you all: Love one another as you would those closest to you. Know that all in your lives can be good, if you so desire."

Sophia was duly thanked for imparting so much of that lifetime. As she withdrew, there was further reference, with fading voice, to her first love:

~ "I did love Sergey, I did. I loved him from the very first part of my being — he was a truly great man and he deserved the title 'great,' not Peter—not Peter, not Peter."

Following Sophia's withdrawal, a control spoke, suggesting we compare the history book views of this great lady; also declaring that we had been honoured by such a visit—this lady being but a fraction of that great ongoing soul. And those memories that she recounted will have long since been dealt with and are no longer in any way troublesome. We certainly felt honoured to have been in receipt of such a visit—I think we were all quite spellbound as that evening concluded. Historians do a grand job of listing facts, but of course they cannot know the inner workings of mind or what happens later in spirit. Thank you Salumet and Sophia for a magnificent presentation of knowledge involving both this world and the next!

PART 4

Concepts and Problems but Angels Prevail

"Consider the universe: we are agreed that its existence and its nature come to it from beyond itself... it dominates, despite all the clash of things: the creation is not hindered on its way even now; it stands firm..."

PLOTINUS, FIFTH ENNEAD.

CHAPTER 20

THE BEAUTY IN MATHEMATICS

A chance chat with a mathematician had led to an unexpected challenge. He proposed I ask Salumet to explain a theorem enunciated by Fermat in the year 1637—he saw this as a forthright test of Salumet's all-knowledge! At first I felt most unhappy about such a prospect—how would a spiritual master react to being tested in such a way!? How could one possibly ask for explanation of an abstruse detail of yesterday's intellect? But then would it be so outrageous? After all Red Cloud, speaking through Estelle Roberts27 had made the statements:

~ "The mathematician who arranged the laws of matter, spirit and etheric, is the most perfect mathematician that ever was"—and then—"For home with God can only be in beauty, whatever way you seek it."

These are wise words; so perhaps to seek mathematically for beauty of spirit might just be considered acceptable; so perhaps therefore we should not be entirely dismissive. Fermat's Last Theorem states that no three positive integers—'a, b, c' can satisfy the equation: $a^n + b^n = c^n$, for values of n greater than 2. Well who cares about that? Well, Fermat—he had clearly cared. So let's consider the case where n = 2. This leads us to what the ancients called 'Pythagorean Triples', an example being: $3^2 + 4^2 = 5^2$, i.e. 9 + 16 = 25. Perfectly correct! The squared numbers add to 25 as they should, and satisfy the equation. So '3, 4, 5' is a 'Pythagorean Triple'; likewise the set of numbers '5, 12, 13' is another Pythagorean Triple. And if we make triangles of these lengths, the angle opposite the longer side is always a right angle. And now we begin to see elements of order and beauty in geometric form—as has been built into certain ancient architecture. So was Fermat onto something?

Next, rather than get bogged down with unnecessary complications, let us just accept that there is firm connection between the workings of Fermat's Last Theorem and what is known as the Fibonacci Series[28]—brainchild of an Italian gentleman who actually preceded Fermat by 435 years; although the mathematical series was known in very much earlier times. But it was first published in book form and called the Fibonacci Series in 1202. The series runs 0, 1, 1, 2, 3, 5, 8, 13, 21, 34, 55, 89 ..., and its basis is: any two adjacent numbers add together to produce the number that follows. See for yourself how it works! Now, an interesting fact is that graphical presentation of this number sequence aligns to so many beautiful forms within nature as well as out there in the universe—describing the spiral form of seashore shells, sunflower seed-heads, pine cones, galaxies, flower petal arrangements, planetary orbits, weather patterns, even the DNA double helix of our body cells. Intriguing!

But if we then plot the numbers against their successive number ratios, the reducing-wave-form graph quickly approaches and aligns to the value 1.61803—known as the 'phi-ratio' or the 'Golden Mean Proportion'. Perhaps we have now reached our intellectual goal. This ratio has long been recognised as pleasing-to-the-eye and has been built into such majestic works as the Athenian Parthenon, the Taj Mahal and the Great Pyramid of Giza. The phi (Ø) ratio is, in fact, amazingly pervasive throughout all nature and all creation. It also responds in a very singular way to further mathematical manipulation. Its square, for example, adds exactly one to its value: $Ø^2 = Ø + 1$, whilst dividing it into one, subtracts exactly one from its value: $1 / Ø = Ø - 1$. And then

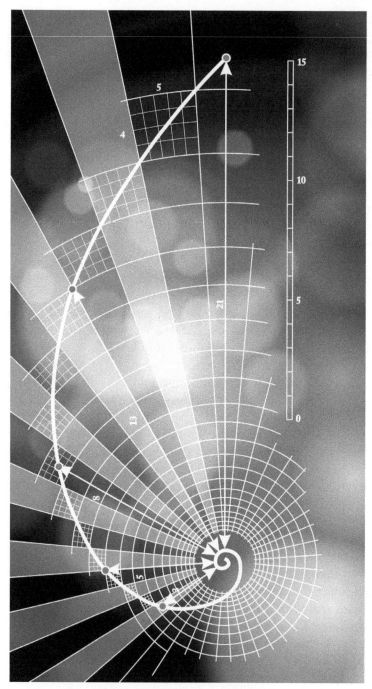

Phi-ratio, graphical presentation.

($5^{1/2}$ + 1) / 2 = Ø. Curious! So there is something odd and very special about phi, which incidentally, Leonardo Da Vinci called the 'Divine Proportion'.

Salumet was with us on 15th November 2010 and had just concluded a section of his teaching with the words:

~ "You are part of that much greater whole—you are 'existence.'"

I felt this to be a suitable point at which to identify 'mathematics' as having a place as part of that 'existence', and proceeded with no small degree of hesitation, to say just sufficient, giving due mention of Fermat's theorem, the Fibonacci Series and Red Cloud's quotation—sufficient to be able to request our teacher's comments:

~ "Yes, I take your words, my dear friend. Let me just say: do you feel (that) the Universal Power—that great source of all life—is just random? You have to remember the *Intelligence behind the Creation*, and of course that is what you are speaking about."

Exactly so—we speak of intelligence behind it all. I replied that these mathematicians seem to have felt that intelligence.

~ "And where does that intelligence come from?—where do the mathematician's numbers come from? It is simply impressed from spirit."

George: "Ah! The understanding of the numbers, impressed from spirit."

~ "Yes, from that Great Intelligence—that all-consuming power that we all belong to. It is simple, my dear friend, but so many on your planet try to complicate issues. The beauty of all existence—as you say: take a leaf, take a flower—look at the perfection that it gives and where does it come from?"

George: "It is nice to have a record of understanding by these mathematicians who have been impressed."

~ "Yes, they are being impressed by the beauty of simplicity, because it is beauty."

I suggested that beauty seems to have a structure within.

~ "Yes! They are feeling the beauty of the Creator."

George: "Yes, it is not all of us that can find a way of describing it, but—"

~ "Try not, my dear friend, to describe, but to *feel*—to look with those eyes that have been given to you—to use all of those senses that you have been given. Use them for the purpose of growing spiritually stronger—and, once again, I will say to you all, my dear friends: find that stillness and you will once more become part of the whole, and as always, I leave that Earthly responsibility with each one of you. But, I do thank you, my dear friend, for your questions. I also have been given the opportunity to speak a little more about creation, whereas, last time, I was ready to dismiss it very quickly. So, I will say to you: I have learned much myself."

Lilian: "That's interesting!"
I made the point that we all now have much deeper feelings as a result of these discussions and so, thanked our teacher for his words.

~ "It is too easy to complicate everything—to use words which seem to be words of wisdom; but, instead to use one word instead of ten is much more acceptable. Do you not agree?"

There was general agreement to this, and perhaps there is a case for confining maths to mathematicians and not inflicting it on general public—or Salumet!

~ "So, with that, my dear friends, I take my leave. I leave you, cloaked in my love and that of spirit. We endeavour to help you whenever we can, but we cannot do it alone. We need your love and your cooperation. But, know that you are part of all things."

So we return to Salumet's initial statement, that humankind is part of a much greater whole—we are existence. So we are encouraged to feel the beauty of creation, without formulating the detail of its structure. That is unnecessary; and yet, that mathematical knowledge has enabled great architects to incorporate the phi ratio into grand designs to good effect. But then it may be possible that beauty of design could be perceived naturally, without recourse to the mathematics?

CHAPTER 21

HAARP AND CHEMTRAILS

W
e have the free will to either appreciate the beauty of creation, or as we become more intelligent, to interfere with it.
Science and scientific thinking have gathered pace with not
a little confusion since the mid-20th century, and are looked upon by
some with considerable misgivings; not that general public have had
full knowledge of what happens at the time. There were, for example,
certain 'high-altitude scientific projects'. These were funded largely by
US military. In Project Argus (1958), nuclear bombs were exploded at
heights of 160 and 480 Km and worldwide effects noted. In further ionosphere tests, codenamed Project Starfish (1962), megaton bombs were
exploded at similar high altitudes; seriously perturbing the Van Allen
Belt—a charged particle layer held in place by Earth's magnetic field.
UK's Astronomer Royal Sir Martin Ryle, realizing possible dire consequences, had filed objection to this project. Later that same year Russia
continued with similar detonations. The combined series of tests has
permanently changed the Van Allen belt. In the following year (1963),
President John F Kennedy and President Nikita Khrushchev agreed a
Limited Test Ban Treaty (LTBT); thus, all such nuclear tests with the
exception of underground testing were banned. The LTBT was signed
and ratified by US, Soviet Union and UK governments—ending that
particular reckless pursuit. The later developed Orbit Manoeuvring
System (OMS, 1981), facilitated space-lab passes over ground-based
observatories, to study the effect of ejecting gases into the ionosphere.

It was discovered that this produced ionosphere holes. Experiments of this nature have continued. A six second OMS release 68 Km above Connecticut (1985) produced an air-glow extending 400,000 square Km across the sky. The space shuttle is propelled by solid fuel rockets. Over the years, solid fuel rockets have ejected more that 200 tons of the ozone-destroying element chlorine into the stratosphere, home to our planet's protective ozone layer. These are happenings concerning Earth's ionosphere and stratosphere that precede the development of HAARP—High-frequency Active Auroral Research Program.

HAARP is a system and ground-based apparatus for generating a huge 3.6 Gigawatts of energy and beaming circularly polarized electromagnetic radiation into selected ionosphere regions; thus heating those regions to around 50,000°C—this for the purpose of distorting and lifting. This forms the basis for developing a *world weather controlling system* which also has other implications. This I know sounds like wild fictional fantasy but it is not. So it is very necessary that we begin with irrefutable fact—because there has been so much denial and reference to *conspiracy theory hocus-pocus* from pseudo authoritative sources; also there has been avoidance of this desperately important matter by national news channels and Press.

A set of filed patents should represent sufficient proof of such a serious undertaking; so we will begin at the United States Patent Office:

US Patent 4686605, (1987): This describes an apparatus and procedure for altering selected regions of Earth's atmosphere, ionosphere and/or magnetosphere. In one embodiment, circularly polarized electromagnetic (EM) radiation is beamed upwards through the target region, heating and exciting charged particles. This ionizes neutral particles, thus increasing overall charged particle density. Weather modification is possible by altering upper atmosphere wind patterns or by introducing plumes of atmospheric particles to act as a lens or focusing device.

US Patent 5038664, (1991): A method is described for producing a shell of relativistic high energy particles at an altitude of around 1500 Km above the Earth. Circularly polarized EM radiation is transmitted at a first frequency to produce heating of plasma at 250 Km or higher. This lifts the plasma to at least 1500 Km where it is subjected to a second frequency to expand it. The modified plasma will be trapped between adjacent magnetic field lines, to form a shell of relativistic particles around the Earth.

US Patent 4712155, (1987): A method and apparatus for creating an artificial electron cyclotron heating region of plasma.

US Patent 5068669, (1991): This patent describes a power beaming system.

US Patent 5218374, (1993): This patent concerns a power beaming system which has printed circuit radiating elements with resonating cavities.

US Patent 5202689, (1993): A lightweight focusing reflector for space.

US Patent 5041834, (1991):An ionosphere mirror composed of a plasma layer that can be tilted.

US Patent 4999637, (1991): This patent concerns the creation of artificial ionization clouds above the Earth.

US Patent 4817495, (1989): This patent describes a defence system capable of discriminating between armed and unarmed objects re-entering from space.

US Patent 3813875, (1973): This describes a rocket fuel system designed for barium release to produce barium ion clouds in the upper atmosphere.

US Patent 5003186, (1991): Concerning the addition of metal oxides, for example aluminium oxide, to jetliner fuel for emission at cruising altitude—this it is stated, is for the purpose of reducing infra red radiation to work against global warming.

US Patent 4412654, (1983): This patent refers to a method of aerial spraying of liquids from the wings of aircraft. The liquid drops flow from a slot at the trailing edge of the streamlined body to discharge into the slipstream.

The fact is that the above twelve patents clearly refer to the HAARP system and to the ejection of metal ions into Earth's atmosphere and stratosphere. A 'chemtrail' is a trail of chemicals deliberately discharged into the atmosphere from aircraft, favoured chemicals being barium titanate and methyl aluminium. 'Contrails' will also be seen in our skies. These, by comparison are harmless condensation trails left by jetliners flying at high altitude. BUT if the question is asked: what is the difference between a 'chemtrail' and a 'contrail'?—in view of the last two patents listed, the answer could sometimes be 'none'. But chemtrails, by virtue of their composition, spread more and take longer to disappear than the contrails. Furthermore, chemtrails are usually seen as parallel arrays across the sky—sometimes grids.

Having established beyond any doubt the reality of what is going on as a clandestine and frequently denied operation, I can now briefly summarise in more digestible form:

Jetliners deliberately spray chemtrails containing barium titanate, methyl aluminium and potassium salts into the stratosphere. The plumes of chemicals reflect and absorb the energies/frequencies beamed by HAARP, such that the high altitude jet streams are manipulated to change world weather patterns. This manipulation can result in storms, drought, extremes of hot and cold and more. Clearly, such manipulation can be with good intent, bad intent, can go wrong, and might also have very serious side effects. The United States has been a lead nation in attempting to control weather in this way, but a number of world governments are also now heavily involved. Information has been withheld from public, and I must confess I knew nothing of this until Serena asked the question of Salumet on 6th May 2013: 'What are Chemtrails and what are they for?' Salumet, of course, knows all, but clearly felt obliged to go slowly and to make no differentiation between chemtrails and their big brother HAARP (this correctly so because of course, as we can now see, they each form part of a single project that extends worldwide). Salumet responded:

~ "What are they? They are—I will not use the word 'invention', because I do not like that word. All thoughts (inspirations) stem from spirit, but what happens is that mankind uses information—either for good or for bad; or sometimes they take information and unfortunately not meant for bad, but they do not realise that sometimes what they achieve is *not* for the betterment of man. I want to say to you that much has been happening since human beings have had air travel.

Unnatural sky patterned by chemtrails.

That is my first reply to your question. This is not something new; it is something that has been happening for some time. It is of course the interference of many energies; trying to achieve something that I have to tell you my dear friends, is not at this moment in time, possible. It can and will be we feel, destructive. What is happening is happening within *all* countries — it is happening throughout your world. And it does not even belong to the 'common scientists' of your world, but belongs to *space travel and travel within your world*. They have been able to use energies, put them together and (they) tell you as a human being, that it is for the best. I am here to say it is *not* for the best — but we are aware of what is happening."

We listened intently—this was a serious statement, phrased as a view of our planet from afar. I had recently read of bizarre CIA experiments in mind control, and for clarification, asked if I would be correct in thinking there to be no connection here:

~ "I would not say completely, *no* — but yes, you are on the right track—of man interfering with what could be used for good. Not just that organization (CIA), but many throughout your world — they have the knowledge but they are misusing it. It is again I have to say, some matter of control, control of the masses, and of course — I do not like to use the word 'wars', but it can be used against each other."

George: "Well thank you for that Salumet, I had read about experiments in 'mind control', that sound absolutely awful, and I didn't know whether to believe it or not, but I think you're confirming that there are such experiments going on."

~ "Yes — as always, mankind has always assumed they have a higher knowledge and I have told you in times past, that mankind interferes in so many ways, and I know you understand that what has been meant for good, can also be used for 'evil', though I am not happy with that word."

Mark: "Would these sprays also be harmful to nature?"

~ "Any prolonged use of these subtle energies of course could be harmful to some. And again, as in all things, it may not be harmful to begin with — but we are trying to deal with it, so do not be too concerned."

Sarah: "The people who are trying to combine these energies, are they aware of the danger?"

~ "They *think* they are doing something good — it is mostly related to military."

Sarah: "Oh right! — with nuclear power, you've said that's actually a good energy, but we're using it the wrong way."

~ "It should have been used for *good* and was *abused*, as this is at this time."

Paul inquired about awareness:

~ "Most people are <u>un</u>aware—there have been murmurings within your world, but because it is *military* it is being kept quite quiet."

225

Paul: "I'm still not clear on the effect that it's having on the populations."

~ "It, if used constantly, will have the effect of changing the whole unification of the human body, as it would in animals, as it would change your atmosphere — so many different ways that it could create change."

Paul: "And they presumably think—"

~ "They feel that they are helping. But I have to say to them: it is just experimental at the moment."

Paul: "It is mankind interfering again, not having enough intelligence—"

~ "—Enough knowledge—yes. As in all things, until it is used, you do not have a result. It sometimes takes time to find the correct result— as many things within your medical profession have seemed to be good medicine and would seem to be wrong for *some* — you cannot say: it is always wrong for all. BUT WHAT IS HAPPENING NOW WILL HAVE A SUBTLE ALTERATION TO THE ATMOSPHERE OF YOUR WORLD."

Sarah: "And will it be able to change back again, or is it irreversible?"

~ "Nothing is ever irreversible, but of course it will have to be addressed."

Mark: "I was just wondering what it is that these people think they're achieving, or think they might be able to achieve?"

~ "Mankind has always been inquisitive."

Mark: "So they are having a go to see what happens?"

~ "Well, I will say—and perhaps you will speak to the dear gentleman of scientific mind—that whatever is looked at, they always have to go a little further. It is that inquisitiveness which drives them forward and of course many good things come from scientific experiments. So you cannot always say it is bad, because that would not be true."

I think Salumet refers to the feeling of personal satisfaction that a scientist has from extending humanity's knowledge, making new discovery etc. I suggested that it is bad if the principle is used for mind control to suit one's own ends:

~ "Yes, you do not have the right to interfere *in any way* with any other human being. IF THEY ARE MISUSING ANYTHING, IT SHOULD BE KNOWN BY THE POPULATION OF THE WORLD."

Well, that with certainty endorses the work of whistle-blowers, who have risked much in the cause of truth and openness. It has indeed been suggested by some that they ought to be in receipt of peace prize nominations—I and our group would all add our names to that recommendation!

There was opportunity for further commentary from Salumet at our 10th June meeting:

George: "You spoke to us about '*chemtrails*' and you very correctly and logically spoke of chemtrails plus a device called HAARP—High-Energy Auroral Active Research Program—a device that projects high energy into the ionosphere around our planet, to produce a heat effect which distorts it. HAARP and chemtrails can be worked together, and some hope that it can be used to control the weather in an advantageous way. But you were saying that this is insufficiently understood and that there are dangers. Now that we have researched through the Internet articles on this matter, are you able to confirm what I've said and take the matter further?"

~ "I would like to say just this: that in all events that take place in your world, there are always *two sides to the coin*, as you may say. Whatever is used in your world, can be used for either good or for negative reasons. This applies to what is taking place and what has been taking place for a number of your Earthly years. Of course, when good can come from any of these happenings, that has to be applauded—not only by human beings, but by those of us in spirit who have helped and inspired. Of course, when the negative side appears, this too is a concern for us—because we have tried to inspire for the good. But these things take their own course in the same way — let us use nuclear power (as example). Nuclear power has advantages and disadvantages, but it has to be *allowed to evolve*. Are you following what I am telling you?"

We gave assurance.

~ "Yes—so I would say to you: what is happening is well known throughout different countries of your world; it is also well noted in our world. I would say to you my dear friends, do not allow this to create fear within you, because we are doing what we can to create *less of the negativity.*

George: "Well that's very good to know. My concern was really that I know that a university in Alaska is very much involved in this, and I imagine they would represent the positive side."

~ "Yes, of course."

George: "And there is also a great military interest, which I imagine would be the negative aspect."

~ "Yes, and I would suggest to all of you my dear friends, to ask continually for help for those people involved—that whatever *good* can come from these things, (they) must, MUST take place—and that negative aspect be *diluted.*"

George: "I imagine part of the negative aspect would be the metal ions used in the chemtrail work, how they spoil the pureness of the atmosphere and how this will affect growing crops."

~ "Yes, but I again reiterate to you my dear friends: do not allow this to colour your judgements too much, because as I have said, we in our world are aware of what is happening and as in all things, provided it (what humans do) does not interfere with the evolution of your planet, we will do what we can—as with other topics and subjects that probably you are not even aware of at this time."

George: "Wonderful! I think in the group here we seek understanding rather than judgement."

~ "Yes, I am aware of this. But it does not matter what you feel in a physical sense, I want you to think about these things on a spiritual level. I want you to rise above all of the problems on Earth and to create a good and loving situation for all people, all lands—all happenings within your world."

Sarah: "So — take away the judgement. "

~ "Yes."

So we may now summarize this complex matter as follows:

- The HAARP/chemtrail project is undeniable reality and nothing new.
- Chemtrails are used in conjunction with HAARP to affect both weather and people.
- At a physical level there is ample patent office proof of the project details.
- There are attendant proving and irrefutable statements from Angelic Realms.
- The atmosphere of our planet is already being significantly altered.
- There are several procedures used in making the chemtrails.
- This is a worldwide happening known to many in authority.
- Governments and standard news media are withholding information from public.
- Whistle-blowers supporting truth and openness should be revered.
- The happening has become a significant detail of Earthly evolution.
- The spiritual way forward is prayer and non-judgement.
- Do not underestimate the good influence from spirit.

These are the undeniable cross-referenced facts that explain observations seen in our skies and reported worldwide via Internet; also the likely cause of some reported weather extremes and sadly, a number of illnesses. There is more that should be said concerning illnesses of humans and indeed of all mammals. A development has been the extensive use in chemtrails of aluminium nanoparticles. What is a nanoparticle? I will explain. One millimetre (10^{-3} m) can be easily visualised as the smallest division on a metric ruler. One micrometer is one thousandth of that (10^{-6} m). One nanometer is one millionth of one millimetre (10^{-9} m). So what are termed 'nanoparticles' are exceedingly small; and there are patents that describe clever methods of preparation for the nanoparticles. This degree of smallness is beyond *Brownian motion*—such particles vibrate, are rarely static and are both chemically and biologically highly reactive. Particles of this minute size no longer exhibit properties typical of their parent metal, so that distribution of them in the atmosphere opens a Pandora's Box of possibilities, only in small part understood. Our medical literature makes it clear that the breathed particles can adversely affect brain and spinal cord[29, 30]; also there is a link between aluminium and neurological diseases such as Alzheimer's and Parkinson's. Nanoparticles can reach the brain via several body processes and the particles are so minute that they cannot be removed from air by filtration systems. Nanoaluminium inhaled into the lungs will increase the burden of asthma sufferers. Nanobarium has the effect of suppressing the body's immune system[31] and so is equally bad news. The two nanometals acting together is a double whammy for humankind and animals alike. It may be that this explains the observed increase in neurological conditions of recent years.

Whilst these are deeply serious matters, we are advised not to be overly concerned—planetary evolution must take its course and spiritual influences are already in place. Quite so; but as Salumet has indicated, the matter has to be addressed. Perhaps this means that those in spirit will manage to influence our thought direction. Perhaps those funding such waywardness will be encouraged to reconsider funding. Perhaps they will inspire development of our own remedial atmospheric flushing system, or perhaps guide those in authority to be less secretive. I feel that an important aspect is for us to give our heartfelt thanks and support to the whistleblowers—Julian Assange, Bradley Manning, Edward Snowden and others—for simply upholding truth and openness. This has to be seen as honourable stance. Public who fund their governments surely deserve to know exactly how *their* moneys are being spent. How can they be responsible citizens if secrecy abounds and they do not know? To be funding such departure from righteous pathway whilst being kept ignorant of that fact is of course contrary to the tradition: *He who pays the piper calls the tune.* I would have thought such withholding of truth to be a matter for the attention of judiciary.

CHAPTER 22

ANGELS

We should never underestimate the many good urges and influences that come to us from spirit. Spiritual influence has always been, throughout time as we know it—from the very first moment of our Earth's creation. Angels are and have been highly influential in watching over this and other planets. Here on Earth, there have been periods in our past when the spiritual light has been stronger so that awareness of them has also been stronger. In Saint John's Revelation[32] he attempts to describe visions of the angelic hierarchy who watch over Earth and a question was asked of Salumet about this on 21st August 2000:

> ~ "This part of what you call literature is indeed correct—there are such beings in our world. They are supreme beings—they come to many planets in the form of help, and many people have become aware of them in your world—and have given them names, to which I might add, they are pleased to respond."

At a later date this was elaborated further, with explanation that they are 'purity of light', have never incarnated—are not part of any incarnate order, but originate from the source of all life. They are imbued with knowledge, wisdom, understanding and the love of all things. But angels are not all the same and have different stations of work. An example is the 'guardian angel' and we each have one in attendance. On 5th February 2001 Salumet made the statement:

~ "Many of these beings come from a spiritual planet of light, to help with the evolution and lifting of consciousness of humankind. I believe this fact is not widely known. Only those who have come to that stage of quietness and self knowledge—only they and they alone will have a glimpse of these magnificent beings. And remember, they *are* magnificent beings. We are speaking of creation now, in its almost pure form. This is what I wish you to try to understand. Guardian angels— their task is to protect you throughout your life if they can. But that purpose is for the expansion of soul and consciousness and all that is spiritual. They are not concerned with everyday living as your guides are. They are the essence of being. They are the providers for this planet of love, wisdom, power and many other spiritual attributes."

There is one fallacy about angels that should be corrected. As seen by humans, a spiritual light emanates from the upper body which has given the impression to those who have glimpsed, of wings. In fact there are no wings, no feathers—it is a spiritual light that has been seen, consistent of course, with the light-beings that they are. Much has been said about angels of light and of darkness, and it would seem that these are as if mirror images of each other. All, it seems, are a necessary part of our evolution and the lower order angels may exercise free will to good *or* bad effect, as with humans. This has resulted in literature references to 'fallen angels'—yes, they exist. So our evolving consciousness would appear to have a complex angelic counterpart. But there is a 'chain of command' or order, and angels guiding our evolution are overseen by four greater angelic beings. These equate to the four great beings witnessed by John in Revelation. And I find it a joy that there is some agreeing detail between that historic account by an enlightened one of Earth and the teaching of our guide: Salumet.

These details relate to Planet Earth and connect as they do with an enlightened part of recorded history. But prior to stating these facts about the angelic influences upon evolving consciousness, Salumet had made it abundantly clear (21st February 2000) that we are just one very small part of a much more extensive development that is now in progress.

~ "The galaxy to which this Earth planet belongs, is now in a state of its own spiritual growth—to that end there will be many changes. You will find that the men of this Earthly planet will come to recognize that within your space-time much is happening. Not only are you in times of much development but you are in a time of great evolution, not known to you before, but which will take effect and will make its self known to you quite soon. You, of course, depend upon the knowledge given to you by those you call 'scientists'. You depend much upon their knowledge. I can tell you, my dear friends: those in my world are already working with them. The time has come for expansion and growth to be recognized, not only on this planet, but by those who are closest to you. And, yes, there is much knowledge that can and will be gained. Therefore I say to you, my dear friends this time, that as you listen to my words I would like you to take them with you and think upon them—and allow yourselves to become part of the cosmic consciousness rather than of the Earthly one. You can achieve this and the time is now ripe for this to take place."

So it is time for us to look to much wider horizons, meaning that we should become aware not only of angelic realms, but also of our galactic neighbours. We have to break out from limited Earthly thinking and recognize that the creation extends far beyond this. Why stay with the small single-planet consciousness when so much more beckons?

The evening of 12th November 2007 was unusual in that we were asked by an unnamed communicator to each *think* of a question without actually voicing it. And those in spirit seemed to be picking up on our thoughts. As to my own thoughts, the truth is that I had more than one question buzzing around in my head, and that must have been a little confusing for those in spirit. My concerns were for the evolution of this sector of this galaxy, whilst at the same time there were struggles and turbulences here on Earth. Were we letting down the galactic team? These thoughts were picked up:

~ "This Earth planet *is* going through a slightly turbulent time, but there is much light at the other end of the tunnel. Although we have seen much trouble and strife, it is but part of evolution, and without these problems you will not go forward. So I know you have much concern for other countries and their populations, but allow me to tell you that it is with much light at the end."

Well that makes sense—as various factions become more aware, we can perhaps understand that this will lead to challenges between groups, religions, traditionalists and others. But the session did not end with this answer. Eileen stirred and Salumet, to our surprise and delight, spoke quite unexpectedly to answer my other unspoken question:

~ "Good evening—I could not leave you this time without answering the question my dear friend has put out about the difference between myself and angelic beings. I do not wish him to struggle with this until next time. Therefore, my dear friend, it is quite simple. I and others come to you from that divine source of energy, as do those angelic beings. And to put it simply for you in your Earth language, let me say: it is only the difference in a 'job description'."

So Salumet and the angels are from the same light-being source and the difference is simply 'job description'. Now I knew from previous communications that Salumet's concern is with *all universes,* not just this one, so I checked with him that that other word in our language 'omnipotent' also suits—it does. I therefore asked if the angels might be less widespread in *their* influence:

~ "Not at all—it is only your association with them and your recognition of them that is different."

George: "So *their* tasks would extend to other universes as well?"

~ "Yes—in the same way as we as divine energy, are more knowing of *all* things."

I thanked our teacher for this clarification and explained it was something I had pondered. He knew this of course and said that he therefore felt the matter should be left no longer.

Five years later (28th January 2013), Salumet again spoke on angels, firstly making it very clear that they are not beings who have once lived here on Earth:

~ "What I wish you to discount is: angels are people who have lived upon this planet and returned as angels—this is not correct. So I would like you, my dear friends, to move away from those thoughts. The true angelic energy is of 'pure love'. They are a perfect example of 'unconditional love'. They come to you always to help, to uplift and to try to instruct."

There was more to be said on those termed 'archangels':

~ "The archangels do much work with human beings, they are a little way down the ladder. Most people assume that because they are named 'archangel' they are the most important. This is not so. But, the Archangels Michael, Raphael and others—each has a mission which they help to perform in your world."

And there was more on 'guardian angels', and some of us are able to see them:

~ "Yes, some people are able to. That is not, I would say, the majority, but those people whose souls have opened and are aware of the guiding light. But you all have what you call a 'guardian angel'. These have been with you throughout time. They will never leave you."

Sara wondered if we might feel their presence in the heart chakra:

~ "You will experience their presence in all parts of your being. It would be a very deep and satisfying love."

One of us expressed concern for population growth and would there be enough guardian angels to go round—to meet all needs? But that is of course thinking about spirit in a purely physical way and that simply does not work:

~ "You are thinking on a physical level. There is no area—there is no number. Energy has always been and some energy is purer than others. You have to widen your view. But it is a good question and one that we come across so often. But yes, just the fact that you consider the question shows that you are growing."

Jan asked about when we return to spirit—will we be able to see our guardian angel then?

~ "If you so desire—of course!—and the recognition will be instant. You will immediately recognise them, and what a joyous occasion that will be!"

To suppose they have gender is again of course, thinking at a physical level, but they might well 'appear' as male or female. Finally that evening, Rod had described a special occasion, many years ago, whilst out walking with family. He had this beautiful intense feeling that seemed to run right through him—never experienced before or since, but never forgotten. Would that have been a spiritual upliftment, he wondered?

~ "That is likely to be your guardian angel, who for some reason that day, would have made himself felt. A feeling as powerful as you have described is usually down to your guardian angel."

And that of course, tallies with the answer to Sara's earlier question.

During our meeting of 2ⁿᵈ September 2013, there was further discourse on light-beings, when I checked that there would be no influence or impact from purely physical parameters:

~ "That would be a correct assumption—there would be no such thing as hot or cold or here or there. It is just existence."

Noting that there is reference in our literature to 'Angels of the Sun', I then asked Salumet if he would have a *preference of location*.

~ "I find that a very odd question!"

I had replied midst much laughter that well, I am an odd person.

~ "Yes—I have to say—I just—what is the best way I can say it to you?—I have no preference of locations. I am just existence. I do know perhaps, that one place I would not like to be for too long, is within this atmosphere now. Of course, you understand that; and again, I can feel your curiosity and your questioning, but no, I have no preference of location—only to that place where I belong."

Perhaps I was being odd in thinking that those in spirit could favour a location?

~ "Yes, you are thinking along physical lines again. Are you sure you understand that?"

George: "I think I understand that physical places are locked within space-time. And time and place relate to space-time really."

~ "Yes—yes. You cannot make comparisons. It is too complicated."

I suggested there are the connections between physical world and spirit, but we could never fully understand.

~ "There are many things, my dear friend, that you will never understand whilst you are human. You can access much more information in our world of course, where your understanding becomes greater; but even there, some people find that it takes much time to fully understand the workings of spirit."

But nevertheless, perhaps it is helpful that we discuss these things.

CHAPTER 23

'THOU SHALT NOT KILL'

Certain biblical narrative is inviolable spiritual law, and that includes the above commandment delivered to Moses on Sinai. It is a clear statement—no ifs, no buts. So artillery, bombs, warring, executions, shoot-to-kill policies—even suicides; all would appear to be in violation of this spiritual law as handed to Moses. A question placed to Salumet (12th January 2004) referred to this, and concerned 'capital punishment' and how that might possibly be passing a problem on to spirit world. Salumet first explained that the instruction to Moses was given on the understanding that mankind should always love his fellow man. But of course, throughout Earth's history there has been much killing—in the name of religion, in the name of war, in the name of justice:

~ "How then can we deal with such an issue? I would say this to you my dear friend: killing another human being *cannot* be justified. But we have to then think: for some upon this planet, they feel that what they are doing is for the betterment and safety of others; so again we have to look at the *motive* for such killings. I would say to you: for everyone who has raised their hand against their fellow man, it will be a source of regret when they come to our world. Of course, you are quite correct in your assumption that these problems do not end on your planets but indeed come into our world where many have these problems. Let us give you an example of one who is legally killed—and I use 'legally' lightly—by your institutions, by your governments because they feel that they are protecting the majority of the people. Imagine the anger and the hatred of the one who is being killed, and then think of the one who uses his hand to do such an act. That soul will come to our world still engaged with anger and hatred which then has to be seen and recognized within our world. That soul will be lost in anger and hatred for some time. You know—you have had many 'rescues' in this group—you understand the problems that people bring with them to our world. So, yes you are correct, KILLING CAN NEVER BE RIGHT but we do take account of the motive behind these things."

So it would seem that capital punishment increases the problem through the generation of more anger, either here or in spirit:

~ "Yes, there is no question about that."

Sarah: "And regimes who make boy soldiers and people who don't really want to fight but are *made* to fight—account will be given to them too because they have done the killing unwillingly or have been brainwashed into it?"

~ "That is why, my dear friend, there is never a clear answer to these questions. You cannot judge one human being against another, because you know not what is in that thinking—what they carry within. And, yes, there is much injustice in your world but all must be accountable for whatever deed."

So wars would seem to be just chapters of disasters, and we can only really consider ourselves sane and mature once we learn to avoid them.

Lilian spoke of animal pets being put down in severe illness:

~ "Every soul, every being upon this planet is here for a purpose. I will say to you only this: that the animals in your world who come within the scope of your love, are dependent upon you human beings for their lives here. They are apart from the animals of the wild—who look after themselves. They *need* the love-bond from the human being. I know what you speak of when human emotions come into play, and they do not want their beloved animal to suffer. And for them, they are doing it for love. But I would say to you all: energy has its time and its place upon this planet, and no man should take any decision which curtails the lifetime of that energy."

Lilian: "Even though they are in pain?"

~ "There are many who are in pain, but again it is motive. You understand? Because it is done from love, then the human being sees it as being right; but when you come to our world, you will see the fuller picture."

So we have the basic spiritual law—the ideal; but clearly, motive also has its lesser part to play.

We returned to the subject of warfare. Early in 2009, a most flagrant example of violation of the basic spiritual law was still fresh in our minds— the 3-week Israeli punitive war against neighbouring Gaza. Ongoing hostilities between Israel and Palestine came to a head when Israeli Prime Minister Ehud Olmert issued a warning on Christmas Day, followed by air attack on 27th December involving at least fifty F-16 fighter jets and Apache helicopter gunships. Artillery and naval bombardments followed and tank incursion—leaving 1,380 dead and 5,380 wounded; those figures sadly including hundreds of children. Israeli casualties were slight, and American-supplied high-tech weaponry had made its contribution to the obvious one-sidedness of conflict. Such aggression in the season of good-will by the *children of Israel* seemed to us scarcely believable. And so, on 16th February 2009, Salumet's appraisal was sought:

~ "All disputes within your world are based on many things—the peoples that you speak of are still imprisoned by the values of religion; values of wanting to retain lands, or take land—which belong to all people. All land belongs to the Earth planet, not to individuals. Of course, much spirituality has been lost. I feel I can tell you that in coming time, the problems in the country that you speak of will begin to decrease so that understanding will come."

I declared that to be good news.

~ "But there has been a great loss of true love, true understanding of their fellow men, and in this situation it becomes 'an uncertainty of spirit'. Perhaps that is the best way I can put it to you. All men are uncertain of what to do, and that brings to mankind 'fear', which you know, my dear friends is what I tell you so often, is happening in your world. But understanding is slowly beginning to take hold in these lands."

George: "Thank you for clarifying the Israeli situation—that does help. And I think we *all* felt a great compassion for the families who were being hurt."

~ "Yes—yes, always there has to be love—compassion—not only for those who have suffered but for the perpetrators also. Do not forget them, because they also need your love and your prayers for understanding. But, I can assure you: there is understanding growing in that area of your world."

So we have the balanced view from deeper spirit on what we see here as an ugly happening, that many I know, have found hard to digest.

On 28th November 2011—that was that occasion when we had gathered in Eileen's conservatory prior to the meeting, and found her listening to the recording of Salumet speaking through her. She looked up and welcomed us and I had then read that self-contradictory Chairman Mao statement ending with the words:

"—in order to get rid of the gun it is necessary to take up the gun."

The statement seems to demonstrate so well our present day political thinking. Having suggested we might read the quote to Salumet and seek his thoughts on the matter, we had then moved into the inner room; and as stated, there was no need to read the quote again—and Salumet went on to make the point:

~ "It is all too simple to say, at times: we are all one, we are of the same energies—that is to simplify matters too much. Rather than think of *yourselves* this time, I would like you, my dear friends, to focus upon some words that are used in your world today, especially those of Christian denomination. Those words are pure and simple, and they are: *'Peace and goodwill to all men'*—simple words, but words which mean so much."

I suggested: it is one thing to say the words—another, to *feel* them strongly inside.

~ "Yes, they are words that are used freely, especially at this coming festive time of your year in your world, but, I would like you, as you say: to *feel* and understand what those words mean—not only to those you love, but to every man who has his feet firmly planted on this Earth plane—not only physical man, but also those in spirit, who are in need of your understanding, and your love."

George: "Of course, with goodwill towards all, there cannot be any wars—would you agree, Salumet?"

~ "There should never be war, but I have been listening to your conversation before we entered this room, and of course, the ideal in your world would be that no man should go against another; but again, I have to say to you: until mankind uses his freewill for the good and betterment of mankind, there will always be problems; but as I have told you on many occasions, the most powerful thing that you can do, is to use the power of your thought. Give out love and compassion to those who do wrong. In that way, energy can be transmuted. I am not saying it is easy, but that is the way to go."

Paul observed that to be something that needs to be practised more.

~ "If you *believe*, my dear friends, that thought is the most powerful asset you will ever have in this world—then why not use it?"

George: "Yes, I think you are saying, Salumet, that the best way to stop wars, is to use power of thought and love; and I think the thought and the love work together."

~ "Of course—thoughts of love, you can almost see *grow* in our world. Mankind is, at this present time, unable to see the effect of those powerful thoughts, but I can assure you, my dear friends, there is no stronger force than the thought of love. No matter the situation, the thought of love for another, and especially those who wish to do wrong and hurt another human being—that thought becomes so powerful, that as I have said, that energy is transmuted."

Sara: "So that's the best thing to teach our children, when they are being threatened—"

~ "Yes. It is not easy. It needs to begin from a very young age. I understand that it is not always easy, but show by example. You can also help your child by sending thoughts to *him* and to those that you feel are not so friendly towards him. Good thoughts are always *used*."

I observed that it seems to have been the policy amongst politicians and leaders to feel that war can only be stopped by war, which is really quite absurd.

~ "I have to say: when I listened earlier—I have to say: it made me smile."

We all laughed at this point and enjoyed the concept of a bodiless light-being smiling.

~ "Yes, you were not aware of me, but I have been listening, yes, because it is an important topic that you chose to speak about in a sensible manner. So many people when they think of wars and disagreement become so irate with other people that they do not always realise that they are harming themselves."

It is indeed an important topic, and one that deserves thoughts that lead to wise rhetoric.

What about the more personal forms of killing?—suicide, euthanasia and the putting down of ailing family pets?—all forming part of life's complex pattern. During our 16th January 2012 meeting there had been discussion about *power of thought* and how in dire circumstance, an ailing hospital patient had accelerated own death by wishing it. Thought is indeed that powerful. This had led to the topic of euthanasia and the question of asking a doctor to end a life painlessly.

~ "Why should you curtail that lifespan because you think it is right? You do not see the wider picture, once again. So why do you feel it is right to curtail that life? It is not correct."

Jan had queried: "In no circumstance whatsoever?"

~ "It is never right, and I will stress NEVER right! When the spirit is ready, they (that one) will go naturally. Very often, in the time of discomfort, does the spirit come to the fore."

Jan: "It seems to soar, doesn't it?"

~ "Yes, and although I understand that human beings find this distressing—I understand the love that you have—but you do not have the right to shorten your own lives. You can use your mind to help you along, but it should be a natural end."

Jan had then asked about the putting down of elderly pets, and it seems that the same rules apply:

~ "They belong to spirit in the same way that you do. So I would say: no."

We said how good it was to have this guidance because there had been so much media discussion of these matters.

~ "There is much controversy I know, but always I have to say: that is where I stand—that is what I know."

Rod mentioned how people through extreme depression are sometimes driven to suicide.

~ "Of course, my dear friend, but that still does not make it right. It still is not part of 'universal law'. I have to say—and I know that some people become upset and offended, when I say that suicide is the most selfish of acts. It is a selfish act and also—I wish you could see the despair they feel at what they have done."

I referred to those Tibetan monks who torch themselves in protest to their country being taken over by another. As a political act it seems in one sense unselfish. But how would Salumet view such an act?

~ "In a way, I understand what you are saying, but it is selfish in that they deprive those who have loved them, of that love. Remember: love is everything and just to hurt deliberately one human being, can never be accepted. No one on this planet is a sole entity—all of you are intertwined in one way or another; be it to a husband, a wife, to children, to parents. No one stands alone. So I have to say: yes, it would still be considered as a selfish act; although, as I say, I understand that they *feel* it is unselfish. Their view will change when that whole picture is shown to them. I cannot deviate because it is the truth."

In the final analysis then, answers are so very simple. The two Ls—Love and Life—are each inviolable. Life is the most precious gift to be nurtured and cared for in love; that love should be given out by all. In reality there is no solitude—all is connected. There is no place on Earth that should harbour warfare or contrived untimely death. We must learn to offer love not war. Love is the essential essence of all sentient beings. It is the key to our cosmic progression.

'THOU SHALT NOT KILL', as given to Moses, is spiritual law.

PART 5

Moving Forward with Help and a Blessing

"...The stream of knowledge is heading towards a non-mechanical reality; the universe begins to look more like a great thought than like a great machine. Mind no longer appears as an accidental intruder into the realm of matter; we are beginning to suspect that we ought rather to hail it as the creator and governor..."

SIR JAMES JEANS, *THE MYSTERIOUS UNIVERSE*, (1930)[12].

CHAPTER 24

DNA UPGRADE AND GENETIC CHANGE

How do DNA and genetic modification relate to spiritual progress? Is there a spirit connection? In past years, the ravages of warfare and the ensuing armistice deals have left their mark on this planet, resulting in the national boundaries and political blocs of today. Whilst these changes have taken place and are plain to see, the *fundamental nature* of living things has remained essentially unaltered—this up to and continuing on through the 20th century. It is true that in agriculture, there have been manipulations such as 'selection' and 'grafting' to improve crop yields. But the underlying genetic make-up of species has remained as it always was—has been left to *nature's* process of selection. It has been *natural selection* that has always prevailed. But now, in the 21st century, scientific humankind has the audacity to question nature's process that she has so meticulously evolved through countless millennia, and man-made genetic modifications are being clumsily superimposed; this in an attempt to secure better plant hardiness, bigger crop yields, extra food production and more financial gain. The United States has led the world in this venture while many of us are less enthusiastic or perhaps more circumspect, as the case may be. Yet, by 2012, our world had 17-million farms spread through 28 countries, growing GM crops on what amounts to 12% of our planet's arable land. So biotechnology has arrived and has established its questioned presence. An increasing alternative (re-introduced) system in agriculture is 'organic farming'. Nearly 1% of Earth's arable land is currently farmed organically, scattered throughout most countries. Organic growers equate naturally grown crops to 'health', whilst at the same time the system of growing provides excellent habitat for bees, butterflies and all nature's evolved wildlife.

When the genetic modification of crops was first mentioned to Salumet, he described it as *an unnecessary step for mankind but one that had already been taken.* It had therefore already become part of our evolution, whether we care to question or not. Later (13th October 2003), he warned against being judgemental:

> ~ "Since the Earth has existed, mankind has made many errors—shall we call them."

He went on to point out that within an excursion into 'error' there will inevitably be some good outcome. Therefore we should be wary of judging. We must of course always be true to ourselves and should offer opinion, but avoid being judgemental of another. We pointed out to our guide that in some places people were burning crops, grown experimentally by GM devotees. Salumet used a rather clever double-edged sentence in his reply:

> ~ "But what you sow you must reap. Remember, whether they feel right or wrong, the time will come when they must face themselves as to whether their judgement was right or wrong. Remember, I have taught you there are two sides: white ↔ black — love ↔ fear."

I suggested that destroying crops must stem from fear:

~ "It is fear. Remember—it is simple—all of existence stems from fear or love. That is why people on Earth are disturbed and create disharmony. Therefore, what you must do is send them love. Surround them with love and in so doing, their thinking will change, and then you will have created that harmony upon this Earth that will ultimately bring a little more happiness."

So it is now too late to stop this venture, but all is not lost, and we can direct our good thoughts towards some useful application coming from it.

There is a good friend in spirit who has visited from time to time via Sarah—a knowledgeable one where farming and nature are concerned. An aspect of this soul had once supplied grain to an Egyptian pharaoh. He first came to us in that guise and gave us his Egyptian name 'Ond Kulla', meaning 'Big Feet'; so that is the name we have come to know him by. But there have been a number of his incarnations since, so this was now quite an advanced and knowledgeable soul who on this occasion spoke with us (1st June 2009):

~ "I promised I would come back, and this time I am coming in a different guise. Tonight I wish to bring with me many who have guarded the crops that you grow—many who have helped in all forms of nature. We have been quite concerned about your nature, and there are many who have been helping those—I was looking for the word—'elementals'—they are being influenced from our side. So I have come to tell you that the work that is being done with your crops—the genetically modified crops—"

Ond Kulla's reference to this subject took us all completely by surprise. Our dear farmer friend from yesteryear was now actually involved in the GM crops issue! Wonderful! He went on:

~ "We are working closely with those who are experimenting with your crops and trying to guide them to work in a more natural form."

We asked if he saw genetically modified crops as a problem:

~ "There are two sides to this. The consumption of modified crops is not perhaps the best way, but also, the experiments being done with the crops are teaching those who are performing these acts quite a lesson, and this lesson will be of use in another way."

I asked if the GM crops were a problem to nature's elementals:

~ "Yes, they are finding this most difficult, but as I said: it is not all doom. They (the scientists) are learning—and there are often periods of not-such-good-times whilst learning is taking place. There will be much good coming from these experiments, but like most things, it takes time on your planet. So my purpose this time is to remind you that you should not ask for genetically modified crop experiments to stop, but merely to ask that what they do, leads them in the right direction."

So this aligns to Salumet's teaching, that we should think the good thought towards happy conclusions. We then asked if GM food will damage the health of those who eat it:

~ "I would say that if you were to eat only genetically modified product all your life, this would be bad for you—but small quantities will not damage you long-term. That is my knowledge, but I am not from the highest level. But overall, for the planet, this is not the best way forward."

These are wise words from one whom we know from his several visits, progresses well in spirit. And he will of course have awareness of the many contributions by those in spirit as well as the work of nature's elementals.

How do genes and genetic modification relate to DNA, and what is DNA? Firstly, DNA is a chemical abbreviation for deoxyribonucleic acid, which is a molecule of lengthy spiral form. The chromosomes within a cell nucleus are made up of DNA molecules and these contain the genetic codes that fix details of character in plants, animals and humans. In animals and humans, genetic code determines such things as colour of eyes and hair. In plants, genetic code would relate to such properties as disease susceptibility and drought resistance. But with 24,000 genes per cell, the research becomes highly complex. Objects of gene manipulation that might be seen as useful are drought and disease resistance of crops. In searching for these objectives, there

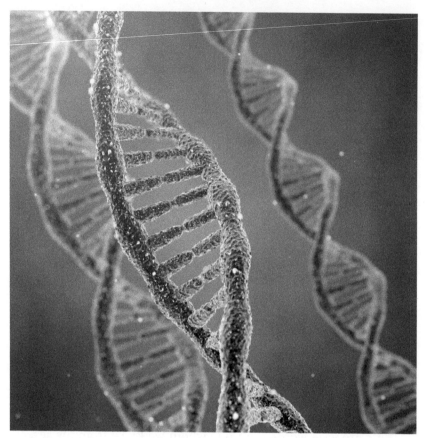

Genes are short sections of the helical deoxyribonucleic acid (DNA).

would of course be much learning along the way. And clearly, there is the connection of chromosomes, genetic code and DNA, with all existing at the very fount of the physical life format—chromosomes containing DNA-bound proteins.

It again took us by surprise when Salumet launched into a discourse on DNA at our meeting of 5th March 2007. He had earlier spoken of the raising of consciousness:

~ "Not only is the consciousness of man being raised – and I would say it is partly being raised because of the lives of many good people upon this earth who *show* their love and their knowledge by example—that is the way forward. But what we in my world are trying to achieve now, is to alter all of the 'stuck' knowledge that is within your DNAs. This is little known at this time, but there are those upon your Earth who are gaining knowledge of this particular aspect of change."

He then paused and announced:

~ "I feel some questions at this point—"

Graham: "Could you expand a bit on what you mean by DNA and stuck knowledge in DNA?"

~ "In the same way as all conditions of your life are within your DNA pattern, so also are thoughts."

The principle of thought-connection to DNA pattern was entirely new to our awareness.
Graham: "Gosh! That is interesting!"
George: "Does this change and connect to a noticeable degree in genetic change?"

~ "Not particularly—it is something that has always existed, but mankind down through the ages in the many areas of living has become 'stuck'—I believe that is your common word—and it remains so. Rather similar to those of you who reincarnate with problems from past lives, so too does humankind come with DNAs which are stuck."

George: "So I think you are saying that there is a particular spiritual connection to the DNA helix—"

~ "Of course, of course!—although it has the physical connotations, all of spirit has to be involved in these things. That is the way forward— to release people from past thoughts and actions. It is something for you to think about."

I suggested it is not quite like wiping the slate clean of our past ways:

~ "That cannot be; that would be much too easy, would it not?"

George: "But it is a factor that would make our way forward a little easier—"

~ "—In changing your lives and thinking—to become that more spiritual being."

Sara: "Re-programming the mind with better thoughts—more positive thoughts."

~ "That is exactly what it would achieve."

Sara: "So that clearly relates to what was said recently about the fact that any condition can be overcome; not necessarily taken away, but overcome by the power of thinking."

~ "Yes. Again it demonstrates the power of the mind. Do you see how thinking joins in all aspects of your lives and how powerful it is? It is that part of you which will always exist."

I ventured that we had not really thought about a DNA link to consciousness.

~ "No, it is something that is very new to your knowledge. DNA, in the amount of years that it has been discovered—but of course in our world it has been known for ever—so it is not new. So, I hope my dear friends it has given you a little more to consider."

Graham: "DNA is linked with our future evolution, so if we are stuck with past consciousness in our DNA which we have at the moment— if we can let that go and move forward with our spiritual learning and awareness, then we will physically evolve."

~ "Yes. Would you like to sit here?"

Salumet's humour brought much laughter, as Graham replied that he did not feel quite qualified yet.

~ "You started this conversation and now you have given a very apt explanation. It just shows how much you have all grown."

So once again a topic had been introduced of which we in the group had no prior knowledge.

It was 1953 when James Watson, Francis Crick and Maurice Wilkins discovered the double helix structure of **d**eoxyribo**n**ucleic **a**cid that we now know more simply as DNA. Much has progressed in this field through half a century and scientific endeavour continues forward. Data posted on the Internet by Sophia Fotopoulou in the e-magazine 'Newsfinder', just three days following our meeting included the statements:

'The human DNA is a biological Internet and superior in many aspects to the artificial one. The latest Russian scientific research directly or indirectly explains phenomena such as clairvoyance, intuition, spontaneous and remote acts of healing, self healing, affirmation techniques, unusual light/auras around people (namely spiritual masters), the mind's influence on weather patterns and much more. DNA can be influenced and reprogrammed by words and frequencies. Only 10% of our DNA is being used for building proteins. It is this subset of DNA that is of interest to western researchers and is being examined and categorized. The other 90% are considered "junk DNA". The Russian researchers, however, convinced that nature was not dumb, joined linguists and geneticists in a venture to explore those 90% of "junk DNA". Their results, findings and conclusions are simply revolutionary! According to them, our DNA is not only responsible for the construction of our body but also serves as data storage and communication.'

I referred those recent research details from Newsfinder magazine to Salumet when he was with us the following week (12th March 2007), concluding with: "I think the meaning there, is that information can be put *into* the DNA, and information also comes *from* the DNA, to have its influence."

~ "Yes, that energy, whether going in or out, is transmuted. Yes, you are correct—it is beginning to enter the consciousness of man—it is now becoming more available to human thinking."

George: "Certainly there is the evidence on the Internet that, as you say: it is entering the consciousness."

~ "Yes, that is the purpose for it, and of course, that mankind might have better control of his own spiritual being."

George: "It is openly declared that thought and words have that influence and—"

~ "—As you well know my dear friend. That, I have told you on many of your years now."

George: "Indeed—and I think that thought can come from the individual himself, or it can come from a healer, or it can come from those in spirit, or as I think you were saying last time, it can enter from *deeper* spirit. All those thought places would, I think, have their effect."

~ "Of course, your words are completely right."

George: "Thank you, it is good to have your confirmation on that."

~ "I applaud the fact that you have gone on and found for yourself what is being made available in other areas. That, my dear friend, will and should satisfy your own need for what you would call 'proof'. Do you not agree?"

And I very happily agreed to that!

In response to a further question from Sarah, Salumet made it clear that whilst DNA energy can be transmuted, the change is not so great that a physical individual's identity becomes obscured. Identity of the individual remains clearly stamped within the DNA.

Several months later, I had chanced upon the intriguing book: *Bringers of the Dawn*[33], and I began ticking paragraphs that aligned to Salumet's teaching. On reaching page 40, I found I had ticked every paragraph! Wonderful! Then I got onto confirmation that DNA modification is a very important happening; and there were further details of the upgrading from double helix character. These details were queried with Salumet during our meeting of 30th July 2007. Our teacher first affirmed that our group is not the only one to be receiving this information, and he reminded us of his previous assurance that his words would be confirmed from other sources. He then continued:

~ "Of course, when you speak of the expansion of the helix—reaching out to other galaxies—that is the energy connection which is needed for mankind to connect further and further; and although you have mentioned a number of twelve (chakras), I will confirm for you now that there are many more, but not known of at this present time. Do not be surprised at this information—the human form is just one mass of energy."

I mentioned the scientific realization that 10 % of DNA has good purpose while 90 % has been referred to as 'junk DNA':

~ "May I interrupt and say to you, that your scientists will soon be considering another 30 % 'good DNA'—that is to come."

Wonderful! I suggested the 90 % would all in fact be found to have purpose, which Salumet affirmed. And likewise, with that part of the brain which is not seen to have application—that also will be found to have purpose:

~ "You only have to think of all those seers and mystics, as you call them in your world. They are using more. Is it not logical that this must be so? But yes, I agree that, on the whole, so much is not utilised."

I responded that it all seems to make so much good sense.

~ "I am pleased that my words can help you. But it is not an easy topic for most to understand. That is why it has been my purpose in a group such as this, that we go slowly, in order for each one to digest such information."

That of course we all appreciate. And we must recognise that if our teacher were to state all he knows, just like that, it would fall upon deaf ears, because it would simply be beyond our comprehension. But following Salumet's 2007 statement on 'junk DNA', it was revealed in the Press six years later that there had been a break-through in our understanding of DNA. That part known by its acronym 'Crispr', previously thought of as 'junk DNA', is no longer considered to be junk. It instead represents a store of genetic information relating to invading virus, and this has led to a valuable and precise method of correcting inherited disorders and disease. So we have much less of what is considered 'junk DNA' in 2013.

Just prior to that Press revelation, during our meeting of 28th October 2013, the subject of DNA came up again in a totally different way—this time in such a way that I felt it to be *very nearly* beyond our comprehension, but not quite. I had been reading about the Anasazi people of North America, this in a new book by Dr Semir Osmanagich—*The Mystery of the Anasazi Civilization*³⁴. By boring into the rock of a canyon wall, they seem to have devised a system of 23 chambers connected by tunnels, the whole arrangement being in the shape of a helix. And each chamber has within it an artefact. All seemed to be modelled on the DNA helix; leaving me with the impression that the people that we know as Anasazi, understood about the DNA helix and chromosomes.

~ "Yes, again it is a case of understanding energy. It is a case of those beings who are much more spiritual than those of you today, using the energy and gaining knowledge. It is my dear friend as simple as that; we can have as many examples as you like about different areas of your world, but what it all comes down to, is that each and every one of you are spirit. You have lost a great deal of knowledge over time, and it is now up to each one of you, if you so desire, to regain that knowledge, to be used for the betterment of mankind."

George: "That's a wonderful thought—what I wanted to go onto was to point out that the Anasazi people mysteriously disappeared as a race, as did the Maya. And it just occurred to me that perhaps they made a collective decision that it would be better for them to continue in spirit instead of reincarnating on the Earth."

~ "They were spiritual beings who had decided that they had something to do upon this Earth, and when that time was up they too returned to spirit—yes."

George: "And that would have been a collective decision?"

~ "A collective decision, yes—I do not like to use the word 'power', but it is the power of the spirit, when you can attain that degree of knowledge."

George: "Yes of course, mankind thinking in a very material way—"

~ "Yes, I would always try to steer you from that way of thinking. I am always very simplistic in my views—"

I had replied that the physical explanations put forward can sometimes be almost laughable. But then I was reminded that we have received much helpful guidance to assist in our own understanding. How very true!

Reverting back to 12th March 2007, we had, following the DNA exchange, drifted on to the topic of children and how school meals were being re-thought at a physical level, but unfortunately not on a spiritual level. That subject ended and our conversation wavered just a little:

> ~ "But you have allowed me to continue most aptly to what I wish to say to you this evening. It has led very nicely to my topic. Since the beginning of this millennium there has been much spoken about children coming into this world who are much more spiritual in nature and who in fact have come to this planet to bring much knowledge. This my dear friends I have to tell you is what is happening *now*; that as we progress through the next one thousand of your Earthly years, much change is coming to mankind—mainly through those small children who have spiritual gifts and knowledge which will in many cases a*stound* the human race. Over your next few years of Earthly life you will be made aware, whether it be by mouth or through your media—there are many children who bring to you much love and truth and they are and will be the forerunners on this planet to help make the change in human consciousness."

I asked if we could think of this as an injection of different-from-the-usual soul material:

> ~ "Yes, it comes from our world. When first I came to you I told you my dear friends that this time we could not—I use your Earthly word 'fail'—but that is not to say that we have failed, but that mankind has strayed just a little from the spiritual pathway."

Sadly, this is all too apparent from our history of warfare, weaponry, irrational investment in the nuclear arms stockpiling and financial greed!

> ~ "But I wish to tell you to watch out for these children; they will appear in all parts of your world, they will deliver to mankind the love, the hope and the change that is needed for mankind to go

forward. Their spirituality will shine forth from them. It will not be denied. These spirits or souls have come for this purpose, but it has been decided that it is the children who shall take the forefront of this knowledge because children have an innocence and a beauty which many adults lose."

Paul observed that it would be very fitting to let the children lead the way.

~ "Yes, all conditions will be suitable. But it is one way forward—not the *only* way."

Sarah: "It will be very exciting to see that in *our* lifetime."
Lilian then referred to the report of a small child with terminal cancer. She had said to her pregnant mother: 'don't worry mother, wherever I am, I will help you with the new baby', and she had remained cheerful.

~ "—A spirit with much knowledge."

Lilian: "Yes. That impressed me."

~ "—A small example of a child who knows the truth and who is bathed in love. There will be many cases—exceptional cases, of children."

Lilian: "The mother would obviously repeat that story."

~ "The mother could not deny the words of the child, and how can a small child know of these things unless it is truth? That is what you must ask of yourselves, not *you* of course my dear friends, but those who have lost their way, who do not know what to believe—and children are always a great gift to humanity."

So we may think of DNA within the cell nucleus as an *interface* between our body's physical structure and spirit. It seems that the changes mentioned above are more subtle than to modify the gross characteristics that identify an individual—this from arrangement of DNA chemical compounds within chromosomes. And it is becoming steadily clearer that the mission projected from spirit to uplift this planet, has so many parts. A list would include:

(1). Teaching by masters such as Salumet.

(2). Easing the 'stuck' condition of DNA.

(3). Introduction of children having spiritually 'sourced' soul origin.

(4). Influence from spirit towards political leaders and scientists.

(5). Inspiration for striving individuals.

(6). Revelations such as achievements of ancient civilisations and the Bible Code.

(7). Extraterrestrial and interplanetary communications that reveal Earth's true place within the pattern of creation.

(8). Light signs reported worldwide (Salumet, 14 July 2003).

One may see all these as facets of the one grand movement mounted from spirit to raise spiritual awareness on the Earth. How fortunate we are to have such wonderful support!—this in what is becoming more obvious by the minute, both a time of need and a time during which Earth moves forward to a much more enlightened future.

CHAPTER 25

LOVE, TRUTH, PEACE
AND GOODWILL

Prior to Salumet's visit of 7th September 2009, we had been chatting and airing our views on frustrating matters—the ease with which concrete and decking are taking over from nature, yet small household wind-power units meet with a minefield of restrictive legislation. And we endeavoured to make sense of confusing world politics and Middle East wars. This period was followed by silence, then the healing prayers as usual. On joining with us, our teacher made it clear that he had been listening and began to speak on judgment of others. I had apologised:

~ "No my friend, it was an introduction to my words."

He went on to say of judgement:

~ "Do not judge another, for you have not walked in their shoes. If you find fault with others, then look within—remember those words. That is one of the things I intended saying. The other was: the offer of prayer for those who are spiritually poor. That includes, my dear friends, not only those in this world, but in spirit also. Part of your mission has been to help those who remain in spiritual darkness in this lifetime."

He went on to speak favourably of our efforts in this regard through both spoken and written word. We should also remain open to truth in all facets of living, and he reminded of 'free will'. One always has the free will to accept or decline truth. And these things connect with that important matter of 'forgiveness'. Our teacher felt we still need to work at this:

> ~ "—Forgiveness of the past, because it *is* past. How can you be open to truth or going within, without first having that forgiveness of past things? Of course, you *are* the past, but it is gone. Until you forgive all past issues, you cannot go forward. And again, we enter into this conversation the word 'fear', which is so much part of your human makeup—fear is part of the condition of being human. But you must let all fear go, because whilst you have fear, you do not have that purity of love, which is your right, which is your spirit. Do you understand what I am saying to you?"

Lilian: "Yes, I find the fear thing quite difficult."
George: "Yes I think you speak of ordinary fears that we should be able to control. Perhaps I could mention there are 'intense' fears which don't seem to be within our control, and our minds—"

> ~ "Let me stop you there. *All* fear is within your control, whether it is fear outside of yourselves, or fear that is deep within—you have that control."

George: "Yes, I was thinking of those occasions when the memory is actually *blanked out* as a result of that intense fear."

> ~ "Yes, I understand. I am speaking in a simplified way. But we move then to what we call 'mind'—that all-powerful thing that you all possess. The mind has the ability to reject fear."

Sarah: "But this intense fear that the mind blanks out—is that a way of controlling the fear, if you are deleting it?"

> ~ "No, you are not putting it behind you. You are saying: it does not exist; but it is still there."

I explained how, during National Service training in the 1950s, my first parachute jump from a balloon car, had involved free-fall through dense cloud—I was much relieved as the parachute flapped open just below cloud-base! The 'intense fear' experienced during that free-fall was deleted from memory. BUT—it was most unexpectedly detected during a psychic reading forty years later! So where mind's control of intense fear is concerned, it is precisely as Salumet says: *'It is still there'.*

~ "It is a human condition of course—in the same way as those who are in danger for their lives allow the fear to build. It is part of the human condition, but you still can control any fear that you experience— and in allowing the fear to dissipate, then we can come close to help. Whilst you grip fiercely this feeling of fear, what you are doing my dear friends, is blocking us from helping you."

Sarah: "So, if you were fearful and had the knowledge that it was going to be alright, would it be appropriate then to ask for help?"

~ "Of course—we are always here to help, but sometimes your fear is so great that it stops us."

Sarah: "And people like Joan of Arc who was burned at the stake and who appeared to be completely peaceful—it was her faith that was keeping her calm—"

~ "Of course, it was the inner knowledge of what she knew to be truth. That is why you have what you term 'brave people' in your world. It is this inner calmness and knowledge which they possess—that sure knowing that all will be well."

We moved on to the need to see the wider picture of existence, and I ventured that a part of that wider picture has been communication with those on other planets, and whilst that has been a wonderful aspect of these meetings—

~ "That was an exercise for you my dear friends because I felt your love and your dedication to this work deserved to know just a little more."

George: "And since your last visit, we have received one from 'Planet Glong'. This is one known to Bonniol, and through Bonniol, they have *heard of* Salumet, but very wisely stated that Salumet was for this Earth and not for *their* planet, which is on its own quite different course. Is there anything you would wish to say about Planet Glong?"

~ "All I can tell you my dear friends—I did not instigate this—but if it has been brought to you through Bonniol then I would say that it is good that you have more information."

I commented that this would seem to be a very advanced planet, in that they had become of single unified mind. It seems that they were able to join with Bonniol on some visits, which we did not know about at the time, and hence their follow-up visit.

~ "Yes, mind transference is an interesting thing is it not? My purpose with Bonniol was to demonstrate to all of you that this is possible. There is so much you can never know, my dear friends—so much that belongs, not only to *this* universe but to many, many others that you will never fully understand."

Sarah: "It was one that came through *me* Salumet and I did feel it was a real one, but I know you've always said to me that I should not question—and I believe it was right but—"

~ "You are a doubter—"

We had laughed heartily at this:

~ "But if you are to progress my dear friend, you must become more aware of those who are using you and at times you will *feel* if it does not seem right."

Sarah: "It *did* feel right!"
George: "It seemed an enormously powerful mind, a very logical mind and it went on for about an hour—quite a lengthy discourse."

~ "Yes, well that can only be for your good—there always has to be reason behind communication. So—perhaps I should say 'well done!' to our doubter, in allowing it to happen."

There followed our laughter again and Sarah's thanks.

~ "The last thing I wanted to remind you of—that all-encompassing 'love'. Love can never be learned, and I might hear some of you say: 'but of course it can'. It cannot. Love exists, and you have never been at any stage of time without that knowledge of love. And in fact, my dear friends, you do have a saying on this planet Earth—*love makes the world go round*. And I fully endorse those words—not only this world but every world that exists. Love always has been. Love is the centre of all things."

George: "I think also there was a 'Beatles' song—*'Love is all you need'*."

~ "Yes—love is important in all of your lives. It is natural for each and every individual to feel the power of love. And if you stop for a moment, you can feel the power of love within the heart area of your physical being. But it is much deeper love than that. It is the purity of love, which can never die. It is an expression. It is a need that you all have. And I will end it again by saying—*Love is all that you need*—and I will remember those words, because it finishes nicely what I wanted to remind you all of."

We voiced appreciation of Salumet's gentle reminders, and as our guide withdrew this time, we were left encompassed in pure love—a deeply wonderful feeling.

Moving on to 21st June 2010, we had been asked during the previous meeting to think on 'What is Truth?' We had since thought. Jette, who has several times sat with us, emailed from Denmark the wisdom she has received. 'The truth is true always—there is only love—lots of it.' Her contribution was read out first—a profound start? We each then followed with our individual thoughts. Salumet finally broke his silence, remarking firstly on the diversity of our thinking—then continued:

~ "I will say only this to you, my dear friends. You have spoken much on truth. You have each given what you feel to be truth. I will say to you: 'cosmic truth' cannot be transmuted in any way, and yes, you are right—truth *is* love but the purest form of love, which you each, as individuals, have not encountered. Love is subject to many emotions when you speak as individuals, but 'cosmic love' cannot be changed. It is the very 'being of existence'. As the gentleman, here, by me, has said:

it is a 'word'—love is only a word, used to describe the indescribable. When we speak of truth—yes, it changes with each individual life and your perceptions of it—as someone here has mentioned. But what is your own individual truth in this lifetime? It is your very being, your heart, your soul, and someone too has mentioned 'instinctive feelings'; all of these things play a part in individual truth; and I feel, my dear friends, that you have captured, between you what truth truly is—but what I would have liked to hear is a little more of your own personal truths in this lifetime. Each has touched upon it briefly. One's own truth may not be another's truth. You are correct in that assumption. That is why, on this Earth plane, there are so many disagreements among mankind, because man cannot agree with what another feels and thinks to be truth. I'm sure you would agree."

Agreed! But Sarah suggested there cannot be unity so long as we each stay with different interpretations of truth.

~ "Whilst mankind is clothed in physical garb, there will be difficulties. But never doubt that we in spirit work tirelessly for knowledge of 'cosmic truth' to be given to each one—not 'individual truth', but 'cosmic truth', and that will take much time. But as the gentleman has already said, your scientists are now beginning to find that all-that-has-been-believed-to-be-true is changing, and that is as it should be. That is because of the influence from our world. But 'truth' is 'love' in the purest sense. Truth can never be changed, because *truth is existence*—purity of existence, creation and all that it encompasses."

So the many disagreements in our world are just a part of the growing-up process, and we would do well to recognise this. There is the need both to recognise and to see that *it is folly to go to war over such trivia.*

~ "Yes. Each individual—you need to find that 'core being' to truly understand yourselves, first and foremost; and then to look outwards and to extend that love from within. That is the way forward to recognising truth. It must first come from within."

We drew attention to those who live in fear—who suffer from harsh political injustice, and who dare not speak out:

~ "Yes, we do not deny the difficulties and the troubles of your world, but remember, each one of you, as spirit, has a responsibility for your own thought. I am sure, each and every one of you must be aware of those individuals who would seem to rise above all terrors that exist in your world and their light shines forth. That should be the aim, no matter what circumstance you find yourself in. You must keep that light shining brightly. No one says it is easy, and we do understand the fears, and the terrors and injustices of your world—man has created these things for himself. But the light within, as you go through this lifetime, or any other lifetime, needs to be nurtured—needs to be made strong, so that link with your own soul outshines all injustice."

Sarah pointed out: "We're lucky—we've had your teaching. There are many others who are not as fortunate."

~ "But they are never alone, but because of situations, they cannot find themselves—that is the sadness."

In conclusion, I had declared the exercise to have been of immense value. We had hitherto thought at personal levels—mere personal levels within the dwarfing, detailed complexity of creation. It had helped all to realise just how complex—how wonderful the whole system is—with its different segments, the material space-time creation, the spirit part which has form, the more fundamental formless spirit guidance—the lines of communication and feedback that connect all; the whole adding up to an incredible recipe for an ever-on-going-evolution. This 'thinking exercise' has left us so much more aware. So thank you, Salumet!

~ "I thank you, dear friend. What I wish to say to you now, before I take my leave, is this, my dear friends: remember, no matter what your lifestyles, no matter what your thoughts, your feelings—however you may describe yourselves; deep within, you are sparks of pure love. Keep this in mind and always you will be guided on the right pathway, not only in this lifetime, but when you return home—that knowledge of who and what you are, can rejoin that purity of spirit."

Later in that same year (15th November 2010), this statement was extended:

~ "If you take all of existence; mankind, as you are upon *this* planet is basically 99.9% non-material. You, my dear friends, are made from all existence—that LOVE, that powerful 'being' that is called the 'universal power'. All universes, all beings, everything which exists is made from that energy. Even people who assume they are spiritual beings on this Earth, still look to that *physical part*, as being the main contender of life—not so!"

The 99.9 % non-material being, does of course include soul, the sourcing of soul and the mind. All make up the non-material. Clearly then, our material being is both small and short-term when compared to all that non-matter.

~ "The truth is simple: you are spiritual beings and that small percentage of you that is material body is indeed a very small part. You, my dear friends, are part of a whole. Do not isolate yourselves. You see before you single entities, but let me tell you, the most part of you is unified— part of that much greater whole—you *are* 'existence'."

As Christmas approached, and prior to the meeting of 12ᵗʰ December 2011, we had been asked to think on *'peace and good will to all men'*; then to air our views. Exactly how should this phrase of our festive period be interpreted? Our individual views were once again some-what diverse. Broadly, two aspects were described—the personal and the more widespread picture. In the former, you wish no harm to an-other. You wish them a good life with enlightenment and with peace. And by cultivating inner peace, it might be said that 'love' and 'good will to all' automatically follow. In its wider concept there is no room for warfare, bad thoughts between nations or political fear—no fears, not even ones directed towards those beyond this planet. Salumet lis-tened patiently. He then finally spoke:

~ "Yes, I am pleased that you have mentioned other planets, other peoples and not just people of the Earth plane. To offer these good thoughts for others, you are, in effect, using your *spiritual* self, and it is the *spiritual* self which must feel that love and peace and goodwill to all. Yes—can you, my dear friends, see the connecting link that you have all made? You can, yes, I know. You have come to recognise your own, what you would term 'failings', but which I would call 'striving to know yourselves'. They are not failings, my dear friends. They are happenings in an Earthly life which needs to be changed in order for the spirit to grow even more. You are *beings of love*. Therefore, feelings of 'peace and goodwill to all men' should be natural to you, but of course, being human beings, makes it a little more difficult—but that is why you are here."

We have of course evolved from animal ancestry, and of necessity, it takes time for us to move beyond animal survival instincts, into the more spiritual ways.

~ "But, I would like you to always retain those words in your minds, and, whenever you encounter upsets and troubles in your lives, remember those words, and automatically, you should find that that spirit within will come to the fore and uplift not only yourselves, but all of those people you know. So my message to you at this your festive season, my dear friends, is to shine within that love which is eternal. Feel that love. *Feel* the peace which emanates from that love, and I will tell you, now: you will experience the utmost love and joy in this your everyday lives. I hope you understand my words this time—and I am saying to you and to all of creation: 'PEACE AND GOOD WILL TO ALL.'"

Our teacher took his leave to be midst his familiar cosmic connections until next year. There were fond farewells, to which I added: "We can't imagine where and how you will be—"

~ "And I can't explain it to you!"

And as we all laughed, Jan added: "Safe journey!"
The journey seen by Salumet of course as:

~ "—A blink of the eye!"

Following Salumet's departure we had chatted amongst ourselves, but there was more to come. It soon became clear that another was with Eileen.
Lilian: "Good evening and welcome! You've been listening?"

~ "It's so lovely to be with you. It's been a long time—a very long time. I've been with you before."

Lilian: "Yes—can you remind us of your name please?"

~ "I am Sister Agnes."

There were delighted murmurs of recognition from several. A number from Holy Orders have visited across the years, but Sister Agnes had preceded Salumet's mission; also had preceded our transcribed records! But Leslie had often spoken of this dear one who had brought illumination in those earlier times.

George: "Sister Agnes! *Yes*, I do remember the name!"

~ "Yes, I was so attracted to your energies tonight and I wish to come just to wish you all a beautiful Christmas."

Sarah: "Thank you very much."

~ "Although, I don't need to honour the Christian religion anymore, I still do enjoy this time of year because of the love and the singing—I don't call them 'hymns' now—singing of love and joy and what you were speaking of—'peace'. It's just so beautiful."

George: "And it goes beyond any single religion, no doubt."

~ "Hold on—I wish to give you these beads. I want you to give them to your lovely lady wife."

As Sister Agnes' hand—Eileen's hand—reached across, I cupped mine to receive the beads ... and later transferred them to an envelope. Both Lilian and Jan declared that they could see their rainbow colours.

~ "Please accept them from me."

George: "Wonderful! Thank you so much!"

~ "Each one I have blessed. Please make sure she has them."

George: "I will, I will. These will be treasured—much treasured!"
Lilian added: "She will be very, very pleased!"

~ "Yes, I used to be most fond of them. They are most beautiful, but they are imbued with not only the love that I give, but all of those sisters who are standing behind me."

The fuller import of this will be realised if I explain that my dear wife, on account of illness, could not be present this evening.

George: "This is wonderful, and, going back in time, Ann was educated at a convent."

~ "So, she will appreciate the rosary bead, yes?"

George: "She will, indeed!"

~ "Yes—oh, I can't express to you my pleasure at being with you again. I really did not think I would ever visit you, but it is my great joy to be with you tonight."

Lilian: "It's been a pleasure!"
George: "It's wonderful for us too, to receive you Sister Agnes; and you are now beyond any single religion? Could I put it like that?"

~ "Of course, but as you are well aware as a group, we do sometimes return in the old garb that we became so used to—and, my goodness! Was it not garb?—so itchy!"

And as we laughed at that description:

~ "I was so pleased to dispose of it! Although, it took me many of your years to even allow that thought to enter my head."

George: "Yes I can imagine."

~ "Yes, but it is wonderful the freedom that you feel."

Sarah: "Do you ever visit nuns who are still wearing the garb?"

~ "Not too often—I have really gone past doing that. This has been a very special visit—this one."

Lilian: "We're honoured!"

~ "Because our acquaintance goes back such a long time—your time I mean, not ours. And I just felt I needed to just say 'hello', and because of the teachings that you have had, I felt it appropriate tonight."

Sarah: "Well that's lovely, thank you!"

George: "We're so blessed with all those teachings, and it's a wonderful, if I could use an expression 'icing on the cake' for you to come through to us again."

Laughter had followed use of such a metaphor, but Sister Agnes had replied:

~ "How generous of spirit!"

Sarah: "I think the last time you came to us we were in Leslie's house. Have you come across Leslie since he's been over?"

~ "I have encountered that dear gentleman, who spent so many hours speaking with us. Yes, of course, his contact with, not only myself but the other sisters goes back much longer than you would know. Yes—yes I have met him. I believe he keeps himself very busy."

Sarah: "I am sure he does."

And of course, those of us who knew Leslie are well familiar with his dedication to spiritual progress.

~ "And now, I really don't want to go, but I have to. It's been lovely. I don't know what else to say, but one of my old sayings—'God bless you all'."

We are truly blessed—that blessing coming as it does from one who has moved on in spirit life to beyond Earthly religion status. There have also been the visits to us over the years of Sisters Anna, Marian, Marietta, Rosetta and Veronica, each an apostle of love, peace and good will. Sister Agnes is the link between pre-Salumet developments, Leslie our group founder, and our group's continued 21st-century endeavours. *Love, peace and good will* equate to: no wars, no nuclear stockpiles, no munitions factories, no thoughts of hostility, and always honouring that principle which is embodied in the *original teachings* of each Earthly religion: *'Thou Shalt Not Kill'*. Ideally, love extends across all international borders, datelines, class groups, age groups, ethnic and

monetary divisions; it also permeates throughout nature and all Creation—not just on this one single planet, but throughout the entire
universe—other universes too. And let us not forget all those in spirit
realms—associated with each and every planet of the countless galaxies. The Creation—of God—Creative Principle—Life Force, that all
sentient beings must acknowledge—extends so much further than just
one single religion, or the one single little planet of our most immediate knowing! And as the simple spiritual ways that beckon become
wholeheartedly accepted, then minds and knowing will become huge-
ly extended. It is a time for so much joy and fuller understanding that
awaits humanity.

"We can get to the stars any time we wish once we learn to open our
minds..."

MAURICE W COTTAM, *MY SILENT POOL*[35].

APPENDIX I

A CROP CIRCLE EXPERIENCE

It was 20th August 2013 when three of us visited the freshly made Etchilhampton crop circle. The formation had been reported on the previous day. The residual energy was unmistakably still there and could be felt. We lay on our backs and relaxed into meditations. Meetings and conversations experienced whilst in the circles are sometimes quite remarkable. On this occasion we met Marvin and learned that his 89-year-old uncle Maurice had published a book. His book includes within its pages the subject of 'interplanetary communication'. I have since read that publication and a quote from it concludes this book.

We also met in the circle that day, a lady with a really impressive looking camera and I had commented on that. Marvin, within the circle, had been taking a number of photos of parts of the formation and I had remarked to the lady, whilst pointing to the sky: "we really need a photo from up there!" She was in fact Lucy Pringle, whom we had not met before. In reply, she clicked back to a photo on her camera replay, explaining that she had been in the helicopter that had passed over about an hour earlier. Wonderful! Lucy is of course an expert where crop circles and their photography are concerned, and gives illustrated lectures around the world. As has been indicated, the designs that arrive in our cornfields invite inspection, feature in our planetary way forward and are most certainly worthy of our interaction.

Etchilhampton crop circle, 20th August 2013.
Photo: Lucy Pringle

Etchilhampton crop circle, two-directional lay of corn.
Photo: Marvin B Naylor

APPENDIX II

THE KINGSCLERE GROUP – PAST AND PRESENT

Usually 8-10 of us, sometimes more, meet on Monday evenings—in the early years it was at Leslie's bungalow in Kingsclere. Then from 2000 to 2011 we met at Lilian's home, also in Kingsclere; while for the past three years it has been Eileen's home in nearby Whitchurch. The present team continue to meet on Monday evenings, travelling from homes scattered across five southern counties—a 60-mile journey for some. A few notes on each might be appropriate. We are:

Leslie Bone: Our group founder and leader to whom we owe so much. Leslie made his journey to spirit in 1999 but has dropped by several times since for a chat. It was Leslie of course who paved the way and first welcomed Salumet in 1994. Now, twenty years on, Salumet's enlightening visits continue.

Lilian Pearce: Lilian has led the group following Leslie's departure and has been our warmly welcoming host since then until 2011 when that role transferred to Eileen. Lilian has continued to have a particular ability where 'rescues' are concerned and has assisted many from a 'stuck' position between worlds—a task that she originally shared with Leslie.

Eileen Roper: A wonderfully versatile medium having the necessary full-trance facility needed for Salumet's teaching, 'he' bringing so much love, wisdom and spiritual knowledge for all humanity. In the more customary trance medium mode, many others have spoken via Eileen, including historic figures, each in their own voice-character and in a variety of moods ranging from grief-stricken to extreme frivolity. And Eileen frequently has awareness of their visual appearance, clothing and immediate environment. Eileen is also a healer and member of the National Federation of Spiritual Healers; and from 2011 has hosted our evenings.

Sarah Duncalf: Trance medium through whom several speak with individual voice character that we have got to know. These have included South American tribal connections from the time of the Inca Empire, an Egyptian head farmer from the days of the Pharaohs and much valued inter-planetary communications. One most remarkable episode was a loud clear speech in an extinct pre-Inca tribal language that the visitor was delighted to have recorded for posterity. Sarah has also shared in the voluminous task of transcript typing over the years.

Sue Grandjean: Trance medium through whom many interesting ones have spoken. These have included North American Indians, Sisters of Holy Orders and a member of the murdered Romanov family. In the early years of Salumet, Sue was compared to a 'battery' providing extra power to aid the transmissions.

Jan Pearce: A trance medium, who on occasions, has received and delivered the most remarkable clairvoyance and clairaudient messages. These gifts have contributed wonderfully during some of the Bonniol interplanetary communications. Jan has been able to sketch objects of clairvoyant vision that have been confirmed by Bonniol. There have also been times when, during the Bonniol dialogue, Jan has 'received' parallel and elaborating information, from Bonniol's team. More recently, Jan has sometimes contributed clairvoyance followed by speech in medium mode.

Richard Pearce: Jan's son Richard is likewise remarkably clairvoyant. There have been occasions during the Bonniol visits when both Jan and Richard were present and received clairvoyant images of Planet Aerah scenes, such that they were able to compare details during the session.

Sara Martin: During sessions, Sara from time to time 'receives' guidance in leading the group in meditation journeys; this usually at the request of Salumet and sometimes others. It is clear that Sara also receives inspiration as a musician and hotel pianist.

Graham Martin: Sara's husband graham is both a special needs teacher and accomplished portrait and landscape artist. He has been able to place some of our more searching questions to Salumet and Bonniol.

Paul Moss: Paul is a professional gardener who goes off on instructive world travels for a month or so in the cold off-peak season. Our dear friend the Aeran being Bonniol has chosen Paul as his medium. Paul has built our extensive website for the group, has transcribed a huge backlog of pre-2000 meetings held as tape recordings, has produced CDs and CD-ROM of all meetings from June 1994 to the present, has made our first three books available on Amazon Kindle—and is currently working through all transcribed meetings of the Kingsclere Group, placing them in their original format on Amazon Kindle as a set of 3-year volumes.

Mark Moss: Mark, a special needs teacher, has been with the group for most of the Salumet years, coming to the earlier ones, missing a period in the middle while living on the Isle of Wight—even then arranging to be picked up off the Portsmouth ferry at times; and regularly attending meetings again now that he and family are back on the mainland—near Stonehenge.

Jim Howship: A retired chemist from a well-known international company who joined us during the Bonniol era, having studied much of our literature. Jim's clear thinking and scientific reason has been a much appreciated input. Jim made his journey to spirit in 2008 and has since got a message through to say that all is well where he is now.

Rod Taylor: With a passing resemblance to his silver screen namesake, Rod, a retired Horse Guards sergeant brings warmth, laughter, as well as searching questions to our meetings; having joined us during the Bonniol era.

Daphne Taylor: Daphne usually accompanies Rod and brings good cheer. Daph and I go back a long way, and as a senior girl, she helped keep me in order when we were both at primary school.

George Moss: As a retired scientist I am well familiar with report writing. In the group, it is my job in the first place to see that everything gets recorded, to place a few searching questions, and then later I do a useful amount of the transcribing. I have an office facility with trusty computer, printer, copier and the inevitable rather untidy pile of papers. And I endeavour to transpose much of the material into books and papers for publication. More recently I have become aware of an increasing need to place words on 'truth of existence' in the form of articles and blogs onto valuable Internet news & discussion sites such as 'Wordpress', 'Disqus', 'Victor Zammit's e-journal' and 'Facebook'.

Ann Moss: My dear wife has been a pillar of strength, has helped with transcribing and has been able to come along to several years of meetings. Ann made her journey to spirit in June 2012, but of course continues to 'be around'; and dropped by for a beautiful chat via Jan on 9th December 2013—what a Christmas present that was!

Serena Coombs: Healing arts practitioner—bodywork, nutrition, energies and shamanic principle. A regular visitor and volunteer at 'White Eagle Lodge', Liss, Hampshire UK. Serena's interests include Earth-healing and sustainability, growing food locally and she keeps updated with the controversial and often challenging issues of the day.

Emily Duncalf and Natalie Moss: It is so nice to have 'youth' represented, and these two have joined with us when their busy schedules permit. Emily clearly cannot commute from Australia!—where she now lives, but occasionally visits UK and sits in. On those occasions when with us she has shown potential as a medium.

The Kingsclere Group – members past and present.
Row 1 ... Leslie ... Eileen ... Lilian ... Sarah ... George ... Ann
Row 2 ... Jan ... Richard ... Sue ... Mark ... Sara ... Graham
Row 3 ... Jim ... Rod ... Daphne ... Serena ... Paul ... Emily ... Natalie

APPENDIX III

WHAT NEXT?

S o is that it? Where do we go from here—within? It is of course always good to go within and to meditate. But there is also input available to help steer our thinking, input from both the remote past as well as from Salumet's ongoing presentations. The Earthly story has been lengthy and complex, and as to our remote past I will refer to the Mayan wisdom which in turn has its links to those still earlier civilizations of Atlantis and Lemuria. Our pyramid excavation friend Dr Sam Semir Osmanagich has published a most intriguing work that accounts the Mayan wisdom[36]. He concludes his book with reference to the several Codices that escaped the disastrous havoc wrought by Spanish conquistadores and Catholic Church, when so many artefacts, documents and even temple-pyramids were destroyed. Modern humanity is thus blessed with a few treasured details from that truly superior civilisation that remain to be studied. A 5,200 year cycle and a 26,000 year cycle of the Mayan cosmic calendar have recently concluded, and we now navigate 'The world of the Fifth Sun' of the Mayan prophesy. They knew of this period of rapid change that Earth now experiences—a period of transformation. They knew, because they were a society, spiritually and astronomically equipped for the knowing. They knew that energies would be upgraded and the greyness and grittiness of pre-2013 centuries would now be left behind. Regrettably, so many later peoples following the Maya, have lived lives that have been markedly less noble, less peaceful, less spiritual and less knowledgeable in real terms. Purely materialistic knowledge has a certain waywardness that needs moderation. As we have seen, knowledge and application of 'spiritual science' is necessary before we can significantly understand energies and aspire to space-travel.

Salumet's mission to Earth continues. He was with us again on 20th January 2014, reminding of the 'Millennium Children' who have and are coming to Earth, bringing with them various spiritual gifts. And:

> ~ "All people, not only millennium children, take great pleasure in coming to this world at this time; because we have amongst them so many wise souls. These children will grow and will provide the knowledge and the wisdom of spirit. They feel honoured that they have been given this opportunity."

He also spoke during that evening of the communications from extraterrestrial sources reported on the Internet. Not all are trustworthy, but some are genuine and originate from beings who wish to help us on our way forward. Salumet has stated that communications from the one known as 'Bashar', channelled via the medium Darryl Ankar in California, are genuine. It is good to know that this powerful and clearly spoken source is indeed genuine. Bashar's website is http://www.bashar.org/ and of course, we shall continue to update our own Salumet website http://www.salumetandfriends.org. This site has many pages, including a ''Scientific Inquiries' page where informative articles on a number of topics will be found.

REFERENCES

1. George E Moss, *A Smudge in Time*, Gemma Books, E Wittering, UK, 2000.

2. Bruce & Andrea Leininger + Ken Gross, *Soul Survivor – The Reincarnation of a World War II Fighter Pilot*, Grand Central Publishing, New York, 2009.

3. Barbro Karlén, *And the Wolves Howled – Fragments of two Lifetimes*, Clairview Books, London, 2000.

4. George E Moss, *Salumet – His Mission to Planet Earth*, Trafford Publishing, Victoria BC, Canada, 2005.

5. Richard Gough, *The History of Myddle*, 1834, Penguin Books Edition edited by Richard Hey, Penguin Books, Harmondsworth, Middlesex, UK, 1981.

6. www.salumetandfriends.org

7. Michael Drosnin, *The Bible Code,* Weidenfeld & Nicolson, London, 1997 (Followed by Bible Code 2 and 3).

8. Jeffrey Satinova, *The Truth Behind the Bible Code*, Sidgwick & Jackson, London, 1997.

9. Prof Volodymyr Krasnoholovets, *The Great Pyramid as an Aether Wind Trapping Site'*, Hera Magazine, Rome, 2002.

10. E W Silvertooth, *Experimental Detection of the Ether,* Nature Vol. 322, 590, London, 1986.

11. E W Silvertooth, *Motion Through the Ether,* Electronics & Wireless World, May 1989.

12. Sir James Jeans, *The mysterious Universe,* Cambridge University Press, 1930.

13. Sir James Jeans, *The Universe Around Us,* Cambridge University Press, 1930.

14. Rev. G Vale Owen / Zabdiel, *The Highlands of Heaven,* The Greater World Christian Spiritualist Association, 1913.

15. Prof Ervin Laszlo, *Science and the Akashic Field,* Inner Traditions, Rochester, Vermont 2004.

16. Bonniol, Salumet, George E Moss, *The Chronicles of Aerah – Mindlink Communications across the Universe,* Trafford Publishing USA/Canada, 2009.

17. Sheila Ostrander & Lynn Schroeder, *The Handbook of PSI Discoveries,* Sphere Books Ltd, 1977.

18. Peter Tompkins & Christopher Bird, *The Secret Life of Plants,* Harper and Row, 1973.

19. Cleve Backster, *Primary Perception: Biocommunication with Plants,* 2003.

20. Albert Einstein, *The World As I See It,* Translation of *Mein Weltbild* by Alan Harris, John Lane, the Bodley Head Ltd, 1935.

21. *The History of Herodotus, Book II* – Euterpé 142-144: also included in: Great Books of the Western World Vol. 5, Ed. Mortimer J Adler, Encyclopaedia Britannica Inc., 1990, p. 79-80.

22. Akbar-Ezzeman MS, Abu'l Hassan Ma'sudi, Bodleiean Library, Oxford.

23. Dr Sam Semir Osmanagich, *Pyramids Around the World and Lost Pyramids of Bosnia,* Archaelogical Park: Bosnian Pyramid of the Sun Foundation, Sarajevo, Bosnia-Herzegovina, 2012.

24. Henry C Roberts, *The Complete Prophecies of Nostradamus,* 1947, Revised Lee Roberts Amsterdam & Harvey Amsterdam, HarperCollins Publishers Ltd, 1984.

25. John Hogue, *The Last Pope,* Element Books Ltd, Shaftsbury, 1998.

26. Masaru Emoto, *The Hidden Messages in Water*, (English translation), Beyond Worlds Publishing Inc, Hillsboro, 2004.

27. Estelle Roberts, *Red Cloud Speaks*, (First published 1938), SNU International, 2013.

28. Fibonacci (Leonardo of Pisa), *Liber Abaci*, Biblioteca Nazionale di Firenze, 1202.

29. Russell L Blaylock, *Aluminium Induced Immunoexcitotoxicity in Neurodevelopmental and Neurodegenerative Disorders*, Current Organic Chemistry, 2012; 2: 46-53.

30. T-T Win Shwe, H Fujimaki, *Nanoparticles and Neurotoxicity*, International Journal of Molecular Sciences, 2011; 12: 6267-6280.

31. Pecanha and Dos Reis, *Functional heterogeneity in the process of T lymphocyte activation*, Clinical Experimental Immunology, May 1989, 76 (2): 311-6.

32. The Holy Bible, *Revelation*, Chapters 5-22.

33. Barbara Marciniak, *Bringers of the Dawn – Teachings from the Pleiadians*, Bear & Company, Santa Fe, New Mexico, 1992.

34. Dr Sam Semir Osmanagich, *The Mystery of the Anasazi Civilization*, Archaeological Park: Bosnian Pyramid of the Sun Foundation, Sarajevo, Bosnia-Herzegovina, 2013.

35. Maurice W Cottam, *My Silent Pool – The Gateway to what the Bible calls The Higher Life – Our Evolution Forward*, Trafford Publishing, Canada, 2004.

36. Dr Sam Semir Osmanagich, *The World of the Maya*, IP "SVJET-LOST" d.d. Sarajevo, Bosnia-Herzegovina, 2004.

37. Prof Ervin Laszlo, *The Self-Actualizing Cosmos: The Akasha Revolution in Science and Human Consciousness*, Inner Traditions, 2014.

Paperbacks also available from
White Crow Books

Elsa Barker—*Letters from
a Living Dead Man*
ISBN 978-1-907355-83-7

Elsa Barker—*War Letters from
the Living Dead Man*
ISBN 978-1-907355-85-1

Elsa Barker—*Last Letters from
the Living Dead Man*
ISBN 978-1-907355-87-5

Richard Maurice Bucke—
Cosmic Consciousness
ISBN 978-1-907355-10-3

Arthur Conan Doyle—
The Edge of the Unknown
ISBN 978-1-907355-14-1

Arthur Conan Doyle—
The New Revelation
ISBN 978-1-907355-12-7

Arthur Conan Doyle—
The Vital Message
ISBN 978-1-907355-13-4

Arthur Conan Doyle with
Simon Parke—*Conversations
with Arthur Conan Doyle*
ISBN 978-1-907355-80-6

Meister Eckhart with Simon Parke—
Conversations with Meister Eckhart
ISBN 978-1-907355-18-9

D. D. Home—*Incidents in my Life Part 1*
ISBN 978-1-907355-15-8

Mme. Dunglas Home; edited,
with an Introduction, by Sir
Arthur Conan Doyle—*D. D.
Home: His Life and Mission*
ISBN 978-1-907355-16-5

Edward C. Randall—
Frontiers of the Afterlife
ISBN 978-1-907355-30-1

Rebecca Ruter Springer—
Intra Muros: My Dream of Heaven
ISBN 978-1-907355-11-0

Leo Tolstoy, edited by Simon
Parke—*Forbidden Words*
ISBN 978-1-907355-00-4

Leo Tolstoy—*A Confession*
ISBN 978-1-907355-24-0

Leo Tolstoy—*The Gospel in Brief*
ISBN 978-1-907355-22-6

Leo Tolstoy—*The Kingdom
of God is Within You*
ISBN 978-1-907355-27-1

Leo Tolstoy—*My Religion:
What I Believe*
ISBN 978-1-907355-23-3

Leo Tolstoy—*On Life*
ISBN 978-1-907355-91-2

Leo Tolstoy—*Twenty-three Tales*
ISBN 978-1-907355-29-5

Leo Tolstoy—*What is Religion
and other writings*
ISBN 978-1-907355-28-8

Leo Tolstoy—*Work While
Ye Have the Light*
ISBN 978-1-907355-26-4

Leo Tolstoy—*The Death of Ivan Ilyich*
ISBN 978-1-907661-10-5

Leo Tolstoy—*Resurrection*
ISBN 978-1-907661-09-9

Leo Tolstoy with Simon Parke—
Conversations with Tolstoy
ISBN 978-1-907355-25-7

Howard Williams with an Introduction
by Leo Tolstoy—*The Ethics of Diet:
An Anthology of Vegetarian Thought*
ISBN 978-1-907355-21-9

Vincent Van Gogh with Simon
Parke—*Conversations with Van Gogh*
ISBN 978-1-907355-95-0

Wolfgang Amadeus Mozart with Simon
Parke—*Conversations with Mozart*
ISBN 978-1-907661-38-9

Jesus of Nazareth with Simon Parke—
Conversations with Jesus of Nazareth
ISBN 978-1-907661-41-9

Thomas à Kempis with Simon
Parke—*The Imitation of Christ*
ISBN 978-1-907661-58-7

Julian of Norwich with Simon
Parke—*Revelations of Divine Love*
ISBN 978-1-907661-88-4

Allan Kardec—*The Spirits Book*
ISBN 978-1-907355-98-1

Allan Kardec—*The Book on Mediums*
ISBN 978-1-907661-75-4

Emanuel Swedenborg—*Heaven and Hell*
ISBN 978-1-907661-55-6

P.D. Ouspensky—*Tertium Organum:
The Third Canon of Thought*
ISBN 978-1-907661-47-1

Dwight Goddard—*A Buddhist Bible*
ISBN 978-1-907661-44-0

Michael Tymn—*The Afterlife Revealed*
ISBN 978-1-970661-90-7

Michael Tymn—*Transcending the
Titanic: Beyond Death's Door*
ISBN 978-1-908733-02-3

Guy L. Playfair—*If This Be Magic*
ISBN 978-1-907661-84-6

Guy L. Playfair—*The Flying Cow*
ISBN 978-1-907661-94-5

Guy L. Playfair —*This House is Haunted*
ISBN 978-1-907661-78-5

Carl Wickland, M.D.—
Thirty Years Among the Dead
ISBN 978-1-907661-72-3

John E. Mack—*Passport to the Cosmos*
ISBN 978-1-907661-81-5

Peter & Elizabeth Fenwick—
The Truth in the Light
ISBN 978-1-908733-08-5

Erlendur Haraldsson—
Modern Miracles
ISBN 978-1-908733-25-2

Erlendur Haraldsson—
At the Hour of Death
ISBN 978-1-908733-27-6

Erlendur Haraldsson—
The Departed Among the Living
ISBN 978-1-908733-29-0

Brian Inglis—*Science and Parascience*
ISBN 978-1-908733-18-4

Brian Inglis—*Natural and Supernatural:
A History of the Paranormal*
ISBN 978-1-908733-20-7

Ernest Holmes—*The Science of Mind*
ISBN 978-1-908733-10-8

Victor & Wendy Zammit —*A Lawyer
Presents the Evidence For the Afterlife*
ISBN 978-1-908733-22-1

Casper S. Yost—*Patience
Worth: A Psychic Mystery*
ISBN 978-1-908733-06-1

William Usborne Moore—
Glimpses of the Next State
ISBN 978-1-907661-01-3

William Usborne Moore—
The Voices
ISBN 978-1-908733-04-7

John W. White—
The Highest State of Consciousness
ISBN 978-1-908733-31-3

Stafford Betty—
The Imprisoned Splendor
ISBN 978-1-907661-98-3

Paul Pearsall, Ph.D. —
Super Joy
ISBN 978-1-908733-16-0

**All titles available as eBooks, and selected titles available in Hardback and
Audiobook formats from www.whitecrowbooks.com**

Lightning Source UK Ltd.
Milton Keynes UK
UKHW04f0616241018
331108UK00001B/193/P